Adolescents
and Inclusion

Transforming Secondary Schools

by

Anne M. Bauer, Ed.D.

and

Glenda Myree Brown, Ed.D.

University of Cincinnati, Ohio

with invited contributors

·P·A·U·L·H·
BROOKES
PUBLISHING Cº

Baltimore • London • Toronto • Sydney

Paul H. Brookes Publishing Co.
Post Office Box 10624
Baltimore, Maryland 21285-0624

www.brookespublishing.com

Typeset by Integrated Publishing Solutions, Grand Rapids, Michigan.
Manufactured in the United States of America by
Versa Press, East Peoria, Illinois.

The name of the high school used in this book is real, but all of the students named in this book have been given pseudonyms and some identifying details have been changed.

Library of Congress Cataloging-in-Publication Data

Bauer, Anne M.
    Adolescents and inclusion: transforming secondary schools / by Anne M. Bauer and Glenda Myree Brown, [editors].
        p.   cm.
    Includes bibliographical references and index.
    ISBN 1-55766-515-X
    1. Inclusive education—United States. 2. Handicapped youth—Education (Secondary)—United States. 3. Purcell Marian High School (Cincinnati, Ohio)—Case studies. I. Brown, Glenda Myree. II. Title.

LC1202 .B37 2001
371.9′046—dc21   2001025738

British Library Cataloguing in Publication data are available from the British Library.

Contents

I   What Does an Inclusive High School Look Like?

II   How Does an Inclusive High School Work?

Contributors

Anne M. Bauer, Ed.D.
Professor
Division of Teacher Education
College of Education
University of Cincinnati
Box 210105
Cincinnati, Ohio 45221

Glenda Myree Brown, Ed.D.
Adjunct Professor
University of Cincinnati
1615 South Dixon Circle
Cincinnati, Ohio 45224

Roseanne Bays, M.Ed.
Department of Human Services
University of Cincinnati
522 Teacher's College
Cincinnati, Ohio 45221

Rachel Davis-Haley, Ph.D.
College of Education
The University of Georgia
254 Holmes Avenue
Athens, Georgia 30606

Nicki Brainard, M.Ed.
Biology and Environmental Sciences
    Teacher
Purcell Marian High School
2935 Hackberry Street
Cincinnati, Ohio 45206

Jason Haap
English Teacher
Purcell Marian High School
2935 Hackberry Street
Cincinnati, Ohio 45206

Christine Bredestege
Math Teacher
Purcell Marian High School
2935 Hackberry Street
Cincinnati, Ohio 45206

Richard Hague, M.A.
English Department Chairperson
Purcell Marian High School
2935 Hackberry Street
Cincinnati, Ohio 45206

Dave Campbell, M.A.
Director of Campus Ministries
Purcell Marian High School
2935 Hackberry Street
Cincinnati, Ohio 45206

Kathy Heekin
Religion Teacher
Purcell Marian High School
2935 Hackberry Street
Cincinnati, Ohio 45206

Louis A. Castenell, Jr., Ph.D.
College of Education
The University of Georgia
G-3 Aderhold Hall
Athens, Georgia 30602

Rick Hennegan
Religion and Language Arts Teacher
Purcell Marian High School
2935 Hackberry Street
Cincinnati, Ohio 45206

Kimberly Moore Hill, M.Ed.
Department of Human Services
University of Cincinnati
2439 Clybourne Place
Cincinnati, Ohio 45219

Margaret Jenkins, M.Ed.
Consumer and Family Science
  Teacher
Cincinnati Public Schools
3030 Erie Avenue
Cincinnati, Ohio 45206

Allan Karol, M.A.
Theatre Teacher
Purcell Marian High School
2935 Hackberry Street
Cincinnati, Ohio 45206

Doug Kennedy
Vocational Specialist for "Jobs for
  Cincinnati Graduates"
Purcell Marian High School
2935 Hackberry Street
Cincinnati, Ohio 45206

Jan Kennedy, M.A.
Principal
Purcell Marian High School
2935 Hackberry Street
Cincinnati, Ohio 45206

Sister Kristin Matthes, M.Ed., M.A.
Religion Teacher
Purcell Marian High School
2935 Hackberry Street
Cincinnati, Ohio 45206

Karen Matuszek, M.Ed.
Director of Student Support Services
Purcell Marian High School
2935 Hackberry Street
Cincinnati, Ohio 45206

Mark D. Motz
Sports Reporter
The Community Press–East Group
394 Wards Corner Road
Suite 170
Loveland, Ohio 45140

Lisa Mueller
Math Teacher
Purcell Marian High School
2935 Hackberry Street
Cincinnati, Ohio 45206

Cliff Pope
Religion Teacher
Purcell Marian High School
2935 Hackberry Street
Cincinnati, Ohio 45206

Randy Reeder, M.S.
Dean of Students
Purcell Marian High School
2935 Hackberry Street
Cincinnati, Ohio 45206

Tom Stickley
History Teacher and Football Coach
Purcell Marian High School
2935 Hackberry Street
Cincinnati, Ohio 45206

Lee Widmer, M.S.
Physics Teacher
McNicholas High School
5464 Edalbert Drive
Cincinnati, Ohio 45239

Karen Willig, M.A.
Language Arts and Resource
  Teacher
Purcell Marian High School
2935 Hackberry Street
Cincinnati, Ohio 45206

Preface

Two years ago, in order to immerse ourselves in the Purcell Marian High School experience, we attended freshman and transfer student orientation. These 2 days introduced us to being a Cavalier. We were told to look around us and note that the person on either side of us probably didn't look or act like us. We were told that we each had gifts and that we should use those gifts to be students instead of just attending high school. People used the word *diversity*. Teachers talked about disabilities. Teachers talked about students being African American, Caucasian, or Latino, instead of silently pretending racelessness. Teachers talked about supporting each other instead of competing against each other. As we helped our fellow students, some with significant disabilities, complete a "spider web" obstacle course, we were told no one wins unless we all win.

We sat in classrooms on the first day and saw students reach around and help the student with disabilities pick up his or her bag and get to the next class. We saw teachers talking with students, asking how they could help. There were no special education classrooms or homerooms. There were no clusters of children with disabilities. There were only Cavaliers. We were walking in an inclusive high school. The teachers, students, administrators, and staff recognized and celebrated the diversity of the students entrusted to them.

This book is written with the teachers, administrators, and students of Purcell Marian High School in Cincinnati, Ohio. It is grounded in a 2-year action research project in which we observed, interviewed, read, and participated. Through that project, we were able to identify many facets related to teaching in an inclusive high school. We offer no recipes, no simple solutions. We offer what we observed, how it worked, and what teachers, administrators, staff members, and students said so that you can begin to think about how to make inclusion work for you.

In Chapter 1, we provide snapshots of interactions in an inclusive high school. Through these snapshots, we refute some of the concerns expressed by teachers and administrators. Through these vignettes, we hope to communicate the "feel" of walking down the halls of Purcell Marian High School. In Chapter 2, we further explore this feel by describing the qualities of an inclusive high school. The key role of the principal and the school mission emerge in this chapter. In Chapter 3, we discuss issues related to change and the continual evolution of inclusion. Rather than an object to be obtained, inclusion is viewed as an ongoing, evolutionary process. In Purcell Marian High School, inclusion means "here comes everybody," but "who" comprises that everybody? In Chapter 4, we look at adolescents who are typically developing, as well as their peers with disabilities. In addition, we explore issues related to students on the margins, as well as those from diverse cultural, ethnic, or language groups.

Chapter 5 follows with a description of the nature of community in an inclusive high school and ways to support such a community. In Chapter 6, we begin to discuss "teaching." Although we recognize that it is sometimes difficult to differentiate and design instruction, manage the classroom, design accommodations, and conduct assessments, we present a series of chapters related to these essential teacher activities. In Chapters 7–9, our teacher collaborators provide a voice of reality. Through their materials and examples, we demonstrate various aspects of each of these issues. In Chapter 10, we describe participation in individualized education programs and legal issues. We explore the rights of parents and students, as well as the general education teacher's role in planning for students with disabilities. In Chapter 11, Richard Hague, Chair of the English Department at Purcell Marian, provides notes on helping new faculty members "join up." He offers suggestions for working as a member of an academic department, one of the important communities within an inclusive high school.

In Chapter 12, challenges confronting an extracurricular activity monitor in a high school where "everybody can play" are described, as well as ways to support student participation. Chapter 13 presents a student's point of view. It reminds us that inclusion is more than disability and describes issues related to African American students and achievement. In Chapter 14, we ask the essential question, "Where do students go after high school?" and discuss some of the issues and questions that emerge as students complete high school and enter the work force and the community.

We hope that this book, a product of a community of leaders, communicates the sense of belonging and family in an inclusive high school.

Anne M. Bauer
Glenda Myree Brown

A Personal Note from Anne M. Bauer

When my husband and I began looking for a high school for our son (pictured above with two of our other children), we knew what we wanted—a place where he would be welcomed, a place where he belonged, a place where he would be challenged to learn and achieve, and a place where he would have friends. We have found that place in Purcell Marian High School. The teachers at Purcell Marian do not view accommodations and adaptations as anything unusual or unique; rather, accommodations and adaptations are the norm. There is an emphasis, regretfully uncommon in secondary schools, on students, faculty, and staff being kind to each other. There is a sense of community that verges on being a sense of family, the result of an ongoing effort on behalf of students, faculty, and staff to have each individual be a part of the community. As a parent, I never thought I would find such a secondary school for my children. As a teacher educator/researcher, I had to get in there with my doctoral students and figure out what was going on. This book came from 2 years of "hanging out"; talking with teachers, staff, and students; going to plays, concerts, and games; and even attending freshman orientation. We experienced the same openness and welcome granted each individual who enters the door and express our sincere appreciation to everyone involved. We have used the teachers' voices and included them as chapter contributors. We are thrilled to share what we have learned.

Acknowledgments

Special thanks goes to Jan Kennedy, Principal of Purcell Marian High School; Karen Matuszek, Director of Student Support Services; and the wonderful teachers and students who showed us that inclusion can work. Special thanks also goes to Lisa Benson at Paul H. Brookes Publishing Co., who believed in this project, and to Deb Mills, for her careful attention to detail. And finally, thanks goes to our own children and families for their patience as we learned.

*To the teachers, administrators, students,
and parents of Purcell Marian High School*

and to our families

*Riley, Demian, Tarie, Christopher, Sarah (who longs
to be Demeter), and Mickey*

and Luther and Isaac

*with love and thanks for their support
and encouragement*

Adolescents
and Inclusion

I

What Does an Inclusive High School Look Like?

MISSION STATEMENT
Purcell Marian High School

—Faculty of Purcell Marian High School

Influenced by the charisms of William Chaminade and Elizabeth Seton,
Purcell Marian High School
Is Catholic, co-educational, multiracial, and urban.
As Jesus came to invite all to the table,
Purcell Marian embraces and promotes inclusivity in all areas.
Respecting diverse academic levels, faith traditions,
and socioeconomic backgrounds,
we actively commit ourselves to innovative education
of the whole person.
By our words and actions,
the faculty and staff strive to be an example in the classroom
of what we want our graduates to be:
respectful of others, thirsting for knowledge,
and equipped with tools and a foundation necessary
for a lifetime of learning and service.

1

A Day in an Inclusive High School

Anne M. Bauer
Glenda Myree Brown

"Good morning, Cavaliers," comes the announcement over the classroom speaker.

The students with last names beginning with *G* through *L* scramble to their seats. Some are trying to finish up last-minute homework, others are rooting through their book bags. Joe leans forward to talk with the student in front of him.

"Hey, Ed. I'll see you Friday night at rehearsal."

"I thought rehearsal was tonight."

"No, man," Joe replied, getting out his plan book. "Oh, right. You guys going to wrestling? We're going to whip them."

"They're scared of us, man. We're going to state."

Joe turned to another student. "You got your homework done?"

Another announcement is made: "Please stand for morning prayer." For a moment, the room is silent. At the "amen," the chatter begins again. The homeroom teacher leans against his desk, occasionally hushing the students when the noise level gets too high. The voice over the intercom talks about a trip to a movie for all juniors; the teacher passes out the permission forms. Another announcement is made about a study group to help students with the SAT; again, the teacher passes out papers to the students.

"Cavaliers, have a great day."

A buzzer signals the end of homeroom, and the students pour out of the room. In the hall, Joe greets everyone he knows, and the students respond with, "Hey, man," "Hi, Joseph," or high fives. Joe heads for Room 19, the resource room. His American history teacher is out for the day, and several of the students in the class are off-campus having work evaluations. Joe gets out his notebook and history workbook, and sits with another student. They compare their work. A student comes over to them and helps them check their homework. They work individually for about 15 minutes, then review the study guide that the teacher had prepared for American history. They check their answers and add the information to the study guide. Joe uses a high-lighter to mark the areas that he wants to review later. Toward the end of the class, all of the students work together to identify the important information from the reading and activities on which they had been working. At the buzzer, the students pack up and proceed to their next class.

Joe arrives in his next class and begins talking with one of the girls who had been assisting in the previous classroom. The teacher asks all of the students to "come around" and get out their packets. The students groan and get out their packets as the teacher begins to talk about a just world. The teacher asks the students to get into groups of three or four. She approaches the students who are lagging behind and asks, "Which group are you in?" In Joe's group, one student assumes the leadership role. He spells words for students who ask. He reads most of the material out loud to the group. The teacher circulates among the groups, working with them briefly, emphasizing, "What does this have to do with a just world?" Joe's group continues its work, with the self-appointed leader saying, "You do this one" or "Think about it—what does this mean?" for the questions with which his group was struggling. He asks Joe to complete one item; Joe gives a brief response. The self-appointed leader says, "I see what you're saying—you mean . . ." and elaborates on the response. He assists Joe in writing the response on his packet after finishing his own. The class continues to work in groups, with the teacher periodically checking in with each group. The buzzer sounds; one student says, "Lunch. My favorite bell." The students pack up and leave the room for their various classes. Joe goes down the stairs to lunch and his work-study job.

At lunch, Joe puts his book bag on a chair with a group comprised predominantly of girls, and heads to the vending machines. He pauses, studying the contents. The student next to him says, "What are you getting?" Joe indicates what he wants. The student says, "You know what you need?" Joe replies, "I think so, I always put a dollar in." The student shrugs and says, "I guess that works" and purchases his lunch. Joe returns to his table with his food, then goes back for his drink. While eating, he watches as the group talks about boys, dances, teachers, and homework. When the conversation is about teachers, Joe interjects, "I had her" or "I won't have him" to participate in the chat. The buzzer sounds, and the group says, "Bye, Joe" or "You working, Joe? Lucky—I'm going back to math."

During the next lunch periods, Joe works in the cafeteria, policing the tables, cleaning the floor, and spending a fair amount of time socializing. When he accumulates a pile of litter with a push broom, he appears confused as to what to do with it. A cafeteria worker asks, "What do you need, hon?" Joe mentions his dilemma—that the usual place he sweeps the pile is occupied. The woman tells him to move his pile a bit, keeping it out of traffic, or he'd be sweeping all day. Joe continues to work for the remaining two lunch periods.

With one bell to go, Joe washes his hands and heads for consumer math. The room is set up with tables for group work rather than individual desks. One student sits in a rocking chair as he works. A poster on the wall proclaims "Greats" and lists "Adventures," "Rescues," "Challenges," "Mysteries," "Heroes," "Disasters," "Firsts," and "Escapes" on which students can identify their growth, achievement, and challenges. Students take turns working with partners, working at computers, and working with the teacher as he teaches mini-lessons.

This is a typical day at Purcell Marian High School—an inner-city high school. The students represent diverse cultural, ethnic, linguistic, and ability groups. The student body is about half Euro-American and half African American; about 20% have identified disabilities and another 25% are considered at risk. Joe is one of the students with an identified disability. His label or category that qualifies him for special education is irrelevant; what is relevant is that he participates fully in the school in a variety of classes and has friends. This high school, especially in its inclusion of students with disabilities in the natural flow of the day, may be very different from the high school you attended. In this book we describe ways that teachers can support students such as Joe in inclusive high schools.

If we look closer at this typical day, we can see the qualities and challenges of an inclusive environment. School climate is vital and must support each student as a full participant in the community of learners. Variations among all learners are recognized and celebrated. Students' needs are met through large amounts of group work and natural supports. Everyone teaches or provides support, from the principal to the "cafeteria lady" (see Chapter 5). Natural supports and accommodations are available to increase the students' success, with students assuming the roles of group leader, tutor, or teacher.

Other issues become apparent if we look at Joe's day more closely. There is flexibility, with a back-up plan available that provides adequate support. When his scheduled class is disrupted, Joe is able to use the resource center, which is composed of students with and without disabilities. Block scheduling is in place, so Joe has fewer classes, resulting in fewer transitions and greater instructional time to address various learning needs (see Chapter 12). The students look out for Joe, and he is provided with supports and strategies to look out for himself (e.g., plan book, strategy for putting a dollar bill in the vending machine so he doesn't have to count change and slow down the line). A wide range of classes is available, from fully inclusive classes (e.g., homeroom, social justice) to classes targeting a specific need (e.g., consumer math) to work study. Joe is engaged in extracurricular activities, both as a participant (he is manager of the football team) and as an avid fan. He hangs out at extracurricular events with students who know him because he is in their classes—he is a student just like them. Joe may struggle to read, may provide shorter responses than them, and may get confused about the date, but students without disabilities don't always do well at everything either.

Although this description is of a day in the life of a student with mild to moderate disabilities, students with more intense educational needs also can be served successfully. Through emphasizing natural supports and recognizing the variations among all learners, all students can *participate* in high school, rather than just *attend* high school. We've heard many stories about how inclusive high schools can't work. With a few more snapshots, we provide additional examples of how inclusive high schools can work.

"Our high school building is old and inaccessible. Students with disabilities couldn't get around."

Snapshot: The van pulls up, and the driver moves to the back to the wheelchair lift. A young lady rolls off the lift—book bag in her lap and computer strapped to the back of the chair. Four young men in warm-up jackets and football jerseys move over to her, and one says, "Hey, Shari, you ready to fly?" The student in the wheelchair laughs and nods, and the boys lock her wheelchair brakes and carry her up the stairs to the first floor on which Shari has her classes. When she has "landed," one of the boys says, "See you at lunch," and the others say "bye," and proceed to their classes. Shari gathers her breath and says, "See ya" and begins to push her way down the hall with her foot.

"It might be great for students with disabilities, but what about students without disabilities? What do they get out of inclusion?"

Snapshot: The football team is playing in the regional finals. The score is close, and on a critical play a student fumbles the football. As the offensive team leaves the field, the player who fumbled sits at the end of the bench alone, head in his hands, feeling dejected. The team manager, a student with moderate disabilities, brings him a towel and cup of water. The player says, "No thanks, man" and the student with disabilities simply sits down next to him, sharing the disappointment.

"Teachers want to teach students who can achieve, students who can learn. It's just too hard to teach without throwing in this inclusion stuff."

Snapshot: In conversation, a teacher remarks, "I can't imagine teaching anywhere else. It is just too interesting." Another states, "When I came here, I thought I'd be here a year until a job teaching advanced placement classes in the suburbs opened up. I've been offered that job—and I didn't take it."

"The students won't respond to kids with disabilities. It will bother them having students with problems in the hall."

Snapshot: Luisa uses a wheeled suitcase instead of a book bag due to her disabilities. At the bell, she moves down the hall dragging the case and stops at the steps. The girl behind her, chatting actively with her friends, says in passing, "Hey, girlfriend" and picks up the suitcase, without missing a comment. Another girl in the group takes the girl by the arm and they continue up the steps. At the top of the steps they hand the suitcase back to the girl and continue to their class.

Snapshot: A student's parents had brought her to the first football game and began to remove her from the wheelchair and place her in the stands with them. A young man, his face painted half red and half yellow, comes over and says, "The students in the spirit squad sit over here. I'll take her." The parents back up, and the student wheels her away (maybe a bit wildly) chanting, "Go, Cavs." At the end of the game, two girls return her to her parents. She is giggling wildly and has "Go Cavs" painted on her face, like the students pushing her. "Vinnie's Restaurant after the game" they tell the girl, then to her parents, "It's the one on Madison Road." The parents, not quite knowing what to do, decide they could go to the restaurant and leave quietly if the invitation really wasn't genuine. When they pull into the parking lot, the two girls wave at their van, and after her parents push her to the door the two girls take her to the loud group of students at several long tables. Without even pausing to stop talking, the students help her drink and break a slice of pizza into small pieces for her to eat.

We welcome you to the challenges and joys of inclusive high schools. We welcome you to this book, which is written with the teachers and staff of an inclusive high school. The strategies, procedures, practices, and examples provided are all real and have emerged from a commitment to serve students of all cultural, ethnic, linguistic, and ability groups in a safe and successful environment.

We are interested in you as a learner. To support your learning, at the beginning of each chapter we provide objectives to guide your reading, and at the end of each chapter we highlight the major points presented.

Welcome to inclusive high schools.

2

Qualities of an Inclusive High School

Glenda Myree Brown
Anne M. Bauer
Teacher Contributors: Karen Matuszek and Jan Kennedy

> An inclusive school is a diverse problem-solving organization with a common mission that emphasizes learning for all students. It employs and supports teachers and staff who are committed to working together to create and maintain a climate conducive to learning. The responsibility for all students is shared. An effective inclusive school acknowledges that such a commitment requires administrative leadership, ongoing technical assistance, and long-term professional development. Within inclusive schools, there is a shared responsibility for any problem or any success for any student in the school. (Council for Exceptional Children [CEC], 1994, p. vii)

Although all schools are different, many secondary schools exist as isolated workplaces in which teachers work largely alone in their rooms, interacting little with colleagues, and keeping problems of practice to themselves. In these schools, teachers feel separated from one another, seldom engaging their peers in conversation, professional sharing, or problem solving (Little, 1990; Lortie, 1975). The culture of these schools is not conducive to collaboration and will not effectively support the implementation of inclusion.

This chapter describes qualities of an inclusive high school that have been discussed in the literature and that have emerged through interviews with teachers, staff members, and administrators at an inclusive high school. Certain qualities exist in inclusive high schools that may be markedly different from those found in traditional high schools. In Purcell Marian High School, we identified the following qualities:

- Inclusive school mission (Jorgensen, 1998)
- Strong principal leadership
- Collaborative school culture
- Climate of collegiality
- Shared leadership (Sergiovanni, 1994)

Collaboration and cooperation are the natural school culture for inclusion. In order to implement the intent of the Individuals with Disabilities Education Act (IDEA) Amendments of 1997 (PL 105-17) in general education classrooms, members of the school staff, faculty, and administration must collaborate. Saxl, Miles, and Lieberman (1990) identified six specific skills necessary for creating a collaborative school culture. These skills include 1) building trust and rapport, 2) diagnosing the organization, 3) dealing with the collaborative process, 4) using resources, 5) managing work, and 6) building skills and confidence. In addition, the inclusive climate and mission have benefits for students with and without identified disabilities.

This chapter includes the voices of both the principal and teachers. Through the voices of those who, in spite of daily challenges, are making inclusion work, we provide you with insights into what actually goes on in creating an inclusive high school. After reading this chapter, you will be able to answer the following questions:

- What is the role of mission in an inclusive high school?
- What is the role of the principal?
- What is the collaborative school culture in an inclusive high school?
- How is the climate of collegiality established?
- What is the role of shared leadership?
- What are the benefits and outcomes for students with and without identified disabilities?

INCLUSIVE HIGH SCHOOL MISSION

The mission of an inclusive high school requires that students with and without disabilities attend school and have membership in general education classes alongside their same-age and neighborhood peers with necessary supplementary aids and services (Thousand, Villa, & Nevin, 1994). It is to provide students with and without disabilities optimal academic and social learning opportunities so that they live productive lives as members of society, now and in the future. One outcome of such a student-focused vision is increased teacher efficacy and pride in the learning and achievement of their students (Peterson, 1986). The way in which implementation takes place in the school reflects the beliefs, attitudes, and values of the staff regarding inclusive education. Therefore, an inclusive mission should be closely aligned with the staff's actions so that it guides the daily work of inclusion.

Jan Kennedy's, principal of Purcell Marian High School, commitment to the inclusive mission and the staff's concurrence with that mission became evident during our time in the school. One teacher's thoughts regarding how the program for students with moderate and severe disabilities began and the role that having an inclusive mission played were, "When we were approached about having a program for students with developmental disabilities, it just seemed like a natural progression or extension of our school philosophy and mission statement, which is to serve all students regardless of abilities or disabilities."

Another teacher expressed her thoughts on the inclusive school mission by stating, "I know that the reason that inclusion works well here is because it's part of who we are. It's our mission statement. It's our philosophy. It's ingrained in everything that we do here."

A veteran teacher who led the first program for students with learning disabilities indicated that, "Twenty-one years ago, when the LD [learning disabilities] program was started, it was the only [secondary] program for students with learning disabilities in the city." He explained further why the program for students with moderate and severe disabilities is "no big deal." ". . . our school has always believed in diversity and believes in educating all students, not just students who are college prep or advanced placement. For as long as it has been in existence . . . the faculty has always chosen to teach students who have not been able to be successful at other high schools."

In teacher interviews, this theme of teaching all students, regardless of ability or disability, emerged as a part of the school's identity and mission. The principal, providing her perceptions of staff response to inclusion, stated, "Everyone felt challenged by our mission statement, but it was in place and everyone here at that time had bought into it. All of us recognized that this was going to be a challenge, but this is who we said we were. We knew it was the right thing to do, and we were going to do it. There was fear, but there was a real overall commitment to making it work. No one, no one, tried to sabotage this. The block schedule they did! But no one tried to sabotage this and that certainly was very helpful. I think that's due to the goodness of the people."

Teachers and administrators were in agreement regarding the mission of inclusion. They echo the statement from *Creating Schools* (CEC, 1994) with which we opened this chapter.

PRINCIPAL LEADERSHIP IN AN INCLUSIVE HIGH SCHOOL

Building an inclusive school community can be difficult, especially for principals in high schools in which traditional structures are deeply embedded in the secondary school culture. How does a principal lead a high school with a tradition of teachers working in isolation according to their particular disciplines toward an inclusive learning community in which diversity and collaboration are valued?

Zalenik (as cited in Sergiovanni, 1995) contended that leadership is based on a compact that binds those who lead and those who follow into the same moral, intellectual, and emotional commitment. Sergiovanni (2001) stated that principals develop this compact through purposing. He defined *purposing* as what principals do to bring about a cohesive, shared consensus to bond people together in a common cause and to define them as a community, in a way sufficiently loose to allow for individual expression. Purposing lets the staff know where the school is going in terms of inclusive practices, why it is going in that direction, and some ways of getting there.

Principals must always project the vision of inclusive education and continually reinforce with teachers and staff the "big picture" so that everyone continues to work toward the inclusive mission of the school. It is the responsibility and obligation of the principal to talk openly and frequently about his or her beliefs and commitments regarding inclusion. Sergiovanni (2001) pointed out further responsibilities of the principal and other school leaders regarding vision and leadership when he described their responsibilities for encouraging a dialogue about what the school stands for and where it should be headed. *Vision*, he contended, isn't a "magic plan" or road map charting the way to the leader's specific reality. Rather, he suggested that vision is more of a compass, pointing the direction to be taken, inspiring enthusiasm, and allowing people to buy into and take part in the shaping of the path that constitutes the school mission. This development of the mission requires building a consensus about purposes and beliefs, creating a powerful force that binds people together around common themes. This attachment provides them with a sense of what is important and valuable. With these bonds in place, the school is transformed from organization to community.

A high school principal who wishes to implement inclusive education must create a school culture in which teachers regularly 1) engage in professional dialogue with colleagues, 2) share ideas, knowledge, and techniques, and 3) participate in collaborative problem solving around classroom issues. Inclusive education in a secondary school means change. The principal must adopt new and creative approaches to leadership if people are going to be open to that change. This requires that the principal build a vision of an inclusive school culture in which leadership, information, and knowledge are shared. As the principal encourages the school staff to collaborate and share their expertise and skills, various staff members will find themselves in leadership positions. In a collaborative school culture, everyone on staff realizes that they can be a leader. This can only happen, however, if the principal is willing to empower the staff through the sharing of information, knowledge, and resources and then trusting that they will do the right thing and get the job done.

Conley and Goldman (1994) noted the importance of trust. They called it "a letting go of control" and increasing the belief that others can and will function independently and successfully within a common framework of expectations and accountability. Principals in successful inclusive high schools understand that teachers are best suited to respond to the unique set of problems related to inclusive education. They understand that teachers can make the choices and decisions that will be in the best interest of the school and ultimately in the best interest of all children (Conley & Goldman, 1994).

Principal leadership in Purcell Marian High School was described by both teachers and the principal. Teachers viewed the principal as a dedicated leader who was committed to including all students as members of the school. When asked about the principal's support of inclusive education, one teacher said, "She's very supportive of the program, and she is very forward thinking—sometimes to the extent I'd like to say, 'Hey come back a little bit.'" Another teacher spoke of the principal's commitment when introducing the idea of serving students with moderate and severe disabilities in general education classes. "It was hammered in that this is not some project that if it doesn't work it's going to go away next year. She let it be known that this is part of the school and they are part of the fabric of the school." Another teacher summed up her appraisal of the principal by saying, "Oh, she is wonderful! I think the reason she is so effective as a leader is because she's so passionate about what she believes in. She is so passionate about it that it's pretty easy for people to jump on board." The principal described the confidence and trust she has in the staff to do the right thing for the students. "It's absolutely critical that I allow teachers to do what they can do with minimal supervision and direction from me. If anything, I hope that's what my staff likes. I trust 99% in these folks to do a good job and the right thing all the time. I don't feel the need to be looking over their shoulders. Sometimes it can be risky. When you give people responsibility, they take the responsibility but ultimately you're still responsible. But you have to take those kinds of risks. If you try to stay safe and keep all the power on your desk, nothing is going anywhere."

The principal realized that although it is important to get the vision or the big picture out in front of staff, it also is important that they have a say in how that vision looks and its implementation. She explained why the vision of inclusive education must be everyone's vision. "The vision can't remain my idea. If it remained my idea it will not go anywhere. If you think it's right, and that this is what its supposed to be, then you've got to sell that to people. You've got to get your front runners, and then they take it from there. They are empowered by that. But if it remains your idea, nothing happens. If block scheduling had remained my idea, there's no way it would have gone anywhere. If an inclusive community was just my vision for this place, it would not have happened. Everyone out there, they're the ones who have to do the including."

CREATING A COLLABORATIVE SCHOOL CULTURE

Roland Barth, head of the Principal's Center at Harvard University, wrote:

> The relationships among the adults in schools are the basis, the precondition, [and] the sine qua non that allow, energize, and sustain all other attempts at school improvement. Unless adults talk with one another, observe one another, and help one another, very little will change. (cited in Krovetz & Cohick, 1993, p. 331)

Collaboration was defined by Bruner (1991) as a process for working together to reach goals that cannot be attained efficiently by acting independently. In his view, successful collaboration includes jointly developing and agreeing to a set of common goals and directions, shared responsibility for attaining those goals, and working together to achieve those goals through exploiting each individual's expertise. Pugach and Johnson (1995) suggested that collaboration includes learning and sharing the roles and responsibilities of all those who are collaborating, building a consensus without hierarchical impositions, and conducting group goal setting and decision making. *Collaboration,* then, is a style for direct interaction between at least two equal parties engaged in shared decision making and working toward a common goal. Collaboration defines the way in which people interact to accomplish the work of inclusion. These interactions result in support, sharing, and relationship building among teachers, parents, and students.

Culture is a patterned way of acting, thinking, and feeling that is acquired over time and transmitted through and to members of a group (Branch, Goodwin, & Gualtieri, 1993). Patterson and Purkey (1993) pointed out that culture is the glue that bonds the school together as it goes about its mission. Culture can either assist the school in its implementation of inclusion or act as a hindrance. Implementing inclusive learning in a secondary school requires that principals create a collaborative culture and empower teachers to perform effectively by sharing pertinent inclusion information with them, building their commitment to values of inclusive learning, and developing their skills and confidence in their ability to work with students with and without disabilities.

In a study of change in urban high schools, Saxl and colleagues (1990) found that collaboration is a complex and demanding activity. It requires developing trusting and collegial relationships, dealing with conflict, and maintaining a clear focus. Based on their research, they identified six key skills necessary to reinforce collaborative cultures and move a staff closer to its goal of inclusive learning for all students: 1) building trust and rapport, 2) diagnosing the organization, 3) dealing with the collaborative process, 4) using resources, 5) managing work, and 6) building skills and confidence in others.

Building Trust and Rapport

Leaders must find ways to increase the trust in the group and rapport in working together. In inclusive schools, time is spent forming common goals and discussing why those goals are important to the learning and achievement of all students. Defining the inclusive mission and aligning the school with it is nearly impossible without developing and maintaining trust among all employees (Carr, 1994). Leaders learn to address resistance in the group and find ways to overcome it without coercion. They also engage in open and supportive communication work processes. Leaders develop "shared influence" in the process, encouraging the active participation of everyone. In urban schools, building trust and rapport are key to creating the motivation needed for implementing inclusive learning.

Diagnosing the Organization

Teacher leaders in collaborative cultures support the problem identification and the problem-solving work of colleagues. They know how to collect and analyze student performance data, make a diagnosis of the educational situation and share it in a clear and helpful way, and place their diagnosis within a conceptual framework to aid in understanding the nature of the instructional or curricular issue. The diagnosis of educational problems is a model of deeper analysis that supports rich collaborative problem solving and improvement efforts.

Dealing with the Collaborative Process

Collaboration is a complex and demanding activity. It requires developing trusting, collegial relationships, dealing with conflict, and maintaining clear focus. In urban schools, teacher leaders help the process to succeed by knowing how to build collaborative relationships, how to mediate conflict as it develops, how to deal with confrontation in a productive way, and how to maintain the focus of students. Ongoing research into school culture, change, and improvement is finding that success is more likely when teachers are collegial and work collaboratively on improvement activities (Fullan & Hargreaves, 1991).

Using Resources and Managing Work

Any form of joint work needs resources and some coordination. Effective urban teacher leaders know how to tap into the resource network to gain materials, ideas, time, and people to help. Personal and financial resources often are at a premium in urban schools, so teacher leaders will need to know how to seek resources, find time, and connect to key resources outside of the school. Learning to "work the bureaucracy" can bring needed resources to the school.

Collaborative work also requires more planning, organizing, scheduling, and coordination. Teacher leaders maintain the flow of collaborative activities by helping manage this work, smoothing the work flow, and facilitating the direction and progress of work. Leaders who help plan and organize joint work are important, given the demands of urban school leaders.

Building Skills and Confidence in Others

Leaders also assume the key tasks of building greater skills and deeper confidence in their co-workers. As leaders, teachers in collaborative cultures help others develop leadership skills, planning skills, and problem-solving skills. They see their role as increasing the skills and knowledge of others through examples, ideas, and support. In addition, teacher leaders in collaborative cultures help increase the confidence that others have in themselves and in the group as a whole.

The principal echoed these components of collaboration: "As an administrator, you have to be able to identify the people that you have to sell. You're not going to sell everybody, so you have to sell the key people and they're not always department chairs and not always the obvious people. So you have to decide who do I need to focus on to affect any kind of paradigm shift that might be needed, and then they'll sell their own constituencies. They have their own constituencies, and if you can sell them then they go out and sell it. You have to establish those relationships with the key folks in your community. You don't know that from looking at a handbook. You only know that after you live with them for a little while—who the key people are. I think it's just as important to identify those people who probably are not going to go along with you and establish a relationship with them that is respectful and friendly."

COLLEGIAL CLIMATE

Sergiovanni defined *collegiality* as "the existence of high levels of collaboration among teachers and between teachers and principal" (1995, p. 135). He characterized collegiality by mutual respect, shared work values, cooperation, and specific conversations about teaching and learning. Sergiovanni suggested that high levels of collegiality generate a strong professional work culture held together by shared work norms. These norms are aligned with school purposes and contribute to increased commitment and extraordinary performance.

Given the historical nature of the traditional high school, a collegial climate in an inclusive high school does not develop overnight. Rather, it is shaped by the way the principal, teachers, and other staff members reinforce and support underlying norms, values, beliefs, and assumptions regarding inclusive education. In inclusive high schools, a collaborative climate exists in which the underlying norms, values, and beliefs support, encourage, and reinforce teamwork, collegiality, and interactions about problems of practice. It is a climate in which teachers share ideas, materials, problems, and solutions in order to foster greater student learning and growth. The staff and administrators work together for the good of students, and energy, commitment, and motivation are high (Peterson & Brietzke, 1994). It is exciting and professionally rewarding for teachers who work in a collegial school climate in which reflection is encouraged and instruction and curriculum are regularly being refined, changed, and developed. Inclusive high schools possess a climate in which people take risks and share information and decision making as they work together to increase learning for all students. Pounder (1998) argued that in inclusive schools that practice collaboration, leadership is encouraged, common goals are developed, feedback is ongoing, needed skills and resources are provided, and staff members are rewarded or recognized for what they do. She further stated that as people work and grow together, the patterns of the relationships among staff are more interdependent. This is in contrast to most secondary schools that seem to have climates that favor professional isolation (Pounder, 1998).

The collegial climate and collaboration at Purcell Marian High School have enabled the staff to embrace the inclusion of students with moderate and severe disabilities and allowed inclusive education to continuously evolve. The student services support team, in its leadership role, offers ideas, shares materials, and participates in collaborative problem solving with others on the staff. The department chair of this group described some of the collaborative work they do to support teachers as well as students with and without identified disabilities while building a collegial school climate: "At the beginning of the year, we have an in-service for all of the teachers who are going to be seeing our students with disabilities. We do a slide presentation. We do picture bios of them, talk about their strengths, their weaknesses, their defining characteristics, and tell the teachers that these are the things that we know have worked. These are some things that we know will work and offer them as much information as possible."

The collegial climate is encouraged by the student support team. In this team, three special educators design a schedule so that each of them is available at a different period. For example, if an American history teacher has some difficulties in making successful modifications during first period, he or she knows which team member is available at that time. The American history teacher would work with that "troubleshooter" during that particular period. In addition, the student support team provides evaluation forms to all of the teachers twice each quarter. In addition to the typical academic achievement checklist, evaluative comments regarding intangibles such as the student's work in cooperative groups or the student's social status in the class are requested. A truer picture of the students' performance is acquired through the evaluative comments.

The principal also suggested that faculty should be recognized for their hard work. "People appreciate simple recognition. It's one thing to say it in private but these folks work for so little in monetary compensation that just that little recognition or acknowledgment means a lot: 'I know that you're working really hard, and I appreciate it; the kids appreciate it.'"

The principal also provided trips to workshops and conferences as incentives for those who are doing well with implementation and for those who are having difficulties. "We have what's called "Jan Bucks". . . . It amazes me how important those become to people. It's 5 bucks in an envelope that they can only use in the Spirit Room [the school store in which T-shirts, sweatshirts, and other items are sold], but it's recognition. Doughnuts. Order doughnuts one morning and say 'thanks' for whatever it is. Lunches. That's really simple. Rewarding people is really simple, and it doesn't have to be very expensive. They're not here for the money. It is very important."

SHARED LEADERSHIP

Effective leadership by the principal in an inclusive secondary school is not controlling and authoritarian. Rather, effective principals realize the need to build a collaborative school culture so that the needs of diverse learners can be best met. Peterson and Brietzke (1994) found that in collaborative schools, leadership takes on many forms and emanates from many different people. *Collaboration,* as an interaction style, means that all staff members plan, work, and problem-solve together as they strive to create a school culture that values student diversity and inclusive learning. Staff members are encouraged to step forward as informal leaders who guide, assist, and encourage the staff toward the goal of inclusion based on areas of expertise and interest. Teachers are empowered to become leaders as knowledge and information is shared. The principal's role is to increase the knowledge and commitment of teachers so that they become leaders in moving the school toward a culture of inclusive education and respect for diversity.

The principal in an inclusive school encourages teachers to become leaders. Peterson and Brietzke (1994) agreed but noted that this does not mean that they become school leaders in the traditional sense in which teachers assume the hierarchical authoritarian leadership styles of traditional schools. Rather, teachers engage in collaborative, facilitative modes of leadership. This shared leadership requires upsetting some of the usual structures of secondary school life. Staff members must re-create their roles to an extent that they develop new structures to support inclusive learning in high schools. This transition requires a principal who can handle transformational or cultural change. This effort will require a secondary school principal who understands how change happens and who can persuade staff to give up some of the deeply ingrained traditions of secondary schools and embrace a new way of looking at how we meet the needs of all students with and without identified disabilities in the general education classroom.

The principal has shared and continues to share leadership with the student services support team since the inception of the program for students with developmental disabilities. Members of the support team have taken their leadership duties and responsibilities seriously. The director of the program remembered what it was like getting started: "I think a lot of the teachers here, although they were excited about this program, quite honestly were afraid. They weren't sure how they were going to make their classroom work for students with disabilities. And so it was our job as a staff to help them be less afraid, to help them see how it can be done. We've done a variety of in-services and workshops here. We have also made workshops and conferences being offered locally or nationally available to them. It also helps that the support team has formed many good personal relationships with the other staff members. This has made it much easier for them to lead, collaborate, share ideas, and work together effectively so that increased student learning and socialization take place."

She further explained, "If we go to them and say, 'You know we have a student who I think would do really well but he's going to require a little extra TLC and you're going to have to do something over and above the call of duty, so to speak,' they're willing to do that because of us. We try not to beat any of the teachers over the head with the idea that this is inclusion and by God you're going make this work. Because I think it's hard. I think inclusion at the high school level is difficult, and it requires a lot of trust. It requires a lot of cooperation. It requires a lot of sliding by the seat of your pants sometimes. On any given day being willing just to try something new that you've never thought of before and sometimes it works and sometimes it doesn't, but I'm not going to come at a teacher and say, 'Well you tried such and such and it was unsuccessful.' I'm thankful that they had the courage to try something new."

BENEFITS AND OUTCOMES OF INCLUSIVE LEARNING

Putnam, Spiegel, and Bruininks stated, "The movement toward inclusion will continue, and the belief will predominate that people with disabilities have the right to full participation in settings and activities. . . . Society as a whole will recognize the benefits of integrated education (1995, p. 572). Focusing on the needs of students with disabilities in general education classrooms has caused some educators to examine how successfully the needs of the students without disabilities are being met. Students with and without disabilities benefit from being included in secondary subject area classes (Ferguson, Meyer, Jeanchild, Juniper, & Zingo, 1992). Results from interviews conducted by McLeskey and Waldron (1996) with teachers in inclusive programs indicated that one of the greatest strengths of inclusive learning is the benefits that accrue to students who are not eligible for special education services, especially students who have difficulty in class but "fall through the cracks" of the eligibility system for special education (e.g., a student who is behind in reading but not far enough behind to be labeled as having a learning disability). In fact, McLeskey and Waldron argued that the primary goal of inclusion should be to allow teachers in general education classrooms to better meet the needs of all students. They further contended that this most likely will include not only students with disabilities but also slow learners, students who are perceived to be at risk of school failure, students with attentional problems, and students who learn the curricular material quickly and become bored. This suggests, as Thousand, Rosenberg, Bishop, and Villa noted, "that the presence of youth with disabilities in secondary classrooms, in fact, represents a gift to school restructuring. Their presence requires and pushes implementation of educational goals, theories, and best practices" (1997, p. 279).

King-Sears and Cummings (1996), focusing on inclusive practices of classroom teachers, found the following benefits for all students in inclusive classrooms:

- Increased opportunities to practice and respond to tasks in a given subject area (e.g., math, spelling, reading)
- Increased time on academic tasks
- More frequent student feedback regarding academic performance
- Reduced off-task and acting-out behavior problems
- Increased fluency in basic skills
- Increased rates of correct responses from students

In a case study of collaboration and co-teaching between a special educator and general educator, Trent (1998) discovered benefits to both teachers. The special educator became more familiar with general education curriculum and content, and the general education teacher learned to modify the curriculum to meet the needs of students with and without disabilities. Friend and Cook (1999) cited higher levels of trust and respect among colleagues and a sense of community among staff as positive outcomes of inclusive schools that practice collaboration.

Educators disagree about many issues, including the benefits for students with and without disabilities, teacher workload and preparation, and distribution of financial resources. Farlow (1996) found, however, that when students with severe disabilities are included in the general classroom, all students develop social communication and problem-solving skills, as well as the ability to get along with others in diverse communities. Students, especially at the secondary level, are building networks that can improve the quality of their life through adulthood. When seeking our first jobs, for example, many of us rely on friendships that began during adolescence. Like their typically developing peers, students with severe disabilities also need community support and friendship networks that extend beyond school. If we believe that our students must learn to live in a pluralistic society and that students with disabilities should receive the support of a community network of friends (in addition to professional social services workers), then inclusion deserves the extra effort and energy required of us (Farlow, 1996).

Salend and Duhaney (1999) conducted an extensive review of the literature on inclusion and its impact on all students. In addition, they examined the impact of inclusion on both general and special education teachers. They found that many secondary students with disabilities, especially those in ninth and tenth grades, received poor grades. These data also showed, however, that secondary students with disabilities, particularly with physical disabilities, who took a greater number of general education courses were more likely to

- Attend postsecondary academic programs
- Obtain employment and earn higher salaries
- Live independently
- Be socially included into their communities
- Be married or engaged

In terms of the impact of inclusion on the learning of students without disabilities, Peck, Donaldson, and Pezzolli (1990) also found that placement in an inclusive classroom does not interfere with the academic performance of students without disabilities with respect to the amount of allocated and engaged instructional time, the rate of interruptions to planned activities, or the students' achievement test scores and report card grades.

SOCIAL OUTCOMES

Salend and Duhaney (1999) explained that in addition to examining the impact of placement in the general education setting on the academic performance of students with disabilities, studies also have been conducted to examine the noneducational, social, and self-concept outcomes for students with disabilities educated in inclusive settings. They found that interviews with secondary students with disabilities indicated that they had negative experiences in both general and special education. Negative experiences of secondary students with disabilities in general education classes related to teachers' failure to adapt instruction to meet their needs, and the fear that their special accommodations resulted in their being stigmatized in the presence of their peers. Secondary students with disabilities reported that their negative experiences in special education included receiving low-level, repetitive, and unchallenging academic instruction; having concerns about their status and the loss of friends; and feeling stigmatized.

Hendrickson, Shokoohi-Yekta, Hamre-Nietupski, and Gable (1996) surveyed a large sample of middle and high school students without disabilities regarding their friendships with peers with severe disabilities. The results revealed that the students without disabilities were willing to form friendships with their peers with severe disabilities and believed that inclusion facilitated the development of such friendships. The students also suggested several strategies for promoting friendships among students such as using cooperative grouping arrangements, sharing information about disabilities, and implementing social activities that promote interactions among students.

Students without identified disabilities also have reported social benefits of inclusion. Meyer, Hyun-Sook, Grenot-Scheyer, Schwartz, and Harry (1998), in examining the social relationships between high school students without disabilities and their peers with disabilities, found that the students without disabilities received several benefits from their experiences in inclusive settings. These students reported that they learned from their classmates with disabilities, had positive feelings as a result of supporting another individual, and were able to deal with disability in their own lives.

In another study of students without identified disabilities, Helmstetter, Peck, and Giangreco (1994) conducted a survey to investigate their perceptions of their relationships with students with moderate and severe disabilities. They found that students without disabilities perceived their friendships with students with disabilities as beneficial in terms of increased personal growth. Students also reported that they learned acceptance of others and human diversity. In interviews of students without identified disabilities, Peck and colleagues (1990) found that these students felt that they had improved in the areas of 1) self-concept, 2) social cognition, 3) acceptance of others, 4) advancement of individual principles, and 5) tolerance of human differences. Some students without disabilities also indicated that they were uncomfortable with students with moderate and severe disabilities because of their lack of social skills, their behaviors, their difficulty communicating effectively, and their physical appearance. This discomfort, however, seemed to decrease as the school year progressed.

The benefits and outcomes for students can be summed up in the words of a teacher who discussed some of the outcomes of inclusive education students with and without identified disabilities: "To see the kids interact...before this program it was hard to imagine some of these kids going to the prom, being on the swim team, the soccer team, or being a team manager—to have the everyday high school life. But they do. The other kids see them, and they welcome them, they talk to them, they accept them. And in return they are accepting of the other students as well. It goes both ways. The kids are involved in the drama club, with all kinds of clubs. So it's the full experience. It's real world. It's real life."

The principal spoke of the benefits to students in this way. "I don't know what happens to them. It doesn't matter where they come from. They just become wonderful human beings. They really do. They are kind, they are protective. In fact, we have one student who uses a wheelchair and will sometimes let people do too much for her. They will come up to her and say, 'Oh, what do you need?' and we have to say, 'She can do it herself, she needs no more help getting down the hall than you do.' But they have this notion about being a Cavalier, and Cavaliers take care of one another."

SUMMARY POINTS

- School culture, climate, and mission are keys to successful inclusion in high schools.
- Inclusion in high schools requires that teachers perceive collaboration as their natural way of doing things, creating a climate in which implementation of inclusion can be more successful.
- The challenge for the school leader seeking to implement inclusion at the secondary school level is in transforming a school culture that has a tradition of teachers working in isolation from other teachers, and groups of students working in isolation from other students, into a collaborative school culture that supports inclusive learning.
- Inclusion in high schools benefits both students with and without identified disabilities.

REFERENCES

Branch, R.C., Goodwin, Y., & Gualtieri, J. (1993). Making classroom instruction culturally pluralistic. *Educational Forum, 58*(1), 58–70.

Bruner, C. (1991). *Thinking collaboratively: Ten questions and answers to help policy makers improve children's services*. Washington, DC: Education and Human Services Consortium. (ERIC No. ED 338984)

Carr, C. (1994). Empowered organizations, empowering leaders. *Training and Development, 48*(6), 39.

Conley, D.T., & Goldman, P. (1994). Facilitative leadership: How principals lead without dominating. *Oregon School Study Council (OSSC) Bulletin, 37*(9). (ERIC No. ED 379728)

Council for Exceptional Children (CEC). (1994). *Creating schools for all our students: What twelve schools have to say*. Reston, VA: Author.

Farlow, L. (1996). A quartet of success stories: How to make inclusion work. *Educational Leadership, 53*(5), 51–55.

Ferguson, D., Meyer, G., Jeanchild, L., Juniper, L., & Zingo, J. (1992). Figuring out what to do with the grownups: How teachers make inclusion "work" for students with disabilities. *Journal of The Association for Persons with Severe Handicaps, 17*(4), 218–226.

Friend, M.P., & Cook, L. (1999). *Interactions: Collaboration skills for school professionals* (3rd ed.). New York: Longman.

Fullan, M., & Hargreaves, A. (1991). *What's worth fighting for? Working together for your school*. Toronto: Ontario Public School Teachers' Federation.

Helmstetter, E., Peck, C.A., & Giangreco, M.F. (1994). Outcomes of interactions with peers with moderate or severe disabilities: A statewide survey of high school students. *Journal of The Association for Persons with Severe Handicaps, 19*, 263–276.

Hendrickson, J.M., Shokoohi-Yekta, M., Hamre-Nietupski, S., & Gable, R.A. (1996). Middle and high school students' perceptions on being friends with peers with severe disabilities. *Exceptional Children, 63*, 19–28.

Individuals with Disabilities Education Act (IDEA) Amendments of 1997, PL 105-17, 20 U.S.C. §§ 1400 *et seq.*

Jorgensen, C.M. (Ed.). (1998). *Restructuring high schools for all students: Taking inclusion to the next level*. Baltimore: Paul H. Brookes Publishing Co.

King-Sears, M.A., & Cummings, C.S. (1996). Inclusive practices of classroom teachers. *Remedial and Special Education, 17*(4), 217–225.

Krovetz, M., & Cohick, D. (1993). Professional collegiality can lead to school change. *Phi Delta Kappan, 75,* 331.

Little, J. (1990). The persistence of privacy: Autonomy and initiative in teachers' professional relations. *Teachers College Record, 91,* 509–536.

Lortie, D.C. (1975). *Schoolteacher: A sociological study.* Chicago: University of Chicago Press.

McLeskey, J., & Waldron, N. (1996). Special education teachers responses to questions teachers and administrators frequently ask about inclusive school programs. *Phi Delta Kappa, 78*(2), 150.

Meyer, L.H., Park, H.S., Grenot-Scheyer, M., Schwartz, I.S., & Harry, B. (1998). *Making friends: The influence of culture and development.* Baltimore: Paul H. Brookes Publishing Co.

Patterson, C.H., & Purkey, W.W. (1993). The preparation of humanistic teachers for schools of the next century. *Journal of Humanistic Education and Development, 31*(4), 147–155.

Peck, C.A., Donaldson, J., & Pezzoli, M. (1990). Some benefits nonhandicapped adolescents perceive for themselves from their social relationships with peers who have severe handicaps. *Journal of The Association for Persons with Severe Handicaps, 15,* 241–249.

Peterson, K.D. (1986). Problem finding in principals' work: Values and cognition in administration. *Peabody Journal of Education, 63*(1), 87–106.

Peterson, K.D., & Brietzke, R. (1994). *Building collaborative cultures: Seeking ways to reshape urban schools.* Oak Brook, IL: North Central Regional Educational Laboratory. (ERIC No. ED 378286)

Pounder, D.G. (Ed.). (1998). *Restructuring schools for collaboration: Promises and pitfalls.* Albany: State University of New York Press.

Pugach, M.C., & Johnson, L.J. (1995). *Collaborative practitioners, collaborative schools.* Denver: Love.

Putnam, J., Spiegel, A., & Bruininks, R. (1995). Future directions in education and inclusion of students with disabilities: A delphi investigation. *Exceptional Children, 61,* 553–576.

Salend, S.J., & Duhaney, L.M. (1999). The impact of inclusion on students with and without disabilities and their educators. *Remedial and Special Education, 20*(2), 114–126.

Saxl, E.R., Miles, M.B., & Lieberman, A. (1990). *Assisting change in education: A training program for school improvement facilitators: Trainer's manual.* Alexandria, VA: Association for Supervision and Curriculum Development.

Sergiovanni, T.J. (1994). *Building community in schools.* San Francisco: Jossey-Bass.

Sergiovanni, T.J. (1995). *The principalship: A reflective practice perspective* (3rd ed.). Needham Heights, MA: Allyn & Bacon.

Sergiovanni, T.J. (2001). *The principalship: A reflective practice perspective* (4th ed.). Needham Heights, MA: Allyn & Bacon.

Thousand, J.S., Rosenberg, R., Bishop, K., & Villa, R.A. (1997). The evolution of secondary inclusion. *Remedial and Special Education, 18,* 270–284, 306.

Thousand, J.S., Villa, R.A., & Nevin, A.I. (1994). *Creativity and collaborative learning: A practical guide to empowering students and teachers.* Baltimore: Paul H. Brookes Publishing Co.

Trent, S.C. (1998). False starts and other dilemmas of a secondary general education collaborative teacher: A case study. *Journal of Learning Disabilities, 31*(5), 503–513.

3

Managing the
Changes of Becoming Inclusive

Glenda Myree Brown
Jan Kennedy

> *"I guess the more inclusive we become, the more exclusive we real-*
> *ize we still are, in spite of all our efforts."*   —*Jan Kennedy*

Inclusion means change and new responsibilities for school leaders, such as restructuring so that the needs of all students are met. And, as Villa and Thousand stated, "When change is on the doorstep, some people (teachers, administrators, and students alike) will feel compelled to dig in their heels and resist, at least initially" (1995, p. 56). How willing are people to go the extra mile it takes to make inclusion work in high schools? How equipped are principals and teacher leaders to guide and assist a staff in creating and sustaining an inclusive school community?

In this chapter, we explore the changes that may occur when a high school becomes inclusive. First, we discuss the importance of the transformational leadership role of the principal in creating an inclusive high school community. Next, we discuss the need for structural and cultural change within high schools for successful implementation of inclusion and how change can be managed using Fullan's (1991) model for change.

The concept of inclusion, however, is not static. Inclusion must evolve to effectively meet the needs of an increasingly diverse student population (Thousand, Rosenberg, Bishop, & Villa, 1997). Lipsky and Gartner agreed, suggesting that inclusive education is "the seedbed in which we learn to nurture and live in a democratic society" (1997, p. 258) and that adolescents need high school experiences with others that reflect a range of abilities, ethnic groups, cultures, languages, economic levels, and ages. To conclude the chapter, we discuss the evolving concept of inclusion. After reading this chapter, you will be able to answer the following questions:

- What kinds of leadership styles support change to a more inclusive environment?
- What structural and cultural changes must occur as high schools become more inclusive?
- How can change be managed?
- How does inclusion continue to evolve in a high school?

LEADERSHIP STYLES AND CHANGE

Principals have traditionally run their schools as bureaucracies, emphasizing authority and accountability. In this "technical leadership" (Deal & Peterson, 1994), the principal is the planner, resource distributor, coordinator, supervisor, disseminator of information, and analyst. The principal determines the best course of action and then, as the formal leader, uses authority to carry it out. Liontis (1992) suggested that in this model the leader knows best, and he or she closely monitors teachers' work. Poplin (1992), however, argued that great administrators do not always make great classrooms leaders and argued that principals should become "the servant of collective vision" and "editors, cheerleaders, problem solvers, and resource finders." Poplin contended that hierarchical management of schools has outlived its usefulness. Transformational leadership has been suggested as a way to collaboratively empower the entire school community to become energized and focused, making teaching and learning transformative for everyone (Sagor, 1992).

A transformational principal pursues three fundamental goals (Leithwood, 1992). First, the transformational principal helps teachers develop and maintain collaborative, professional school cultures. Teachers talk, observe, critique, and plan. Teachers' isolation is reduced, leadership is shared, and there is active communication of the school's beliefs. The second goal is that teachers internalize professional growth. Through their commitment to school mission, teachers become participants in school improvement. The final goal of transformational leadership is to help teachers solve problems more effectively. Transformational principals believe that their teachers as a group can design better solutions than the principal could alone.

Deal and Peterson (1994) suggested that transformational leaders rely on persuasion, idealism, and intellectual excitement. They foster group goals, convey high performance expectations, create intellectual excitement, and model these things in themselves (Leithwood, 1993). Leithwood cautioned, however, that transformational strategies require highly developed intellectual skills.

STRUCTURAL AND CULTURAL CHANGES

Principals and teachers in high schools can generally agree with inclusion as a philosophy but may have problems figuring out how to make it work so that everyone benefits. Regardless of how much they may be willing to include all students, adjust their attitudes, or change their instructional approaches, strategies, and techniques to meet the needs of all students, principals and teachers inevitably come up against structural barriers that make implementation difficult. Sergiovanni and Starratt (1998) recognized the influence and power that traditional high school structures have on maintaining the status quo and their ability to act as barriers to an innovation such as inclusion. They suggested that standard operating procedures in schools, like most institutions, tend to take on a life of their own. Because of this, principals and teachers may lose sight of the big picture and the purposes behind the procedures and allow means to become ends. Procedures then begin to define not only the way things have been but also the way they are supposed to be. Values such as uniformity, predictability, efficiency, obedience, and conformity can tend to override other values such as freedom of conscience, creativity, diversity, inventiveness, risk taking, and individuality. The institutional environment becomes inimical to human life.

The way a traditional high school works is an example of how procedures and structures can dominate the school instead of teachers' and students' needs dominating. The 50-minute period or bell, long sacrosanct in high schools, challenges students who have to adjust to seven transitions a day and teachers who are trying to use universal design and cooperative groups in too short of a time period. Tracking students as advanced placement, college preparatory, general education, remedial education, and special education can severely delimit students' interaction across their group; they may, in fact, attend all 4 years with the same 40 people in their classes. After-school extracurricular activities prevent students without transportation from participating. The emphasis on class rank and grade point average can lead to a culture of competition rather than support. These structures are inconsistent with meeting each student's needs but often are held as unchangeable. Rather than ask, "Why do we have 50-minute instructional periods?" teachers say, "I can't include that student because I have only 50 minutes."

Sergiovanni described school culture as "values, symbols, beliefs, and shared meaning of parents, students, teachers, and others conceived as a group or community. Culture governs what is of worth for this group and how members should think, feel, and behave" (1996, p. 89). Inclusive high schools require principals and teachers who can effectively lead the way in making the necessary cultural changes. Villa and Thousand (1995) suggested a new culture must replace the old one to implement a new vision of schooling.

Addressing the philosophical change toward inclusion requires that school leaders guide staff, students, and parents in creating a new and different type of high school culture. This new culture provides students with and without disabilities an equal and optimal educational opportunity. This change is a function of committed people and shared decision making (Fullan, 1991;

Sarason, 1990). Fullan (1991) found that the level and degree of successful educational change relates to the extent to which teachers interact with one another. He maintained that change is a process that requires teachers to reach new understandings about their work, its purpose, how to accomplish it, and how it connects with others. This is a challenge for teachers in high schools who may be accustomed to working alone or within their specific department, but it is exactly the type of cultural change necessary to support learning and living in inclusive high school communities. Yet, Meyen, Vergason, and Whelan (1993) noted that it is not clear whether the difficulty of implementing inclusion at the high school level is a consequence of the way high schools are organized or due to a lack of attention by school leadership.

MANAGING THE CHANGE OF INCLUSION

Facilitating change is a systemic process (Saxl, Miles, & Lieberman, 1990). Because inclusion means change, we use a model offered by Fullan (1991) to understand how change can occur. Fullan offered four broad phases of change:

1. *Initiation:* The process that leads up to and includes a decision to adopt or proceed with a change. Inclusion should be viewed as feasible during this phase.
2. *Implementation:* The first attempt of putting an idea or reform into practice. Successful implementation is critical because it will have a direct impact on the outcomes for all students in an inclusive school community.
3. *Continuation:* An extension of the implementation phase in that the new program is sustained beyond the first year or two or whatever time frame is chosen. Continuation occurs as the culture of the school changes or shifts to support and embrace the concept of an inclusive community so that the staff begins to unconsciously use it to describe who they are as a school.
4. *Outcomes:* Various results, including the degree of school improvement in relation to given criteria. Fullan (1991) explained that change is not linear but a process in which events at one phase can feed back to alter decisions made at previous stages, which then proceed to work their way through in a continuous interactive way.

Leadership strategies are needed as principals and teacher leaders go through the process of getting people to buy into the vision of an inclusive high school community. Sergiovanni (1996) identified four leadership approaches or strategies: 1) bartering, 2) building, 3) bonding, and 4) binding. A definition of each approach in the context of creating inclusive school communities is provided in Table 3.1.

Bartering, building, bonding, and binding are utilized depending on the school's structures and culture in terms of its willingness to create an inclusive school community. Some of the strategies are best used early on, and others are best used later. At some point, more than one strategy may have to be utilized at the same time. The emphasis is not on which leadership strategy is best but rather on which of the strategies is more logical to use based on where the school is in the inclusion and change process.

We use Purcell Marian High School as an example of the change process. Before the Education for All Handicapped Children Act of 1975 (PL 94-142), students with learning disabilities were unidentified, unrecognized, and included full time in general education classrooms. Teachers realized that they were not effectively meeting the needs of some students who needed extra classroom support or even a different type of instructional approach. The learning disabilities program was introduced as a way to support these students. Students with learning disabilities and related programming have become an integral part of the school culture. As one teacher stated "LD [learning disabilities] has always been with us. We just move right along, and most of the time you're not even aware of the fact that this is a student with learning disabilities unless something sort of calls it to your attention. Then, once you are aware of it, you tend to make preparations in accordance for that particular student."

Table 3.1.   Leadership strategies

Bartering	Principals and teachers strike a bargain in which the principal or teacher leader gives to the staff something they want in exchange for their effort toward building an inclusive school community. The emphasis in bartering is on trading wants and needs for cooperation and compliance.
Building	Principals provide the climate and interpersonal support necessary for teachers to feel competent in inclusive classrooms. The emphasis in building is less on trading and more on providing the conditions that enable teachers to experience psychological fulfillment.
Bonding	Principals and teachers develop a set of shared values about the relationships they want to share and the ideas that tie into what they want to create in an inclusive school community. Therefore, together they can become a community of learners and leaders—a community of colleagues.
Binding	Principals and teachers commit themselves to a set of shared values and ideas that ties them together as a "we." The emphasis in binding is on developing common commitments and conceptions about purposes, teaching and learning, and the relationships that bring people together as a community of mind. Binding is recommended as a means to establish the moral authority that enables people to become self-managing.

Initiation

Havelock suggested that change "originates in a 'concern' or a feeling by some-one that something is wrong and that someone should do something about it" (1995, p. 14). When the present principal of Purcell Marian High School took the position in 1992, she realized that the school was failing to serve a large group of students. It was at this point that the principal began to seek assistance from key people within the school. She enlisted the support and assistance of one of the teachers who worked in the program for students with learning disabilities and made her director of a program for students with developmental disabilities. They then began planning how they would initiate and implement the program for students with developmental disabilities. Part of this planning required dealing with the issues of resources, barriers, and structures that could hinder or support later implementation efforts.

At the initiation stage, the principal began to examine the capacity of the school to meet the needs of students with developmental disabilities. Fullan (1991) argued that this can best be accomplished by addressing the issues' relevance, readiness, and reliability during the initiation stage of change. The principal indicated that before and during initiation she and the new director of the program read and attended workshops and conferences related to inclusive practices so that they would have information and resources to share with and empower the staff.

Although the principal had worked many years in various capacities, she was, as a new principal, quiet during her first year and listened to and objectively observed the school culture (Kotter, 1996; Sergiovanni, 1996). Activities centered around favorably influencing the mindset of the staff toward developing a more inclusive school culture. She began initiation by selling the idea or vision of inclusion of students with developmental disabilities to the faculty. Bartering occurred throughout each stage but most heavily during initiation and implementation. She kept conversations going among and with various staff members regarding the richness of the diversity of the school and how they were all privileged to be a part of a diverse school. Once the teachers and staff were comfortable with her as the principal and had focused on who they were and where they were headed as a school, she began to share her evolving inclusive vision for the school. Timing was important. As Bennis and Nanus stated, "An effective vision is right for the times, right for the organization, and right for the people who are working in it" (1985, p. 107).

In the statements that follow, the principal described how she worked during the initiation stage to bind the faculty together by using figurative language to sell the vision of what was unique about their school—its diversity—to the staff to make them feel good about the situation they were in and to get them moving toward more inclusive efforts (Sergiovanni, 1996):

> Here we use the words "this is holy ground and it's really special to be here." It's not easy to work here but it's very special to be here, and I think that you have

to have people who feel very good about the situation that they're in rather than feeling as if other people have it better. So, if they're looking at other schools and seeing wonderful facilities and teachers with only college prep, so you have to sell what you have. Once teachers and staff feel very good about what they're doing and the situation they're in, then it's easier to say, "Okay now, let's make it even better. We have this wonderful diversity, and yet we could be so much more." We can grow this and make it better. But the first role—absolutely—for anyone who comes into a new situation is: You cannot go in like a steam roller. You can do that later, but not the first year. You really have to let them teach you who they are and about the culture because it's valuable to them. Whatever is there, whatever you may think of, it's valuable to them or it wouldn't be there. So you have to learn and see what you can appreciate and what's unique there.

To create a new culture or a new system of operation, we have to struggle with the loss of the old (Kotter, 1996; Schein, 1999). This means that the principal had to create and articulate new shared values, while at the same time celebrating the old values so that the faculty could gradually let them go and put their energies into implementation of inclusion of students with developmental disabilities.

Yukl explained that "the vision should convey an intuitive appealing picture of what the organization can be in the future. The core of the vision is the mission statement" (1994, p. 362). The principal's goal was to have everyone buy into and focus on the inclusive vision. She knew the importance at this point in initiation to bond the faculty around a common ethos, vision, or mission that would serve to bind and inspire them during the challenging times of implementation. Key to this goal was the development of the mission statement.

Writing the mission statement was a team effort. The principal enlisted the school counselor as head of the mission statement committee, which had many discussions as to who they were and their mission. Their job was to write a draft and bring it to the group for discussion. The principal shared what happened:

> The committee met at her [the counselor's] house one evening, and I think it went 6 or 7 hours over dinner. They all came back and said that it was a spiritual experience for them to talk about what this place meant to them and what they saw as its mission in this area. . . . I think we may have made one grammatical change to the statement that came out of that meeting. So that's how it happened and it has to be included in the description of who we are. I really do believe that this is holy ground and whatever decisions that are made here must be responsive to our mission. There was a chairman, the very first chairman of our board who said to us, "As long as you continue to do the right thing the school will be fine." And that really is how we operate.

Janney, Snell, Beers, and Raynes (1995) used the phrase "start small and build" to create opportunities for teachers to see other teachers having success with the change of inclusion. Teachers are more likely to believe their peers' judgments of the worth of an innovation than those of an administrator or outside consultant (Huberman & Miles, 1984). With this in mind, and a mission statement that celebrated inclusion and diversity among staff members, the principal was ready to begin implementation of the inclusion of students with developmental disabilities on a small scale by starting a pilot program with a few carefully selected teachers (Havelock, 1995; Louis & Miles, 1990).

Implementation

Havelock (1995) contended that the principal, as the agent of change, must be able to relate to the key people on the faculty and must have as wide a network of relationships with others in order to buy in to the idea and have successful implementation. When speaking of relationships and the key people she needed for implementation of the initial pilot, the principal said,

> As an administrator, you have to be able to identify the people that you have to sell. You're not going to sell everybody so you have to identify the key people, and they're not always department chairs. They are not always the obvious people. You have to look at the staff and figure out who do I really need as allies? Who do I need to focus on to affect any kind of paradigm shifts? Who has their own constituency? You have to establish those relationships with the key people in your community. You don't know who they are from looking at a handbook. You only know that after you live with them for a little while.

As part of evolutionary planning (Louis & Miles, 1990), the principal put together a pilot program with key people. She explained that some teachers would have to be involved the first year. Although the pilot program was carried out by a few key teachers, all teachers were aware of the fact that eventually they would all be called on to teach students with developmental disabilities. When asked how the program was received by the faculty as a whole, the principal stated that it was received with "great trepidation." Even though the program for students with learning disabilities had been institutionalized for many years and faculty members were comfortable, many teachers expressed concern at hearing that students with developmental disabilities would now be joining their fold. The faculty and staff were philosophically open to broadening the definition of inclusion to mean students with developmental disabilities. However, there was fear and concern about their new roles and responsibilities and their ability to be effective. The academic dean reflected on the reactions of staff when the principal introduced the program for students with developmental disabilities:

> I think everybody was welcoming and excited to have it. Some people were fearful, which I think is a fair thing to feel. Some people felt like, well what am I supposed to do with the students in the wheelchairs in my classrooms? Or is it fair that this person will have a longer amount of time to take a test? Or is it fair that I only ask this person 5 questions and everybody else has to answer 25? You know, is that really a true assessment? Another big issue for me in this position

has been with students who have developmental or learning disabilities making honor roll status or if class rank is an issue. Well how can that person be number 55 when you've got all these college prep students after them who are 56, 57. So, yes, [there were] some real concerns and some genuine concerns.

A teacher echoed the comments of the dean and voiced his initial concerns and questions:

What do I do if they have Down syndrome or if they have a brain injury and you're not sure how they're going to react? What are they going to get out of my classroom? As a teacher I cannot teach the same to them as I do to someone else. How is that going to affect my instruction?

Another math teacher shared:

I was very skeptical when the program started. Being a math teacher, and I was an upper-level math teacher, I was wondering, well how are we going to mainstream these kids? Now are we going to put them in a place where they can't succeed? Are we going to put them in a place where I have to dilute what I figure is a pretty core class? Do I have to dilute that and bring them up or is it going to be pretty competitive?

Implementation may be the point of greatest resistance in the change process because the implications of the change become apparent at this point, and such feelings as fear of failure and of loss of previous security become real and threatening (Havelock, 1995). Louis and Miles (1990) agreed that implementation comes with many problems and challenges, and they stressed the importance of the principal's coping with those challenges during implementation by supplying the leadership with resources needed to make implementation successful. The principal must keep in mind that teachers need more support when the actual implementation begins, and principals have to be prepared to offer this extra support (Havelock, 1995). The principal put the focus of the change strategies on the teachers. Janney et al. (1995) noted that teachers need for their fears and their opinions to be respected and their work valued when trying something new or innovative such as full inclusion. In addition, they argued that during implementation the principal or teacher leader also must focus on building a collaborative culture in the school and assisting teachers to develop the skills required for collaborative service delivery. It was during implementation of the pilot program that the principal began to barter, build, bond, and bind the faculty in earnest.

During the second year of implementation, after a successful pilot program, the principal brought in more teachers and expanded the program schoolwide. At this point in implementation, the teachers needed the increased emotional and informational support of the principal, and the principal needed more buy-in to the program and competency from the teachers. To get the desired results, the principal began bartering in earnest with the staff. This bartering took the form of money, food, trips, and recognition. She explained her methods:

> Money, food, and trips! I really don't have the resources to give bonuses. But I have put in place a tuition reimbursement program. If I ask someone to attend a specific workshop, I try to make it very attractive. We fund seminars in San Francisco, New Orleans, New York, or Chicago, and say, "You know, you have done such a good job with this, I'd like you to go to this seminar or this workshop. It's Thursday and Friday, but we can get a better airfare if you stay the weekend." People appreciate that. They appreciate simple recognition.

The principal also offered a type of reward or recognition called "Jan Bucks." Everyone on the staff can nominate people for Jan Bucks by putting the nominations in the principal's mailbox and indicating what outstanding effort that person put forth to make inclusion of the students with developmental disabilities work. The principal then issues them Jan Bucks. The principal indicated that she also keeps that list of names as an indicator for her as to who is doing the work and putting forth the effort.

When asked what other kinds of things she did to calm the initial fears and anxieties of the faculty once the program went schoolwide, the principal replied,

> Talk to them, talk to them, talk to them. Hold their hand and give them very concrete examples. We did some in-servicing. [The director of the program] is just a tireless worker and she demonstrated some simple modifications and accommodations. She would take a simple English test and say, "Okay now this is how you would give this test to this student. If you want them to fill in a blank, that's okay, just give them a little word bank. Don't make it true or false, make it yes or no." Provide the little tricks. When they have the tools then they can do the job. They just needed the tool box. So it really only took 2 years to get virtually everyone on board.

Over the past 8 years, through implementation and continuation, the program became institutionalized. The principal has supported the program by increasingly broadening the curriculum to include more students socially and academically. Block scheduling provided more time and better support of teachers' efforts in inclusive classrooms. She pushed forward to make the school more inclusive by examining the layout and structure of the curriculum and determining how well it served or included all students. She examined the curriculum to determine how she could change or alter it to be more inclusive and meet the academic and social needs of the total student population. The principal explained, "As an educational leader I always look at the curriculum and say, 'What's missing here? What ought to be here first of all to help the kids who are already here but also to enable us to serve more kids.'"

Throughout implementation, the principal continued to lead and build support for teachers and their inclusive efforts by dismantling other structures and barriers that actually hindered the inclusion of some students. She decided that they needed to make changes in how she made creative use of time and space to restructure the school day. By using a block schedule and utilizing space more creatively, additional options in the curriculum were developed.

The principal described coping and the challenges and problems that come with implementation (Louis & Miles, 1990). Her comments show evidence of her continuous building of structural support for teachers and students so that inclusion efforts were more effective:

> There are all kinds of excuses, you know. "We can't do dance because we don't have time to do that," or "There's nowhere in the curriculum for that, there's nowhere in the school day," and "We can't do these kinds of art classes because we have no room." Time and space become wonderful barriers for people who don't want to change, so you have to adjust them and say, "Look, this is how it can be done. We can redo the whole day and look at what opens up! We can change this room into this and look at the possibilities." We changed the kitchen into an art room. You can do all kinds of things. It's not always easy to do, but it is possible.

In addition, the principal had to deal with "loyal opposition" during implementation. She stated that it is equally important to identify teachers who are not supportive of the change and establish a respectful, friendly relationship. Other faculty members must be comfortable with the relationship. In addition, it's important to recognize influential teachers and spend time with them.

Louis and Miles (1990) found in their study of urban high schools that when it comes to implementation, sharing power is crucial. Hall and Hord (1987) agreed and suggested that the principal create and share leadership with a change-facilitating team. They argued that such a team is the key to successful school improvement. The lead change facilitator would be the principal with three or four other change facilitators on the team. The second change facilitator could be an assistant principal, department chair, or resource teacher. They also found that a third level of change facilitator existed and that they were usually teachers who did not have formal roles and titles but whose roles were seen as crucial by their peers.

Sergiovanni (1996), in describing the roles of members of the change team, noted that these facilitators served as agents of change by modeling the use of new practices, disseminating information to other teachers, cheerleading, and providing support. The principals who were most effective in implementing change were team oriented, working closely with these other levels of change facilitators. Often, structures were built that allowed them to work together as a change facilitator team.

The principal shared leadership responsibilities with the teacher who had agreed to help spearhead the program. The principal formed a special education support team that consisted of the director and four other special educators. Together they made up the special education support team whose purpose was to support inclusive efforts in the classroom by encouraging collaboration, consultation, sharing, modeling, and generally building a sense of collegiality among the staff regarding inclusion. The principal, in making the department chair the director of the program, empowered her to lead others on the staff in making the program work.

In sharing leadership, the principal utilized both bonding and binding with the support team as they built an inclusive school community together (Sergiovanni, 1996). This resulted in their feeling inspired and being empowered. As soon as the support team was in place, they began working with the teachers and offering support through modeling, consultations, workshops, in-services, conferences, and so forth. For example, at the beginning of the school year the team does in-services and gives the biographies and profiles of students to the teachers, answers questions, and models interactions.

The program has been strongly promoted and fully supported for almost 8 years by the principal, who has been instrumental in finding ways to break down barriers and create new structures that support inclusive schooling. The principal and the support team have offered faculty members informational support through workshops, in-services, retreats, collaborative consultations, and so forth (Thousand et al., 1997). This is intended to give them the "tool kit" and prepare them to be effective teachers in inclusive classrooms.

THE EVOLUTION AND BROADENING
OF INCLUSION: DOING AWAY WITH DUAL SYSTEMS

Jorgensen (1998) suggested that inclusion should not be based solely on the benefits for students with disabilities. Inclusive education can be viewed as exclusive when seen only in the context of special education. Schools should prepare to address the many domains of diversity that will be present in the general education classroom. Shapiro-Barnard stated that "inclusion makes sense for students with and without disabilities, for entire school communities, and the future of public education" (1998, p. 3).

In an attempt to provide an optimal educational opportunity for all students, education is slowly moving away from its exclusive paradigm and moving toward inclusive schools that operate within a culture that provides students with and without disabilities an equal opportunity to have their educational needs met within the mainstream of general education. High schools that build inclusive communities in which the concept of inclusion continues to evolve and grow must have a school culture in which diversity is valued (Jorgensen, 1998). "The goal is that all students benefit from learning together with students who are different from themselves including those from different races, cultures, genders, talents, temperaments, and experiences" (Jorgensen, 1998, p. 9). The culture of the school has to become one of collaboration and collegiality as people gain skills and competencies through sharing ideas, expertise, challenges, resources, and common ideals and visions. In an inclusive school community all students are valued, supported, and learn together in general education classes (Sapon-Shevin, 1992). Inclusion moves beyond the context of special education to a school in which all students are valued members (Capper & Keyes, 1999; Sergiovanni, 1996).

The definition of inclusion has moved out of the context of special education and into the realm of educating all students. Before 1978, all students were served within general education. Faculty were concerned because they did not feel that they were able to effectively meet the needs of students who varied from their peers. A veteran teacher reflected, "When I first came here there were a lot of kids who I think the old timers are familiar with—the kid in the classroom who wasn't very smart and who usually sat in the back. As long as he was quiet, he was passed through. I just felt, as I was teaching, that those kind of kids really needed help because life wasn't going to let them sit in the back. So I decided to start a program with kids who some of the teachers thought just couldn't handle too much."

The program for students with learning disabilities began just prior to Purcell Marian's merging with another high school and emerged as a part of the culture of the blended school. Initially, students with learning disabilities received services in special classes with special education teachers and were mainstreamed as much as possible into general education classes. The program evolved and has become so institutionalized within the school that it is a part of the main flow of the school. The program has evolved into choices available to students with learning disabilities, including:

- Full participation in general education classes
- Full participation with support from tutors or specialists
- Participation in specific classes on a full-time or part-time basis
- Participation in the special studies program that emphasizes college preparation for juniors and seniors
- Participation in the occupational work experience program
- Participation in academic programs and vocational training at the appropriate vocational school
- Participation in regional vocational programs

In 1991, under the leadership of the present principal, the school became even more inclusive as the program for students with developmental disabilities was designed to meet the students' academic, social, and transition needs. As the program was being implemented, the definition of *inclusion* began to evolve to mean not just students with disabilities but to mean meeting the varied needs of everyone in the diverse student population. The principal and staff became sensitive to the fact that they were excluding some students without meaning to just by the way the school day was structured. Once the faculty became sensitive to issues such as not having any money for fees or extracurricular activities, not having a car, the need to take public transportation and perhaps transfer buses two or three times, they looked at how practice times, extracurricular activities, and other activities were scheduled. Traditional extracurricular classes (e.g., the school newspaper, yearbook, drama) were scheduled during the school day due to transportation issues for students who would be unable to gain access to those activities outside of the school day.

The evolution of inclusion continues. As a new school year approaches, the program for students with developmental disabilities and the program for students with learning disabilities are being dismantled. Support will now take place within a broader arena under a new structure called the *student support services team,* which offers support to all students who need it. The special education teachers will teach remedial classes. These classes will be open to any student in the building who needs them. A proactive multidisciplinary intervention team will be initiated to support students with and without identified disabilities. The principal indicated that these changes were all made to better reflect where Purcell Marian High School is as a school in terms of its vision of inclusive education for all. The director of the program for students with developmental disabilities pointed out, "We wanted to get away from that term *special education* because there are some students without a documented disability that need just as much support. Education should not be special any more than it should be for everybody. It should be education first."

In this light, inclusion can be seen as a vision or an ideal state toward which schools will continuously strive as the definition of inclusion expands. The expanding vision of inclusion will continue to evolve over time as the principal and staff persist in their attempt to serve the increasingly diverse needs of the student population. As Jorgensen stated, "Absolutely every student regardless of label, color, or status should be included" (1998, p. xiv). At Purcell Marian High School, the premise is that everyone should be included with needed support rather than from the view that they must first prove that they can make it and learn in a general education classroom. Part of inclusion is ensuring that all students have optimal opportunities to be included and participate in the mainstream of high school life. The school prides itself on being real world partly because of its inclusion of students with disabilities but also because of its cultural and economic diversity. The principal indicated that she perceives inclusion to be evolving to include everyone:

> One of the things that has been very helpful to this school since the merger is that its enrollment has consistently mirrored the city racially, economically, culturally, and ability wise. We think that maintaining that is really important in being an inclusive school. We try to maintain that balance by not excluding anyone and by continuing to remain attractive to all of those groups. That is a tough thing to do, but we think that is the secret.

As the school's concept of inclusion comes out of the special education box, teachers are realizing that there are many dimensions of diversity that are so complex that trying to meet the needs of all students is an never-ending process. Each time they feel they have arrived at their goal in terms of inclusion, they realize that they are really not there and that there are more needs to be met, more changes to be made, and more work to do. The school is moving toward a form of inclusion in which there is no need for words like *inclusion* or *included students* because the focus of the school is on meeting and supporting the needs of all of its students within the mainstream of education. As the principal stated, "That is a tough thing to do." Teachers do not speak of included students in inclusive classrooms but rather of "students who are in classrooms." Inclusion is no longer a destination but rather a way of thinking, doing, and being. As one teacher explained, even though there may be some fear as the principal leads them down the never-ending path of inclusion, having the right kind of leadership makes everything work out:

> There was a bit of panic there because, you know, with change there is always that small bit of panic. But it's working out well. We've got the right people. We had the right people in place to spearhead everything. We have an ambitious leader, and she has the right people to get it rolling. Planning is everything.

Thousand and colleagues concurred with the director's statement and noted that "the goal is to erase the negative special education labels placed on students and their teachers as well as to change the paradigm that only 'specialist' can work with students with exceptional labels" (1997, p. 274). Inclusion is becoming a state of mind, an ideal for which to strive.

SUMMARY POINTS

- Unlike hierarchical leadership, transformation strategies rely on persuasion, idealism, and intellectual excitement to motivate teachers through values, symbols, and shared vision.
- Traditional high school structures and procedures must be addressed when evolving toward inclusion.
- Facilitating change is a systematic process and includes initiation, implementation, continuation, and outcomes.
- Transformational leaders utilize bartering, building, bonding, and binding.
- Inclusion is not a static concept but instead continues to evolve.

REFERENCES

Bennis, W.G., & Nanus, B. (1985). *Leaders: The strategies for taking charge*. New York: HarperCollins.

Capper, C., & Keyes, M. (1999). Spirit centered leadership within inclusive schools. *TASH Newsletter, 12*(1), 25–26.

Deal, T.E., & Peterson, K.D. (1994). *The leadership paradox: Balancing logic and artistry in schools*. San Francisco: Jossey-Bass.

Education for All Handicapped Children Act of 1975, PL 94-142, 20 U.S.C. §§ 1400 *et seq.*

Fullan, M.G. (1991). *The new meaning of educational change* (2nd ed.). New York: Teachers College Press.

Hall, G.E., & Hord, S.M. (1987). *Change in schools: Facilitating the process.* Albany: State University of New York Press.

Havelock, R.G. (1995). *The change agent's guide* (2nd ed.). Englewood Cliffs, NJ: Educational Technology Publications.

Huberman, A.M., & Miles, M.B. (1984). Rethinking the quest for school improvement: Some findings from the DESSI Study. *Teachers College Record, 86*(1), 34–54.

Janney, R.E., Snell, M.E., Beers, M.K., & Raynes, M. (1995). Integrating students with moderate and severe disabilities: Classroom teachers' beliefs and attitudes about implementing an educational change. *Educational Administration Quarterly, 31*(1), 86–114.

Jorgensen. C.M. (Ed.). (1998). *Restructuring high schools for all students: Taking inclusion to the next level.* Baltimore: Paul H. Brookes Publishing Co.

Kotter, J.P. (1996). *Leading change.* Boston: Harvard Business School Press.

Leithwood, K.A. (1992). The move toward transformational leadership. *Educational Leadership, 49*(5), 8–12.

Leithwood, K.A. (1993, October). *Contributions of transformational leadership to school restructuring.* Houston, Texas: Paper presented at the annual meeting of the University Council for Educational Administration. (ERIC No. ED 367061)

Liontis, L.B. (1992). *Transformational leadership.* Eugene, OR: Clearinghouse on Educational Management. (ERIC No. ED 347636)

Lipsky, D.K., & Gartner, A. (1997). *Inclusion and school reform: Transforming America's classrooms.* Baltimore: Paul H. Brookes Publishing Co.

Louis, K.S., & Miles, M.B. (1990). *Improving the urban high school: What works and why.* New York: Teachers College Press.

Meyen, E.L., Vergason, G.A., & Whelan, R.J. (1993). *Challenges facing special education.* Denver: Love.

Poplin, M.S. (1992). The leader's new role: Looking to the growth of teachers. *Educational Leadership, 49*(5), 10–11.

Sagor, R.D. (1992). Three principals who make a difference. *Educational Leadership, 49*(5), 13–18.

Sapon-Shevin, M. (1992). *Celebrating diversity, creating community: Curriculum that honors and builds on differences.* Baltimore: Paul H. Brookes Publishing Co.

Sarason, S.B. (1990). *The predictable failure of educational reform: Can we change course before it's too late?* San Francisco: Jossey-Bass.

Saxl, E., Miles, M., & Lieberman, A. (1990). *Assisting change in education: A training program for school improvement facilitators. Trainer's manual.* Alexandria, VA: Association for Supervision and Curriculum Development.

Schein, E.H. (1999). *The corporate culture survival guide: Sense and nonsense about culture change.* San Francisco: Jossey-Bass.

Sergiovanni, T.J. (1996). *Leadership for the schoolhouse: How is it different? Why is it important?* San Francisco: Jossey-Bass.

Sergiovanni, T.J., & Starratt, R.J. (1998). *Supervision: A redefinition* (6th ed.). New York: McGraw-Hill.

Thousand, J.S., Rosenberg, R.L., Bishop, K.D., & Villa, R.A. (1997). The evolution of secondary inclusion. *Remedial and Special Education, 18*(5), 270–284.

Villa, R.A., & Thousand J.S. (Eds.). (1995). *Creating an inclusive school.* Alexandria, VA: Association for Supervision and Curriculum Development.

Yukl, G. (1994). *Managerial leadership and the effective principal.* New York: National Conference on the Principalship, National Institute of Education.

4

Who Are the Students in an Inclusive High School?

Anne M. Bauer
Glenda Myree Brown

Working with adolescents often is a challenge. As teenagers confront the series of events that compose "growing up," their pain, anger, joy, and fear often are thrust upon the adults around them. In this chapter, we explore issues confronting all adolescents, with additional information about students with disabilities, students considered at risk, and students representing diverse cultural, ethnic, or linguistic groups. After reading this chapter, you will

- Recognize the themes that occur in adolescent development
- Describe which students are identified as having disabilities
- Describe students who are at risk
- Recognize issues related to ethnic, cultural, and linguistic diversity

THEMES THAT OCCUR IN ADOLESCENT DEVELOPMENT

Adolescence did not really exist until almost the 20th century. As the western world became more technologically sophisticated, there was a need for a literate, educated population. Free public schooling spread as social reforms began to protect children and young adolescents from being sent to war or from working long hours in factories. Adolescence continues to extend beyond the teenage years as most adolescents now finish high school and the majority attend college or other postsecondary education (Miller, 1989).

Adolescence is a difficult time for most young people and their families. Adolescents are confronted with several tasks, each of which involves problem solving and personal decision making. Adolescents must develop a sense of *identity*—a self-concept of a unique combination of values, attitudes, beliefs, and behaviors—and interpersonal skills. They must adjust to a changing body. As they develop abstract thought, they must formulate a value system and set goals for their future achievement. Perhaps most difficult is the need to establish a new relationship with their family that addresses a growing need for autonomy and lessening emotional dependence.

There are several themes that help us understand adolescents: 1) Adolescence is part of a developmental process, 2) adolescence is a time of continuity as well as change, 3) adolescents demonstrate new ways of thinking and learning, and 4) adolescents are trying to figure out who they are and where they fit in.

Adolescence Is Part of a Developmental Process

Some aspects of adolescence are determined by biochemical processes common to all human beings. This physical maturation, however, does not automatically produce social or emotional maturation (Wolman, 1998).

In terms of physical development, one of the most visible signs of the beginning of adolescence is a growth spurt. Girls usually begin this spurt when they are 10 or 11 years old, and growth reaches its peak around 12 or 13 years of age. When girls are around 14, their growth slows substantially. In boys, the growth spurt usually begins at about 12 or 13 years of age, and reaches its peak at about 15 or 16 years of age. The growth rates for the head, limbs, and trunk vary and apparently are not coordinated at all. For example, on average, the head of a 16-year-old boy may have reached its adult size, but the upper and lower limbs may continue to grow. In comparing boys and girls, adolescent boys are physically stronger than girls, and the difference in strength increases with age. Girls, maturing faster than boys, temporarily have an edge over boys in motor coordination. However, by the end of the teenage years, boys' motor coordination is superior to that of girls (Wolman, 1998).

Boys and girls who physically mature early have some advantages in interaction with their peers. Late-maturing boys are shorter than their peers and are derided. Being short, beardless, and childlike in appearance may adversely affect a boy's self-esteem and self-confidence. Tall boys who grow facial hair early may act in a more self-confident manner (Siegel, 1982). In some instances, though, slow maturation may reduce the gap between physical and mental growth, and adolescents who physically mature later than their peers may have better perceptual and motor skills (Petersen & Crockett, 1985). The implications of early maturation are less pronounced for girls, though at times early maturing girls who are taller than their peers are ridiculed and ostracized.

Adolescence Is a Time of Continuity as Well as Change

Even though adolescence is a time of rapid transformation, there also is continuity. Many of the problems the child encounters, such as identity and relationships with parents, are re-encountered as an adolescent. Even though marked changes in personality can and do occur, continuity, rather than discontinuity, is the general rule of development (Elkind, 1994). An easy-going child will probably become an easy-going adolescent, and a difficult child will probably become a difficult adolescent.

Adolescents Demonstrate New Ways of Thinking and Learning

In order to talk about the new ways adolescents can think and act, we need to revisit the work of Piaget (1970). Piaget asserted that knowledge is constructed by the activity of the child and that intellectual growth is a form of adaptation that, like biological growth, is fairly structured. Piaget maintained that the mental operations of a mature adult have their roots in the simple sensorimotor coordination of the developing infant. This highly active child, who begins with simple structures to make sense out of the world, continually assimilates new information into the structure, which then allows him or her to develop new ways to understand. Piaget identified stages of cognitive development, and each of these stages reflects a particular way of operating on information. Change occurs very slowly as children become more and more aware of inadequacies and inconsistencies in their own thought. This self-driven change often is apparent to teachers. For example, no matter how clearly you think you have presented some new information, it often is returned to you in a way you may not even recognize, complete with inaccurate quotations attributed to you. When this happens, you haven't matched the students' developmental level (Danner, 1989).

Inhelder and Piaget (1958) indicated that around the ages of 11–15 years, the adolescent becomes capable of "formal operations." In this stage, students use logical symbols, think in abstract terms, analyze theoretical concepts, and formulate hypotheses. By the age of 18, most adolescents are capable of intellectual analysis of social and moral problems (Feather, 1980). These intellectual changes allow adolescents to begin to understand social problems and partake in adult social relationships. Adolescents' demands for equal rights and independence and their criticism of the adult society, then, are not a matter of hormonal imbalance and emotional immaturity. Rather, the improvement in cognitive processes enables adolescents to analyze social roles within the family group and the society at large and critically examine the discrepancies between justice as professed and practiced (Lerner & Shea, 1982). Gardner (1983) suggested that the development of formal operations is like a giant cognitive wave that spontaneously spreads its way of knowing across all important domains of cognition.

Elkind (1994) described several implications of formal operations for adolescents. When they attain formal operations, adolescents can think in terms of possibilities, even when these are not in accord with the facts of the real world. They can engage in debate because they can anticipate their opponent's possible arguments and prepare to encounter them. In addition, adolescents can begin to "think about their thinking." Adolescents are able to deal with multiple dimensions at one time and keep many variables in mind simultaneously; because adolescents can think of so many possibilities at one time, they sometimes pick the inappropriate one. Adolescents are more capable of selective attention and can, for example, pay attention to their homework while there is background noise. They also can demonstrate divided attention in which they can listen to a lecture and take notes at the same time. Adolescents understand multiple causation and can use organizational strategies—setting their own priorities and identifying responsibilities.

Danner (1989) cautioned teachers who apply the Piagetian theory that in his zeal to counteract what he felt was simplistic quantitative models of development, Piaget emphasized qualitative differences between the thinking of younger and older children. In his writing, everyone was unambiguously in one stage or substage, and transitions between stages were rapid and complete. Among adolescents, a relatively rapid and universal shift in intellectual competence would surely make life easier. These developmental changes, however, are more gradual, uneven, and uncertain.

Even though adolescents are able to demonstrate new ways of thinking and learning, the early years of adolescence are frequently years of lowering of school grades and often unpredictable academic failure. The transition from grade school into junior high school often is associated with failure in school grades, truancy, and leaving school. These achievement problems may be related to a decline in intellectual interest and academic progress. Many adolescents lose faith in their intellectual abilities, and their academic motivation is reduced (Wolman, 1998).

Adolescents Are Trying to Figure Out Who They Are and Where They Fit In

During adolescence, students make the gradual transition from identification with parents to identification with peers. As members of a peer group, adolescents feel more self-confident, more courageous, and more outgoing. Although peer groups do not usually demand uniformity, they do require an unswerving loyalty and high degree of conformity with group manners and morals. Adolescents develop their self-concept by accepting and sharing the group's ends and means and identifying with the members as a whole. Peer groups take an active part in setting the rules for adolescent behavior (Wolman, 1998).

Elkind (1994) suggested that the adolescent struggle to find an identity is extremely complex in our society in which adult standards, values, and beliefs are so varied. Younger children are confronted with simple struggles for identity, whereas adults' standards are so clear. Rather than attaining identity achievement (a solid sense of identity), some adolescents experience identity "foreclosure" by deciding on an identity early in life and sticking with that decision, sometimes through convenience or pressure. This foreclosure, such as following in the family business, may shut off options for the adolescent. Elkind referred to another alternative to identity development as an *identity moratorium,* in which adolescents leave many identity options open for themselves well into college. They may have a high school identity and then re-enter a moratorium after leaving school and entering college.

Identity diffusion is another alternative to identity achievement that may be experienced by an adolescent. In identity diffusion, identity is not generally cohesive or consistent. The student's identity takes on whatever coloration is most suited to the particular circumstances in which he or she finds him- or herself. These students have no genuine identity of their own.

For young women, identity formation seems to follow a pattern of breaking relationships in order to establish relationships. For young men, identity formation seems to be a pattern of breaking rules in order to establish new rules (Elkind, 1994). The unique challenges to girls in identity development have been explored in a series of qualitative studies. Brown and Gilligan (1992) described that for adolescent girls, saying what they are feeling and thinking often means to risk, in the words of many girls, losing their relationships and finding themselves powerless and all alone. Girls who had been outspoken may become reluctant to say what they were feeling and thinking or to speak from their own experience about what they know. For girls, "being nice to everyone" is a seemingly safe way to navigate the relational waters. Strong voices and disagreements among girls seem to arouse discomfort.

At the elementary school level, gifted girls and boys report similar interests. By secondary school, however, gifted girls develop lower career aspirations than gifted boys (Kerr, 1985). Subtle teacher behaviors have been reported that may socialize gifted girls to lower expectations. For example, a study of science classes found that when teachers needed assistance in carrying out a demonstration, they selected boys to help 79% of the time (Tobin & Garnett, 1987). In addition, the "cultural underachievement" of women appears to be related to women's needs to balance professional interests and higher education while fulfilling traditional sex roles (Davis & Rimm, 1985).

In terms of fitting in, by early adolescence several factors change the way in which the adolescent interacts with both parents and peers. Adolescence presents a range of new social interaction situations and social roles: dating, working with others in a part-time job, or spending time with peers in the absence of adult supervision (De Armas & Kelly, 1989).

Feeling socially awkward is normal among virtually all teenagers (De Armas & Kelly, 1989). Self-reports of loneliness, social anxiety, and other interpersonal difficulties are common among younger and older adolescents. Although feelings of social awkwardness usually pass with experiences in new social roles for many teenagers, some adolescents have more persistent pat-

terns of social anxiety, isolation, and loneliness. Individuals with early life social interaction problems, especially isolation, are at risk for adjustment difficulties later in life. Adolescents who report that they are shy, lonely, or anxious
may lack the social skills needed to effectively and comfortably converse with
others. These adolescents also may be less skilled in the ability to generate solutions to interpersonal problems, conflicts, and dilemmas.

WHO ARE THE STUDENTS WITH DISABILITIES?

When we think of *disability*, we often picture students in wheelchairs, wearing
hearing aids, or with Down syndrome. In education, however, there is a difference between having a specific condition and being identified as having a
disability. There are two ways in education in which students can be identified as having a disability. The first, through the Individuals with Disabilities
Education Act (IDEA) of 1990 (PL 101-476) and its amendments of 1997 (PL
105-17), is specific to education and the provision of special education services.
The second, through the Rehabilitation Act of 1973 (PL 93-112), extends beyond education into the community and employment. Because students may
be identified as having disabilities under one of these laws and not under the
other, we address each of them in turn.

IDEA is the way in which most teachers, parents, and students think
about being identified as having a disability. The IDEA Amendments of '97
state that a student with a disability is a student

> with mental retardation, hearing impairments (including deafness), speech or
> language impairments, visual impairments (including blindness) . . . emotional
> disturbance, orthopedic impairments, autism, traumatic brain injury, other health
> impairments, or specific learning disabilities; and who, by reason thereof, needs
> special education and related services.

In other words, a student with a disability must be identified as having one of
the conditions described and require special education or other services (see
Table 4.1). If a student does not demonstrate one of the conditions described,
then he or she does not have a disability by this law. If a student does not need
special education or related services, then that individual is not identified as
having a disability.

If a student with a disability is one who requires special education or
other services, then those definitions also become important. According to
IDEA '97, special education is

> specially designed instruction, at no cost to parents, to meet the unique needs of
> a child with a disability, including instruction conducted in the classroom, in the
> home, in hospitals and institutions, and in other settings, and instruction in phys-
> ical education.

Related services include

> transportation, and such developmental, corrective, and other supportive services (including speech-language pathology and audiology services, psychological services, physical and occupational therapy, recreation, including therapeutic recreation, social work services, counseling services, including rehabilitation counseling, orientation and mobility services, and medical services, except that such medical services shall be for diagnostic and evaluation purposes only) as may be required to assist a child with a disability to benefit from special education, and includes the early identification and assessment of disabling conditions in children.

Section 504

IDEA is not the only means by which a student can qualify as having a disability. Section 504 of the Rehabilitation Act of 1973 (PL 93-112) states

> No otherwise qualified individuals with a disability in the United States . . . shall solely by the reason of his or her disability, be excluded from participation in, be denied the benefits of, or be subjected to discrimination under any program or activity receiving Federal financial assistance.

An individual with a disability, according to Section 504, is someone who 1) has a physical or mental impairment that substantially limits one or more major life activities, 2) has a record of such an impairment, or 3) is regarded as having such an impairment. Learning is the major life activity in which students with disabilities are affected. Rather than provide services, the emphasis in Section 504 is the elimination of barriers to participation, whether physical or programmatic (Rosenfeld, 1998). Far more students may be eligible for accommodations and adaptations related to Section 504. Rosenfeld suggested that unlike IDEA, which focuses on the unique educational needs of the student, Section 504 looks at comparing the opportunities presented in the educational process for students without disabilities to those with disabilities.

Rather than provide special education, Section 504 provides for making "reasonable accommodations" that take into account the functional limitations of the individual and the alternative methods of performing tasks or activities that would permit participation. Schools must comply with both IDEA and Section 504 of the Rehabilitation Act of 1973. Accommodations must be individualized and modifications made so that the students with a disability are at an equal starting point with the students without disabilities.

In answering our question "Who are the students with disabilities in an inclusive high school?" we may respond by saying that the students with disabilities are those who are receiving special education or related services through IDEA '97 or who receive accommodations and modifications through Section 504. Each of these groups of students have written individualized plans for their education.

Table 4.1.   Definitions in the Individuals with Disabilities Education Act Amendments of 1997 (PL 105-17) regulations

Autism	"A developmental disability significantly affecting verbal and nonverbal communication and social interaction, generally evident before age 3, that adversely affects a child's educational performance. Other characteristics often associated with autism are engagement in repetitive activities and stereotyped movements, resistance to environmental change or change in daily routines, and unusual responses to sensory experiences. The term does not apply if a child's educational performance is adversely affected because the child has an emotional disturbance."
Deaf-blindness	"Concomitant hearing and visual impairments, the combination of which causes such severe communication and other developmental and educational needs that they cannot be accommodated in special education programs solely for children with deafness or children with blindness"
Deafness	"A hearing impairment that is so severe that the child is impaired in processing linguistic information through hearing, with or without amplification, that adversely affects a child's educational performance"
Emotional disturbance	"A condition exhibiting one or more of the following characteristics over a long period of time and to a marked degree that adversely affects a child's educational performance: (a) an inability to learn that cannot be explained by intellectual, sensory, or health factors; (b) an inability to build or maintain satisfactory interpersonal relationships with peers and teachers; (c) inappropriate types of behavior or feelings under normal circumstances; (d) a general pervasive mood of unhappiness or depression; (e) a tendency to develop physical symptoms or fears associated with personal or school problems"
Hearing impairment	"An impairment in hearing, whether permanent or adversely affects a child's educational performance but that is not included under the definition of deafness"
Mental retardation	"Significantly subaverage general intellectual functioning, existing concurrently with deficits in adaptive behavior and manifested during the developmental period, that adversely affects a child's educational performance"
Multiple disabilities	"Concomitant impairments (such as mental retardation-blindness, mental retardation-orthopedic impairment, etc.) the combination of which causes such severe educational needs that they cannot be accommodated in special education programs solely for one of the impairments. The term does not include deaf-blindness."

Table 4.1.   *(continued)*

Orthopedic impairment	"A severe orthopedic impairment that adversely affects a child's educational performance. The term includes impairments caused by congenital anomaly (e.g., clubfoot, absence of some member), impairments caused by disease (e.g., poliomyelitis, bone tuberculosis) and impairments from other causes (e.g., cerebral palsy, amputations, fractures or burns that cause contractures)."
Other health impairment	"Having limited strength, vitality, or alertness, including a heightened alertness to environmental stimuli, that results in limited alertness with respect to the educational environment that (i) is due to chronic or acute health problems such as asthma, attention deficit disorder or attention deficit hyperactivity disorder, diabetes, epilepsy, a heart condition, hemophilia, lead poisoning, leukemia, nephritis, rheumatic fever, and sickle cell anemia; and (ii) adversely affects a child's educational performance"
Specific learning disability	"A disorder in one of the basic psychological processes involved in understanding or in using language, spoken or written, that may manifest itself in an imperfect ability to listen, think, speak, read, write, spell, or to do mathematical calculations, including conditions such as perceptual disabilities, brain injury, minimal brain dysfunction, dyslexia, and developmental aphasia"
Speech or language impairment	"A communication disorder, such as stuttering, impaired articulation, a language impairment, or a voice impairment, that adversely affects a child's educational performance"
Traumatic brain injury	"An acquired injury to the brain caused by external physical force, resulting in total or partial functional disability or psychosocial impairment, or both, that adversely affects a child's educational performance. The term applies to open or closed head injuries resulting in impairments in one or more areas, such as cognition; language; memory; attention; reasoning; abstract thinking; judgment; problem-solving; sensory, perceptual, and motor abilities; psychosocial behavior; physical functions; information processing, and speech. The term does not apply to brain injuries that are congenital or degenerative, or to brain injuries induced by birth trauma."
Visual impairment including blindness	"An impairment in vision that, even with correction, adversely affects a child's educational performance. The term includes both partial sight and blindness."

Variations Among Students

Even though IDEA '97 and Section 504 formally identify students according to various disability categories, in inclusive schools the individual's specific diagnostic classification is generally not helpful in planning and implementing an effective program. Teaching is based on students' strengths, challenges, talents, and gifts rather than their labels. In general, however, students vary from each other 1) in the ways and rates in which they learn; 2) in ways that they interact with teachers, parents, and peers; and 3) in ways in which they gain access to the environment (Bauer & Shea, 1999).

Students Who Vary in Learning Styles and Rates   These students usually come to the attention of teachers because of the mismatch between the expectations and demands of the classroom and school, and the ways and speed with which they learn. Students with learning disabilities may demonstrate a discrepancy between their ability and academic functioning because of the ways in which they learn. The National Joint Commission on Learning Disabilities contended that *learning disabilities* is a heterogeneous group of disorders, manifested by significant challenges in learning, speaking, reading, writing, reasoning, or mathematics. Self-regulation and social skill problems often are associated with learning disabilities (Hammil, 1990). Bryan (1991) suggested that students with learning disabilities have three challenges in social interactions. First, these students have a difficult time acquiring positive notions about themselves and their self-efficacy. Second, students may generate negative attitudes and judgments of others because of their challenges in interacting. Finally, as students with learning disabilities attempt to interact, they may have difficulty responding to rapid, complex, and ambiguous social situations.

Students with mental retardation vary from their peers in the rate they learn. The American Association on Mental Retardation (Luckasson et al., 1992) abolished levels of mental retardation based on cognitive disability and described mental retardation according to the needed levels of supports across four areas. They suggested that mental retardation is not something a person has but a state of functioning. *Mental retardation* is "significantly subaverage intellectual functioning, existing concurrently with related limitations in two of more applicable adaptive skill areas" (Luckasson et al., 1992, p. 2). The skill areas affected include communication, self-care, home living, social skills, community use, self-direction, health and safety, functional academics, leisure, and work.

A third group who vary from their peers by their learning styles or rates are students who are gifted, creative, or talented. Students who are gifted, creative, or talented confront unique developmental challenges (Hilyer, 1988). Among these challenges are 1) facing society's contradictory treatment of learners who are gifted, creative, or talented; 2) labeling; 3) dealing with a more rapid development; 4) experiencing a heightened sensitivity; 5) having a discrepancy between intellectual and social skills; 6) striving for unrealistic goals or expectations; 7) focusing on perfectionism; 8) feeling stress, anxiety, and depression; and 9) finding it difficult to deal with failure and success.

Students Who Vary in Their Interactions and Behaviors   Students may vary in the ways in which they interact according to gender; cultural, ethnic, or linguistic group membership; temperament; or personality. Identifying students who vary in their interactions and behaviors to the extent that special education is required and a disability is identified is difficult. More than half of the referrals for students with emotional or behavioral disorders occur when these students are in third through sixth grade. Almost three fourths of these individuals are boys, and most are identified because of poor peer relationships, frustration, low achievement, withdrawn behavior, disruptive behavior, fighting, refusing to work, and short attention spans.

Students Who Vary in the Ways in Which They Gain Access to the Environment   Most teaching uses spoken language as its medium (Cazden, 1986). For students whose communication, physical, and sensory systems vary from their peers, gaining access to the learning environment may be a significant challenge. Students with orthopedic disabilities or other health problems are challenged in gaining access to the physical environment and are limited in experiences common to others in interactions with objects, places and positions, or mobility. Students with visual impairments are challenged in their ability to acquire concepts that others learn vicariously through observation. Students with communication disorders may have difficulty with the production of spoken language or comprehending or using the signs and symbols of language to express or receive ideas in a spoken, written, or other symbol system. With more than half of the school day devoted to listening, students who are deaf or who have hearing impairments may have a significant problem in receiving the same information as others in the classroom.

WHO ARE STUDENTS ON THE MARGINS?

One group of students that elicits great concern in an inclusive high school is the students who would, in more traditional environments, fall through the cracks. Often described as *at-risk students*, these students on the margins are "a diverse set of students, including those whose primary language is not English, and others who, for whatever reason, are struggling in their academic programs or in their social behaviors in the schools" (Wang, Reynolds, & Walberg, 1995, p. 2). These students may include students from families with low socioeconomic status, students in single-parent homes, students for whom English is a second language, students who exhibit substance abuse, or students who are members of gangs.

Students of Low Socioeconomic Status

There is a connection between a family's economic resources and students' tested performance; students from families of low socioeconomic status tend to have the lowest SAT scores, the lowest achievement test scores, and the highest dropout rates from high school. The combined SAT scores of children whose parents earn more than $70,000 a year are, on the average, 200 points higher than those of children whose families earn between $10,000 and $20,000 (Bronfenbrenner, McClelland, Wethington, Moen, & Ceci, 1996).

Among developed countries, the United States of America has the highest percentage of children living in poverty. The principal source of income for families whose financial resources place them below the poverty line is Temporary Aid to Needy Families (TANF); yet government benefits have been dropping. As the value of TANF benefits in constant dollars has fallen sharply since the 1970s, the number of needy families has grown. Among these families, more young children have been growing up in single-mother families. A critical issue is education. Education is a powerful force in decreasing the risk that a family will end up in poverty. The critical factor is that the child's parent has completed high school (Bronfenbrenner et al., 1996).

The poverty rate for African Americans, Hispanics, and Native Americans is about three times that of non-Hispanic Caucasians. Even Asian Americans, who have a higher average income than non-Hispanic Caucasians, are more likely to live in poverty. Minority families are overrepresented among the "poorest of the poor"—families with incomes less than half of the official poverty threshold ($16,400 for a family of four in 1997). More than half of those in extreme poverty are from minority groups (Population Reference Bureau, 2000).

Students from Single-Parent
Families, Families of Divorce, and Stepfamilies

In 1997, only 48% of American children lived with two parents; in 1980, the figure was 77%. Almost 25% of American children lived only with their mothers, 4% lived with only their fathers, and 4% lived with neither parent. Caucasian children are more likely than African American children to live with two parents. In 1997, 75% of Caucasian children lived with two parents, whereas 35% of African American children and 64% of Hispanic children lived with both parents (Forum on Child and Family Statistics, 1999).

Of the students who are not living with two biological parents, children in never-married, single-parent homes are at greatest risk for school failure (Carlson, 1992). Children in single-parent homes are least likely to experience adverse effects if 1) they are female; 2) their custodial parent is confident, mentally healthy, educated, and authoritative; 3) the family is economically secure and resides in a community with resources oriented to the well-being of children; and 4) relationships between the single custodial parent and other family system members, including the noncustodial parent, are cooperative and free of conflict.

The second highest risk group is those students with families that have experienced divorce (Carlson, 1992). The transition from two-parent to single-parent families is usually accompanied by reduction in income stability, lower income, and a change in residence and school. Divorce remains the single most common psychological stressor for children (Guidubaldi & Perry, 1985). Wallerstein and Blakeslee (1989) described several differences between the impact of divorce and other life crises such as death, illness, and unemployment. Divorce more often involves anger, which may be expressed verbally or physically or both. Rather than strive to ensure their children's safety and emotional security, parents in the process of seeking a divorce frequently give priority to their adult problems. This diminishes their capacity to parent. In addition, during the process of divorce, the usual social supports available to parents and children are less available because relatives and friends tend to withdraw from the conflict occurring within the family.

Students for Whom English Is a Second Language

Students for whom English is a second language face greater challenges progressing in school and, as adults, in the labor market. Five percent of all school-age children in the United States speak a language other than English at home and have difficulty speaking English. The percentage varies, however, by region of the country, with 2% of children in the Midwest and 22% of children in the West speaking English as a second language. Children of Hispanic or Asian origin are more likely than non-Hispanic Caucasian or African American children to have difficulty speaking English because they are more likely to speak another language at home (Forum on Child and Family Statistics, 1999).

Substance Abuse

According to the National Institute on Drug Abuse (1998), *substance abuse* is the use of any chemical substance that causes physical, mental, emotional, or social harm to an individual or those close to him or her. Substance abuse in a family has two primary effects on children. First, typical parent–child interactions do not occur because of parents' preoccupation with obtaining and using drugs. Second, as a result of the parents' preoccupation with activities associated with their addiction, family life is disorganized. Children living with parents who are abusing controlled substances live in unstable, often dangerous, environments and are cared for inconsistently by parents who frequently have psychological and physical problems.

Due to the potential serious effects of substance abuse during pregnancy, children whose mothers used drugs or alcohol of any kind during any time of the pregnancy are referred to as having been *prenatally exposed*. This includes far more children than those born addicted to a controlled substance.

Students also engage in substance abuse. The National Institute on Drug Abuse (1998) reported that in 1993, 67% of the children surveyed reported having tried alcohol, and 26% said that they had already been drunk at least once by the eighth grade. By the end of the eighth grade, 32% reported having tried an illegal drug. Almost 40% of tenth graders and 50% of all twelfth graders have tried illegal drugs (Johnston, O'Malley, & Bachman, 1994). More deaths and disabilities result from substance abuse than from any other preventable cause (Institute for Health Policy, 1993). Substance abuse among adolescents increases health risks, causes automobile and other accidents, increases the likelihood of criminal activity, and decreases productivity (Brooks & Rice, 1997).

Students Engaged in Gangs

In 1993, more than one third of all students in the United States reported that "fighting" gangs were present in their schools. Although the percentage of Caucasian students reporting the presence of fighting gangs in their schools (31%) was less than that reported by African American students (42%) and Hispanic students (5%), the number of Caucasian students exposed to gangs at school was nearly 2 million more than the number of minority students exposed to gangs at school (National Center for Education Statistics, 1993). The problem of gangs in school extends beyond the inner city. The number of students who encounter gangs in school is as great for suburban or Caucasian students as it is for urban or minority students. In addition, gang presence, not a student's ethnicity, culture, or linguistic group, account for most of the differences across students who report different levels of victimization and fear at school. Compared with students who did not report gangs in their schools, students who did were 1) nearly twice as likely to fear an attack at school, 2) more than twice as likely to fear an attack while traveling to or from school, and 3) more than twice as likely to have been victimized within the past 6 months. Students who attended schools with gangs were more than four times as likely to avoid certain areas within their school and more than three times as likely to report that they had brought something to school for protection in the last 6 months (National Center for Education Statistics, 1995). The presence of gangs, then, is a significant disruptive force.

WHAT ISSUES ARE RELATED TO
CULTURAL, ETHNIC, OR LINGUISTIC DIVERSITY?

In 1997, 66% of the children in the United States were Caucasian, of non-Hispanic culture. Fifteen percent were African American and not Hispanic, 15% were Hispanic, 4% were Asian and Pacific Islander, and 1% were Native American. The number of Hispanic children has increased faster than any other ethnic, cultural, or linguistic group, growing from 9% of the child population in 1980 to 15% in 1997. The percentage of Asian and Pacific Islander children doubled from 2% to 4% of all children in the United States between 1980 and 1997 (Forum on Child and Family Statistics, 1999). There is, then, a great need to understand and recognize cultural diversity in schools. Lynch suggested that when trying to understand one's self and culture, it is important to remember that

> Culture is dynamic and ever changing; cultural practices that individuals remember and practice from their place of origins are often different from those occurring in the country of origin today. Culture, language, ethnicity, and race are not the only determinants of one's values, beliefs, and behaviors. Socioeconomic status, educational level, occupation, personal experience, and personality all exert a powerful influence over how individuals view themselves and how families function. In any group, within-group differences are as great as across-group differences. Within any culture there are wide variations in attitudes, beliefs, and behaviors. (1998, p. 48)

Lynch (1998) described values of various groups along several cultural continua (see Table 4.2). We often speak of culture and ethnicity and assume meanings that may not be shared. Our culture is more than an influence on our behavior; our culture plays a role in everything we say, do, or think (Spindler & Spindler, 1994). Kugelmass (1993) suggested that *culture* refers to the covert and overt beliefs, expectations, and values of people and institutions; culture is that which gives meaning to our experience. *Ethnicity* is defined as membership in a group of people who share a unique social and cultural heritage that is transmitted from one generation to the next (Mindel & Habenstein, 1991). Race and ethnicity may overlap (as with Chinese Americans or African Americans) or may be independent of each other (Latinos may be Caucasian, black, Native American, or all three).

Anglo American Students

Students from Anglo American cultures often do not perceive themselves as part of a cultural group because they come from the "dominant" culture of the United States. Yet, for the most part, Anglo American families demonstrate fairly consistent cultural values and practices. Writing about individuals expe-

Table 4.2.   Continua of cultural values

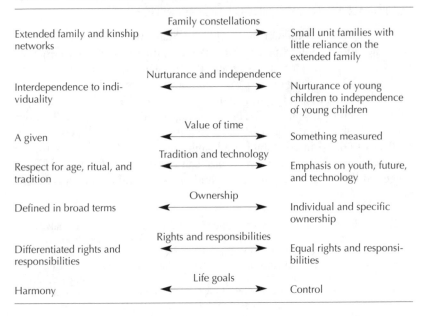

	Family constellations	
Extended family and kinship networks	◄———————►	Small unit families with little reliance on the extended family
	Nurturance and independence	
Interdependence to individuality	◄———————►	Nurturance of young children to independence of young children
	Value of time	
A given	◄———————►	Something measured
	Tradition and technology	
Respect for age, ritual, and tradition	◄———————►	Emphasis on youth, future, and technology
	Ownership	
Defined in broad terms	◄———————►	Individual and specific ownership
	Rights and responsibilities	
Differentiated rights and responsibilities	◄———————►	Equal rights and responsibilities
	Life goals	
Harmony	◄———————►	Control

riencing Anglo American–based culture for the first time, Althen (1988) identified values related to individualism and privacy, equality, informality, an emphasis on the future, change and progress, an assumption of the goodness of humanity, a belief that "time is money," a work orientation, and a directness and assertiveness in communication. In terms of disability, no single cause is ascribed; rather, a variety of reasons based on scientific causes exist, including genetic disorders, environmental agents, and prenatal and perinatal trauma (Hanson, 1998).

African Americans

Since the beginning of the 20th century, the African American population of the United States has remained between 10% and 12% (Allen & Majidi-Ahi, 1989). The differences in cohesiveness between the African American and Anglo American cultures may be viewed as problematic by Anglo American teachers (Hanna, 1988). Willis (1998) described these groups as "my family, my folks, my kin, or my people" to describe individuals who may or may not actually be related. Though private gain is respected, there is an expectation that gain will be shared in a reasonable measure with the larger community.

The child's obedience and respect for older adults may be an early contribution to family maintenance and cohesiveness.

Communication patterns among African American students may serve as another manner of identification (Willis, 1998). Some differences in communicative behaviors, such as eye contact, may be interpreted as inattention by an Anglo American teacher (Allen & Majidi-Ahi, 1989). African American students may be more likely to verbally reinforce one another in conversation (Smith, 1981). Communication skills valued among peers, such as verbal dueling and argument, may be viewed as aggressive and disruptive by teachers (Lynch, 1993).

Latino Students

Latino students are those learners of all races whose cultural heritage is tied to the use of the Spanish language and Latino culture (Fradd, Figueroa, & Correa, 1989). The Latino population is concentrated in urban areas and, as a consequence, isolated in housing and schooling (Hyland, 1989). This isolation is said to be related to linguistic skills—Latino children are usually placed in classrooms or schools primarily with other children who have limited English proficiency.

In the United States, Latinos of Mexican origin compose the largest group, with about 14.6 million or 64.3% of Latinos. Additional large groups of Latino students include Puerto Ricans (about 2.4 million) and Cubans (about 1.1 million) (Zuniga, 1998). Mexican Americans tend to be young, poor, and living in large families while confronting the challenges of illiteracy and lack of facility of English (Ramirez, 1989). The family is a mixture of traditional and contemporary patterns. The home may be child centered, with parents passive and indulgent toward children. There is an emphasis on cooperation and respect for authority. Mexican Americans appear to be more oriented to the here and now and emphasize "doing" rather than "being."

Puerto Ricans in the United States reside primarily in New York City and the Northeast. As American citizens they have voting privileges and ease of travel between the mainland and the island. Catholicism, with its emphasis on a personal relationship with God, is the predominant religion (Garcia-Preto, 1982). Generational change is apparent among Puerto Ricans. First-generation migrants exhibit traditional values, with *barrios* serving to recreate and preserve the native culture. Second- and third-generation Puerto Ricans cope with and adapt to the language and values of the mainstream culture, often generating feelings of failure and stress due to tensions between the traditional and new cultures (Inclan, 1985).

Latino students may enter school with a significantly different social, economic, and cultural background than their peers who understand Anglo

American culture (Hyland, 1989). For example, "copying" may be viewed as a legitimate activity among students. Copying work may be based on home socialization patterns that stress collectivity and social cohesiveness. Rather than representing low ability and lack of motivation, copying may be considered a constructive approach to intellectual exchanges and the acquisition of new knowledge in a social unit composed of peers (Delgado-Gaitan & Trueba, 1985). In addition, the organization of classroom instruction may limit students' abilities to demonstrate their full range of competence in two languages. A lack of English language structural proficiency and a lack of vocabulary in Spanish may be interpreted by teachers as a lack of conceptual ability (Commins & Miramontes, 1989).

Native Americans

In the United States, there are 517 federally recognized Native American entities (196 of which are in Alaska), and 36 states recognize Native American tribes. Each of these entities has unique customs, traditions, social organizations, and ecological relationships to the environment (Leap, 1981).

Native Americans share a history of cultural, psychological, and physical genocide. Once estimated at 10 million, the Native American population has been reduced through cultural genocide to fewer than 2 million. As a consequence of efforts to eliminate them and to assimilate them, many Native Americans experience a sense of alienation from Anglo Americans (LaFramboise & Low, 1989).

Responses of Native Americans to this sense of alienation have been described by Spindler and Spindler (1994) through their work with the Menominee tribe. These responses include reaffirmation, withdrawal, constructive marginality, biculturalism, and assimilation. Among the Menominee, reaffirmation was represented by a group of cultural "survivors" from the past and a larger number of younger people who had seen Anglo American culture in school and work and were trying to re-create and sustain a recognizable Native American way of life. Another group of Native Americans was so torn by conflict that they could identify with neither the traditional nor Anglo American cultural symbols or groups and withdrew, either into self-destruction through substance abuse or through doing nothing.

Constructive marginality was described by Spindler and Spindler (1994) as forming a personal culture that was instrumentally productive but was usually constituted of several different segments, some of which were Anglo American. Among those who assimilated, two groups emerged: 1) those who were more *respectable* than most Anglo Americans and denigrated Native Americans who did not conform and 2) those who were undifferentiated culturally from Anglo Americans but were interested in Native American traditions in a more distant way. Bicultural Native Americans were equally at home in the traditional and mainstream context. Spindler and Spindler described these strategies as defensive because the self-esteem of the people is threatened.

Grimm (1992) reported that several issues challenge the identity of learners who are Native Americans, such as removal from the family for boarding schools and foster placements, high dropout rates (60% among children attending boarding school), overidentification as special education students, a high incidence of alcohol and drug abuse, high suicide rates, chronic health problems, and low income. Perhaps most difficult for Native American students is a conflict between cooperative learning styles and the competitive setting of the school. Native American children often learn by observation rather than by displays of curiosity and verbal questioning and prefer cooperation and harmony. In school, these behaviors are perceived to be a general lack of individual competition and to be a reliance on peer structure (Brod & McQuiston, 1983).

A Native American philosophy of child development has become the basis for working with learners with special needs (Brendtro, Brokenleg, & Van Bockern, 1990). The basic premise underlying this Native American philosophy is that to develop successfully, children must have or feel the spirit of belonging (e.g., trust, attachment, love, friendship), mastery (e.g., success, achievement, motivation, creativity), independence (e.g., autonomy, confidence, responsibility, self-discipline, inner control), and generosity (e.g., self-sacrifice, caring, sharing, loyalty).

Asian Americans

Since 1970, the Asian American population has doubled and continues to increase. The Asian American population is comprised of many diverse groups, including Chinese, Japanese, Korean, and Pilipino Americans; immigrants and refugees from Vietnam, Thailand, Cambodia, Laos, and Indonesia; people from India, Pakistan, and Ceylon; and children with one Asian parent (Ho, 1992). The heterogeneity of this group is exemplified by language, historical, social, and economic differences, as well as changes that occur through generational status (Ho, 1992).

Although cultural values may vary as related to these variables, there are several potential values that may put Asian American learners in contrast to conventional school behavior. Chan (1998) described a cultural value for contemplative, circular thinking and fatalism that may be starkly contrasted with mainstream culture's analytic, linear thinking and sense of personal control evident in schools. Chan contrasted the stoicism and patience of traditional Asian cultures with the optimism and eagerness to act in mainstream Western culture. Whereas Asian cultures value group welfare, mutual interdependence, and conformity, mainstream Western culture emphasizes privacy, autonomy, and challenging authority.

Asian Americans, unlike other cultural, ethnic, and linguistic groups, have a positive stereotype related to school achievement. Dao (1991) contended, however, that changes have occurred in the Asian American population and that many of these children are at risk for school failure. Many children come from families with life and educational experiences vastly different from children from established Asian American families. Recent immigrant or refugee children face the triple burden of learning English and the new school curriculum, adjusting to a new culture, and surviving an impoverished environment. In addition, recent refugees may have had traumatic experiences, including death, piracy, and extreme violence, and may not be emotionally ready to benefit from instruction.

Appalachians

Though not readily identifiable by race, gender, or surname, Appalachians are a distinct cultural group (Sullivan & Miller, 1990). *Appalachians* are individuals who were born, or whose ancestors were born, in the federally defined Appalachian region of 397 counties and 5 independent cities in portions of 13 states, including New York, Pennsylvania, Maryland, Ohio, Virginia, West Virginia, Kentucky, Tennessee, North Carolina, South Carolina, Georgia, Alabama, and Mississippi (McCoy & Watkins, 1980). The term *urban Appalachian* was coined in the early 1970s by Appalachians living in Midwestern cities to describe themselves after realizing that, due to their permanence, the term *Appalachian migrant* was no longer appropriate (Obermiller & Maloney, 1994).

Urban Appalachian youth remain on the economic margin (Borman & Stegelin, 1994), avoiding more challenging opportunities outside of their neighborhoods because such jobs disrupt important social networks of exchange between kin and peers. Without mentors, role models, and sponsors outside of the neighborhood, these young adults remain adrift, keeping afloat through a series of odd jobs and exchange strategies.

An ethnographic study of two working-class Appalachian communities by Heath (1983) described the mismatch of school and home play and communication patterns. Heath found that indirect questions, rather than the direct commands used in the home, were difficult for the children to understand. This mismatch in communication was reported by urban Appalachian adolescents in a later study (Penn, Borman, & Hoeweler, 1994), who stated a need for a more "person orientation" than work orientation.

The impact of the cultural mismatch between school and home for urban Appalachian students is exemplified by studies conducted in Cincinnati, Ohio. Urban Appalachian neighborhood enclaves ranked higher than either predominantly African American or other Caucasian areas both in the high percentage of dropouts and in the percentage of the population between 16 and 25 years of age who are neither high school graduates nor currently attending high school (Penn et al., 1994). Those students who remain in school are achieving at significantly lower levels than their non-Appalachian peers. In schools serving urban Appalachian children, scores on the California Achievement Tests have declined two or three times greater than the declines for Cincinnati public schools as a whole. The Appalachian dialect and the cultural emphasis on individualism are in conflict with standard English and the conformity anticipated in many schools.

SUMMARY POINTS

- Adolescence is a part of a developmental process, marked by continuity as well as change.
- Adolescents demonstrate new ways of thinking and learning and are struggling with their identity.
- Students may be identified as having disabilities through IDEA or through Section 504 of the Rehabilitation Act. Students identified through IDEA receive special education services, and students identified through Section 504 receive accommodations.
- In addition to students with disabilities, there are students "on the margins" in secondary schools. These students may include students living in poverty, students in single-parent homes, students for whom English is a second language, students who may be engaged in substance abuse, and students engaged in gang activities.
- Secondary school teachers need to recognize the uniqueness of each student's ethnicity, culture, or linguistic group.

REFERENCES

Allen, L., & Majidi-Ahi, S. (1989). Black American children. In J.T. Gibbs & L.N. Huang (Eds.), *Children of color: Psychological interventions with minority youth* (pp. 148–178). San Francisco: Jossey-Bass.

Althen, G. (1988). *American ways: A guide for foreigners in the United States.* Yarmouth, ME: Intercultural Press.

Bauer, A.M., & Shea, T.M. (1999). *Inclusion 101: How to teach all learners.* Baltimore: Paul H. Brookes Publishing Co.

Borman, K., & Stegelin, D. (1994). Social change and urban Appalachian children: Youth at risk. In K.M. Borman & P.J. Obermiller (Eds.), *From mountain to metropolis: Appalachian migrants in American cities* (pp. 167–180). Westport, CT: Bergin & Garvey.

Brendtro, L.K., Brokenleg, M.L., & Van Bockern, S. (1990). *Reclaiming youth at risk: Our hope for the future.* Bloomington, IN: National Education Service.

Brod, R.L., & McQuiston, J.M. (1983). American Indian adult education and literacy: The first national survey. *Journal of American Indian Education, 22*(2), 1–16.

Bronfenbrenner, U., McClelland, P., Wethington, E., Moen, P., & Ceci, S. (1996). *The state of Americans: This generation and the next.* New York: The Free Press.

Brooks, C.S., & Rice, K.F. (1997). *Families in recovery: Coming full circle.* Baltimore: Paul H. Brookes Publishing Co.

Brown, L.M., & Gilligan, C. (1992). *Meeting at the crossroads: Women's psychology and girls' development.* Cambridge, MA: Harvard University Press.

Bryan, T. (1991). Social problems and learning disabilities. In B. Wong (Ed.), *Learning about learning disabilities* (pp. 195–231). San Diego: Academic Press.

Carlson, C. (1992). Single parenting and stepparenting: Problems, issues, and interventions. In M.J. Fine & C. Carlson (Eds.), *The handbook of family–school intervention: A systems perspective* (pp. 188–214). Needham Heights, MA: Allyn & Bacon.

Cazden, C. (1986). *Classroom discourse: The language of teaching and learning.* Cambridge, MA: Harvard University Press.

Chan, S. (1998). Families with Asian roots. In E.W. Lynch & M.J. Hanson (Eds.), *Developing cross-cultural competence: A guide for working with children and their families* (2nd ed., pp. 251–354). Baltimore: Paul H. Brookes Publishing Co.

Commins, N.L., & Miramontes, O.B. (1989). Perceived and actual linguistic competence: A descriptive study of four low-achieving Hispanic bilingual students. *American Educational Research Journal, 26,* 443-472.

Danner, F. (1989). Cognitive development in adolescence. In J. Worell & F. Danner (Eds.), *The adolescent as decision-maker: Applications to development and education* (pp. 51–82). San Diego: Academic Press.

Dao, M. (1991). Designing assessment procedures for educationally at-risk Southeast Asian-American students. *Journal of Learning Disabilities, 24*(10), 594–601, 629.

Davis, G.A., & Rimm, S.B. (1985). *Education of the gifted and talented* (4th ed.). Needham Heights, MA: Allyn & Bacon.

De Armas, A., & Kelly, J.A. (1989). Social relationships in adolescence: Skill development and training. In J. Worell & F. Danner (Eds.), *The adolescent as decision-maker: Applications to development and education* (pp. 83–109). San Diego: Academic Press.

Delgado-Gaitan, C., & Trueba, H.T. (1985). Ethnographic study of participant structures in task completion: Reinterpretation of "handicaps" in Mexican children. *Learning Disability Quarterly, 8,* 67–75.

Elkind, D. (1994). *Understanding your child from birth to sixteen.* Needham Heights, MA: Allyn & Bacon.

Feather, D.B. (1980). *Children, psychology, and the school.* Glenview, IL: Scott Foresman.

Forum on Child and Family Statistics. (1999). *America's children 1999.* Washington, DC: Author.

Fradd, S.H., Figueroa, R.A., & Correa, V.I. (1989). Meeting the multicultural needs of Hispanic students in special education. *Exceptional Children, 56,* 102–104.

Garcia-Preto, N. (1982). Puerto Rican families. In M. McGoldrick, J.K. Pearce, & J. Giordano (Eds.), *Ethnicity and family therapy* (pp. 247–283). New York: The Guilford Press.

Gardner, H. (1983). *Frames of mind: The theory of multiple intelligences.* New York: Basic Books.

Grimm, L.L. (1992). The Native American child in school: An ecological perspective. In M.J. Fine & C. Carlson (Eds.), *The handbook of family–school intervention: A systems perspective* (pp. 102–118). Needham Heights, MA: Allyn & Bacon.

Guidubaldi, J., & Perry, J.D. (1985). Divorce and mental health sequelae for children: A two-year follow-up of a nationwide sample. *Journal of the American Academy of Child Psychiatry, 24,* 531–537.

Hammil, D.D. (1990). On defining learning disabilities: An emerging consensus. *Journal of Learning Disabilities, 23,* 74–84.

Hanna, J.L. (1988). *Disruptive school behavior: Class, race, and culture.* New York: Holmes & Meier.

Hanson, M.J. (1998). Ethnic, cultural, and language diversity in intervention settings. In E.W. Lynch & M.J. Hanson (Eds.), *Developing cross-cultural competence: A guide for working with children and their families* (2nd ed., pp. 3–22). Baltimore: Paul H. Brookes Publishing Co.

Heath, S.B. (1983). *Ways with words: Language, life, and work in communities and classrooms.* New York: Cambridge University Press.

Hilyer, K. (1988) Problems of gifted children. *Journal of the Association for the Study of Perception, 21,* 10–26.

Ho, M.K. (1992). Asian-American students: Family influences. In M.J. Fine & C. Carlson (Eds.), *The handbook of family–school intervention: A systems perspective* (pp. 75–85). Needham Heights, MA: Allyn & Bacon.

Hyland, C.R. (1989). What we know about the fastest-growing minority population: Hispanic Americans. *Educational Horizons, 67*(4), 124–130.

Inclan, J. (1985). Variations in value orientations in mental health work with Puerto Ricans. *Psychotherapy, 33,* 324–334.

Individuals with Disabilities Education Act (IDEA) of 1990, PL 101-476, 20 U.S.C. §§ 1400 *et seq.*

Individuals with Disabilities Education Act (IDEA) Amendments of 1997, PL 105-17, 20 U.S.C. §§ 1400 *et seq.*

Inhelder, B., & Piaget, J. (1958). *The growth of logical thinking from childhood to adolescence: An essay on the construction of formal operational structures.* New York: Basic Books.

Institute for Health Policy. (1993). *Substance abuse: The nation's number one health problem. Key indicators for policy.* Waltham, MA: Brandeis University for the Robert Wood Johnson Foundation, Heller Graduate School.

Johnston, L.D., O'Malley, P.M., & Bachman, J.G. (1994). Overview of key findings. *National survey results on drug use from the Monitoring the Future Study, 2,* 5–25.

Kerr, B.A. (1985). Smart girls, gifted women: Special guidance concerns. *Roeper Review, 8,* 30–33.

Kugelmass, J. (1993). The challenge of cultural diversity. In A.M. Bauer & E.M. Lynch (Eds.), *Children who challenge the system* (pp. 117–144). Norwood, NJ: Ablex.

LaFramboise, T.D., & Low, K.G. (1989). American Indian children and adolescents. In J. Gibbs & L. Huang (Eds.), *Children of color: Psychological interventions with minority youth* (pp. 114–147). San Francisco: Jossey-Bass.

Leap, W.L. (1981). American Indian language maintenance. *Annual Review of Anthropology, 10,* 271–280.

Lerner, R.M., & Shea, J.A. (1982). Social behavior in adolescence. In B.B. Wolman (Ed.), *Handbook of developmental psychology* (pp. 129–144). Upper Saddle River, NJ: Prentice-Hall.

Luckasson, R.J., Coulter, D.L., Polloway, E.A., Reiss, S., Schalock, R.L., Snell, M.E., Spitalnik, D.M., & Stark, J.A. (1992). *Mental retardation: Definition, classification, and systems of supports* (9th ed.). Washington, DC: American Association on Mental Retardation.

Lynch, E.M. (1993). Negotiating status and role: An ethnographic examination of verbal dueling among students with behavior disorders. In A.M. Bauer & E.M. Lynch (Eds.), *Children who challenge the system* (pp. 29–44). Norwood, NJ: Ablex.

Lynch, E.W. (1998). Developing cross-cultural competence. In E.W. Lynch & M.J. Hanson (Eds.), *Developing cross-cultural competence: A guide for working with children and their families* (2nd ed., pp. 47–90). Baltimore: Paul H. Brookes Publishing Co.

McCoy, C.B., & Watkins, V.M. (1980). Drug use among urban ethnic youth. *Youth and Society, 11,* 83–116.

Miller, P.H. (1989). Theories of adolescent development. In J. Worell & F. Danner (Eds.), *The adolescent as decision-maker: Applications to development and education* (pp. 13–46). San Diego: Academic Press.

Mindel, C.H., Habenstein, R.W., & Wright, R., Jr. (Eds.). (1998). Culture and ethnicity. In C.H. Mindel, R.W. Habenstein, & R. Wright, Jr. (Eds.), *Ethnic families in America: Patterns and variations* (4th ed., pp. 1–23). Upper Saddle River, NJ: Prentice-Hall.

National Center for Education Statistics. (1993). *National Household Education Survey*. Washington, DC: Author.

National Center for Education Statistics. (1995). *Education policy issues: Statistical perspectives: Gangs and victimization at school*. Washington, DC: Author.

National Institute on Drug Abuse. (1998). *Drug addiction treatment: A research based guide*. Washington, DC: Author.

Obermiller, P.J., & Maloney, M. (1994). Living city, feeling country: The current status and future prospects of urban Appalachians. In K.M. Borman & P.J. Obermiller (Eds.), *From mountain to metropolis: Appalachian migrants in American cities* (pp. 3–12). Westport, CT: Bergin & Garvey.

Piaget, J. (1970). *Science of education and the psychology of the child*. New York: Orion.

Penn, E.M., Borman, K.M., & Hoeweler, F. (1994). Echoes from the hill: Urban Appalachian youths and educational reform. In K.M. Borman & P.J. Obermiller (Eds.), *From mountain to metropolis: Appalachian migrants in American cities* (pp. 121–140). Westport, CT: Bergin & Garvey.

Petersen., A.C., & Crockett, L.J. (1985). Pubertal timing and grade effects on adjustment. *Journal of Youth and Adolescence, 14*, 191–206.

Population Reference Bureau. (2000). *Income and poverty*. Washington, DC: Author.

Ramirez, O. (1989). Mexican American children and adolescents. In J.T. Gibbs & L.N. Huang (Eds.), *Children of color: Psychological interventions with minority youth* (pp. 224–250). San Francisco: Jossey-Bass.

Rehabilitation Act of 1973, PL 93-112, 29 U.S.C. §§ 701 *et seq.*

Rosenfeld, S.J. (1998). *Section 504 and IDEA: Basic similarities and differences*. Hollywood, FL: Edlaw.

Siegel, O. (1982). Personality development in adolescents. In B.B. Wolman (Ed.), *Handbook of developmental psychology*. Upper Saddle River, NJ: Prentice-Hall.

Smith, E. (1981). Cultural and historical perspectives in counseling blacks. In D.W. Sue (Ed.), *Counseling the culturally different: Theory and practice* (pp. 1–35). New York: John Wiley & Sons.

Spindler, G., & Spindler, L. (1994). What is cultural therapy? In G. Spindler & L. Spindler (Eds.), *Pathways to cultural awareness: Cultural therapy with teachers and students* (pp. 1–35). Thousand Oaks, CA: Corwin Press.

Sullivan, M., & Miller, D. (1990). Cincinnati's Urban Appalachian Council and Appalachian identity. *Harvard Educational Review, 60*(1), 106–124.

Tobin, K., & Garnett, P. (1987). Gender related differences in science activities. *Science Education, 71*, 91–103.

Wallerstein, J., & Blakeslee, S. (1989). *Second chances: Men, women, and children a decade after divorce*. New York: Ticknor & Fields.

Wang, M.C., Reynolds, M.C., & Walberg, H.J. (1995). Introduction: Inner-city students at the margins. In M.C. Wang & M.C. Reynolds (Eds.), *Making a difference for students at risk: Trends and alternatives* (pp. 1–13). Thousand Oaks, CA: Corwin Press.

Willis, W. (1998). Families with African American roots. In E.W. Lynch & M.J. Hanson (Eds.), *Developing cross-cultural competence: A guide for working with children and their families* (2nd ed., pp. 165–208). Baltimore: Paul H. Brookes Publishing Co.

Wolman, B.B. (1998). *Adolescence: Biological and psychosocial perspectives*. Westport, CT: Greenwood Press.

Zuniga, M.E. (1998). Families with Latino roots. In E.W. Lynch & M.J. Hanson (Eds.), *Developing cross-cultural competence: A guide for working with children and their families* (2nd ed., pp. 209–250). Baltimore: Paul H. Brookes Publishing Co.

FROM THE PRINCIPAL'S DESK

Each month, Jan Kennedy presents *From the Principal's Desk* on the front page of the Parent–Teacher Organization Newsletter. Here are some selections:

September. The windows are in, the phones are working, student handbooks arrived, and schedule changes are completed! Now it is time to sit back and reflect for a moment on what it is that we're actually about here at Purcell Marian.

First of all, we are a Catholic school. While we wholeheartedly subscribe to James Joyce's definition of Catholic as "Here comes everybody!" we also know that we lose our reason to exist if we are not faithful to Catholic tradition and rationality.

Second, we are a school. This means it is our job to provide the environment and the opportunity for students to become thoughtful and competent adults. While individual academic pursuits are very important, we must never allow ourselves to think that Proficiency Test scores or SAT scores provide us with an adequate measure of our success. Rather, it is the quality of the spiritual, intellectual, social, and emotional lives enjoyed by our graduates that best reflects the quality of a Purcell Marian education.

We are inclusive. How incredibly blessed we are to have a faculty, staff, and student body who appreciate the value of sharing gifts.

We are innovative. We do not introduce change for the sake of change (though it is usually refreshing). However, we recognize the importance of determining the unchanging needs of our students and responding in new ways. Furthermore, as research continues, we learn more and more about the learning process and work to develop instructional techniques that take advantage of new knowledge.

As we move through the year, let us keep the "big picture" in mind, even as we deal with grades and football games, homework and parent conferences, service projects and exhibitions, exams, plays, and proms.

December. There will, of course, be no school on January 18 in honor of Dr. Martin Luther King, Jr. This is an important time for all of us to reflect on our country's continuing struggle to ensure the civil rights of all our citizens. It can be so easy to dismiss one another on the basis of race, religion, ethnicity, or disability. This is a very special day for the Purcell Marian family as we strive to live out our philosophy of inclusion and equality.

January. As many of you are already aware, Purcell Marian was awarded the Inclusion Award in Education by the Inclusion Network, an organization whose mission is to inspire, support, and celebrate efforts in Greater Cincinnati to include people with disabilities in all areas of community life. It was one of my proudest moments as principal to accept this award on behalf of Purcell Marian's faculty and students. It has been our experience that "when all are included, all are rewarded." Unfortunately, there are still many who believe that inclusion in an education setting brings mediocrity and a "watered down" curriculum. I ask you all to help rid our community of this myth.

I would also encourage you to celebrate and recognize National Women's History Month by sharing with your sons and daughters the stories of the women in your families who have worked to keep their families and communities strong and vibrant. It is always important for our students to understand that they really do stand on the shoulders of those who preceded them.

II

How Does an
Inclusive High School Work?

We Are Blessed

—Kathy Heekin, religion teacher

When I heard in the spring of 1993 that Purcell Marian was becoming an inclusive school I groaned inwardly, "Don't we already have enough diversity for any one high school? Now we're throwing another factor into the mix." Translation: more work, more demands. However, our mission statement reads: "As Jesus came to invite all to the same table, Purcell Marian embraces and promotes inclusivity in all areas." That's pretty clear. And so it was to be. Over the years, I have found a new richness in my teaching as a result of these students. Without always being able to give words to it, I know all my students have as well. In addition to the patience and acceptance that special teenagers have taught all of us, they have been a great source of inspiration as well as a challenge to our spirituality.

Let me give you an example, one of my favorites. Last year I taught a young man, "Jack," who is sometimes described as difficult. Who knows why he carries so much anger with him? On his good days, he is golden, but on his bad days, he is impossible. He is, however, an excellent basketball player and that seems to just keep him in check. He doesn't want to lose that. At the beginning of his class with me, "Dawn" would appear at our door asking for help to go down the steps. Dawn uses a wheelchair and needs two or three strong students to carry her and her wheelchair down a full flight of steps. My classroom is located by the stairwell, so it is to my door that she comes. In the beginning of the year, Jack volunteered regularly. After a month of this, he grew tired of it and tried to back out of it. Dawn would have none of this. If he didn't come out to help her, she would sit at our doorway and call for him. "Jack! I want Jack!" There were times Jack would try hiding under my desk. She would not let up . . . and so he would go out in the hallway and lift her down the steps. For almost the full year, Jack continued to carry Dawn down to the basement level. It did wonders for him. She was able to fuel compassion in his soul . . . something none of the rest of us had been able to do! This is just one small example of how these special students have enriched us at Purcell Marian. As a member of our classes, they offer our students an opportunity to witness the loving hand of God in their lives. No one has been unaffected by their presence. As a teacher of religion I am reminded of this quote from our Archbishop (I think): "When educators teach learners to live justly, when they encourage compassion for those most in need, when they raise social consciousness and promote commitment to the common good, they engage and nurture spirituality."

We have been blessed by these students and by their parents who have entrusted them to us.

5

Community in an Inclusive High School

Anne M. Bauer
Glenda Myree Brown

Inclusion seeks to create schools based on meeting the needs of all learners as well as respecting and learning from each other's differences (Salend, 1998). Inclusive schools establish communities of learners by educating all students together in age-appropriate, general education classrooms in their neighborhood schools. Ferguson (1996) noted that although inclusion has focused on individuals with disabilities, it is designed to alter the philosophy for educating all students. One of the overarching conditions in schools successfully serving students at risk is that these schools function as caring, cohesive communities (Irmsher, 1997). The sense of community found in inclusive high schools is far removed from the culture of isolation found in many traditional high schools.

In this chapter, we define what is meant by school community. We describe how community looks and functions in an effective inclusive high school by utilizing the four levels of community described by Sergiovanni (1994). Throughout this chapter we use the voices of the principal and faculty members of Purcell Marian High School to provide insight into what happens in an effective inclusive high school in terms of building a school community that supports inclusive learning. We also offer principles and practices found in effective inclusive school communities, as well as a list of questions intended to guide the planning and work of those who wish to create inclusive school communities. After reading this chapter, you will be able to

- Describe the nature of school communities
- Identify how school communities function
- Identify ways to create a school community
- Describe the benefits of a caring, inclusive community

THE NATURE OF SCHOOL COMMUNITIES

As a result of the dissatisfaction with the current state of affairs in education, restructuring efforts have been forthcoming from almost all aspects of education, including curriculum, testing, instruction, organization, and teacher preparation (Thurlow, Elliott, & Ysseldyke, 1998). And now, with the philosophical change toward social and academic inclusion of students with and without disabilities, some high schools are beginning to look and function more like communities and less like formal organizations (Sergiovanni, 1994). Addressing this philosophical change toward inclusive learning in high schools requires that school leaders guide staff, students, and parents in creating a new and different type of secondary school culture that looks and functions like a community. Schools that function as communities share common values and a common vision. They respect and value the varied gifts, talents, abilities, and experiences of the students, staff, parents, and administrators. Raywid (1993) pointed out six common attributes of schools that function as communities: 1) respect, 2) caring, 3) inclusiveness, 4) trust, 5) empowerment, and 6) commitment.

Sergiovanni (1994) described a *community* as a collection of individuals who are bonded together by natural will and share a set of shared ideas and ideals. Sergiovanni and Starratt stated that school communities are

> Defined by their centers of shared values, beliefs and commitments. In communities, what is considered right and good is as important as what works and what is effective; teachers are motivated as much by emotion and belief as they are by self-interest; collegiality is understood as a form of professional virtue. (1998, p. 45)

Inclusion is effective when school culture emulates a community. Students and adults live and work together on a daily basis by respecting and valuing each other and the wide range of gifts, talents, and experiences they share. The teachers relate that they reflect "real life" as a diverse, urban, school community, and strive to prepare all students to become contributing and productive members of society. Sailor and Skrtic (1996) pointed out that when we consider that schools are a reflection of society, it makes sense that they would prepare students by providing them the opportunity to learn and work together in a school that functions as a community. Thousand, Rosenberg, Bishop, and Villa (1997) noted that for adolescents to be able to successfully navigate the larger, complex, heterogeneous community of adulthood, they need experiences with students who reflect a range of abilities, cultural and ethnic groups, languages, learning styles, economic levels, and ages.

HOW SCHOOL COMMUNITIES FUNCTION

Because community is important to an inclusive school, it is crucial that school leaders who are working to create an inclusive school community understand the forms that it can take and how to create it. Tonnies's (1957) theory of community (as cited in Sergiovanni, 1994) is used to make meaning of and provide a clear picture of the different forms of community found at Purcell Marian High School. According to Tonnies, communities exist in three forms: community by kinship, of place, and of mind. Bellah (1985) added a fourth form, which is called *community of memory*. We provide examples of all four forms of community and describe the meaning of these forms of community in the context of an inclusive high school.

Community by Kinship

"Community by kinship characterizes the special kind of relationships among people that create a unity that is similar to that found in families and other closely knit collections of people" (Sergiovanni, 1994, p. 68). In schools that function as communities, relationships are like family, space and time resemble a neighborhood, and common ideas and values are shared (Sergiovanni, 1994). The web of relationships that stand out in schools that operate as communities are different from those found in more traditional schools that are operated as organizations. Sergiovanni pointed out that the relationships found in communities are more special, meaningful, and personalized and that they result in a connecting quality that has moral overtones. In addition, because of these overtones, members feel a special sense of obligation to look out for each other. One teacher spoke of the influence the principal had in creating a community by kinship, "I think there are probably a lot of principals who are good administrators, but the faculty doesn't sense that this is their family, so to speak."

Another teacher described the school community that exists by kinship in this way: "Everybody is not perfect in a family, and if you have a son or daughter that has special needs you accept them because they are a part of your family. You find ways to make it work. We're a family here, and that's why all of our students are welcome. Because a strong sense of community is embedded in the school culture, inclusion of students with developmental disabilities was well received and accepted overall by the faculty. The principal and faculty spoke often and at length of how the entire staff, including the teachers, students, janitors, counselors, secretaries, librarians, and cafeteria workers are all a family, and family members take care of each other regardless of their abilities or disabilities."

Karen Matuszek, Director of Student Support Services, related, "The other really wonderful thing about this place is the staff members, our janitors, our secretaries, and our cafeteria workers who are so inclusive in their dealings with our students, who make our students feel so welcome that, in fact, this year we went to the Faculty Welfare Committee, and asked if we could start an Inclusion Award to give a teacher here at school who had been a wonderful support academically or socially of our students, who had done just a really nice job. We asked for nominations from everybody on the staff, and we had a whole page of nominations for different reasons, and the winner was not a teacher. The winner was one of our janitors who was absolutely thrilled to death! When we sat down and looked at all of the nominations, of all the people who we felt were the most important to our students this year, he won the award. This person greets all of our students by name and stops and eats lunch with them. If he needs some help with doing something like carrying tables or whatever, instead of going to a senior class with the strongest boys, he'll come here first and ask our students for the help, and they absolutely love him."

The school has a culture deeply rooted in community by kinship. The reason for this sense of community and responsibility for each other, much like a family would have, may be due in part to their mission and belief system that, in the words of the director, "means educating everybody. . . . Everybody should be allowed to have an equal education. I think that's where it all stems from."

The staff and administrators repeatedly spoke of community in the context of family, service, trust, collaboration, and cooperation. In addition, their comments often had moral overtones when they were speaking of their responsibilities to and interactions with all students. As one faculty member stated, "It's the caring, it's a caring attitude. What makes our program successful is that the teachers at this school are really caring. They just reach out to the kids." Another reported, "Basically our faculty is what really helps all the programs in this school. Without their kindness we would not have this program. They could just say, 'No, I don't want these kids in my classroom.' So, I give them a lot of credit."

Community of Place

Community of place "characterizes sharing a common habitat or locale. This type of sharing with others for sustained periods of time creates a special identity and a shared sense of belonging that connects people together in special ways" (Sergiovanni, 1994, p. 68). A teacher gives an example of community of place and the impact it has on students and how they relate to their peers who may look, act, or have needs that are different from them: "This is really a tight-knit place in the sense that it is extremely diverse . . . not just racially, but economically. The majority of our students come from working-class families, and that's one big tie-in that they've all got. They are coming from hard-working homes; whether you are a white kid from Norwood or a black kid from Evanston, it doesn't matter. Everyone knows 'my parents are working hard to send me here, and it's a major struggle.' And you know, people use that to bond, and the kids tie into it. They kind of wear it as a badge of pride that they can all be from different places and still come here to school. The kids are always telling me, 'My friend that goes to [suburban school] wants to know what is it like to go to school with black kids,' and the black kids are going, 'My friends from [inner-city school] want to know how do you go to school with those white folk,' and they say, 'It doesn't matter to us. We are just going to school.' It's a tight-knit group that way. The [students with disabilities] who came in are just another part of the family here. They are really just another group of kids here at the school. They are Cavaliers just like everyone else. They are just part of the family now."

Another example of community of place is found in the following comment by a teacher who speaks of how the graduates identify and connect with the values of the school to the extent that they keep coming back either as teachers or as visitors: "I bet there are 30 grads that work here. From the class of 1960 to the class of 1991. We have a new teacher this year who is class of 1995, whom I taught my first year teaching. He is already back 1 year out of college. He graduated at the top of his theology class and he still wanted to come back here, so it says a lot about how people get attached here. There are alumni in the hallways nonstop. Kids, as soon as they come back from college, this is the first place they go. I get six or seven visitors a week. As soon as they get back in town, they come in and say 'hi.' And I'll ask them how is school, and they will just sit down for a while. There is something here that makes it a special place."

This *coming back* is described by Matusov (1999) as "an inclusion of generations," which helps to maintain the culture of a caring community of learners. A teacher at Purcell Marian explained the strong ties between and among students and staff in terms of how they relate to each other as members of the same inclusive community: "The kids here feel that people care about them here. The kids come back and they tell me, 'you know it's one place where I feel like you gave a crap about what I'm doing 10 years after high school. You told me that you wanted to see me in 10 years doing well.' I know as a group here we want all the children to be successful in life and feel that they got something out of the school."

The faculty consists to a large degree of two main groups of people, both of whom exhibit a special sense of loyalty and attachment to the school. The first group is made up of those faculty members who were teachers at either of the individual schools that merged to form the larger, co-educational high school. These teachers have invested from 20 to 35 years and have chosen to stay on board through the years because of the feeling of family and community. The second group consists of teachers who are graduates and who chose to return there to work because of their attachment to the school community. One veteran teacher noted, "I've been here 35 years, and I enjoy it. I'm sure that any of the teachers here want to be here and be involved in this because of the freedom that you have to work with that type of student and to do everything you can to help them."

Another teacher who is a graduate talked about the students and how they frequently come back to visit because of the sense of family and community that they found there. He speaks of the attachment former students have: "I don't know what it is but it makes people want to come back. My sister, it's all she talks about. She is a freshman at the University of Cincinnati now. I've had five or six cousins graduate from here since I have. One is now the director of Minority Recruitment at Whittingburg University, and he calls once a week wanting to know, 'Who can I get, who can I get?' So there is an attachment." Graduates are frequent candidates for teaching positions, as are individuals who began at the school as instructional assistants and completed their teacher education programs.

A caring school community seems to have a strong, direct impact on the quality of teaching and learning in inclusive classrooms. The director of the program indicated that a caring school community is more important than having everything perfect on paper and having a lot of funding. She stated, "We had the right attitude and the right heartfelt belief that they [students with disabilities] should be here. And so all of the money in the world is not going to buy that, and that's the biggest difference."

Community of Mind

> Community of mind emerges from the binding of people to common goals, shared values, and shared conceptions of being and doing. When put together, the three represent webs of meaning that tie people together and give people a sense of belonging and uniqueness as a community. (Sergiovanni, 1994, p. 68)

It is community of mind among the staff that allows the work of inclusion to be carried out successfully. Teachers share a common ethos and a vision of inclusive education for all students. A shared community of mind was instrumental in the successful social and academic inclusion of students with developmental disabilities. There was some tension, but it did not stop them because they shared a common inclusive mission that said they would teach all students regardless of their abilities or disabilities.

The sense of inclusion and community dominates the school culture. One teacher stated that if you did not believe in inclusion, "I don't think there's any way possible that you could stay at this school and be happy." The school is able to successfully develop an inclusive community because the concept of inclusion is ingrained in their mission statement and in their daily interactions with each other. It is a deeply entrenched part of who they have said they are and how they identify themselves as a school. The principal explained her perception of how the staff responded to the idea that they would now be responsible for teaching not only students with learning disabilities, but students with developmental disabilities as well. In doing so, she provided a good example of how community of mind was essential in assisting the staff in overcoming fear and moving the school forward in its inclusive efforts. She stated that even though there was that initial fear that comes with change, they made a commitment to it because they knew as a staff that it was the right thing to do.

Community of Memory

"In time, communities by kinship, of place, and of mind become communities of memory thereby binding members with images of common memories and common learnings" (Sergiovanni, 1994, p. 69). Sergiovanni further explained that being a part of a community of memory is what sustains people when times are tough, connects them when they are not present, and provides them with a common history for creating sense and meaning. A veteran teacher who started the first program for students with learning disabilities provided an example of community of memory. He explained that because of a community of memory, the teachers were committed and confident in their ability to be effective in an inclusive classroom even though there was initial concern and fear. The school has a long history of meeting the needs of a diverse student population.

The principal explained that the staff responded to the fact that they would be responsible for teaching students with developmental disabilities with some concern about their ability to be effective as teachers. In her explanation, she provided a good example of how community of memory was essential in overcoming fear and moving the school forward in its inclusive efforts. She explained that even though people were challenged and somewhat afraid initially, they were able to keep going because they had the inclusive mission of the school and a history of meeting the needs of a diverse student population to bind them together and help them focus and stay committed. When implementation became difficult, it was community of memory that pulled them through.

PRINCIPLES AND PRACTICES

There are certain principles and practices that are common to schools that function as inclusive communities. Fisher, Sax, and Jorgensen (1998) found that the following principles and practices emerge in schools that function as effective school communities:

- Decisions about inclusive education and school reform originate in an administrative vision that is unwavering in the face of uncertainty and the difficulties of putting principles into practice.
- Inclusion of students is solidly based in changing general education.
- Support for teachers and administrators is provided through internal structures.
- Social justice issues are infused throughout the curriculum.
- Creative use of time through implementation of innovative school schedules is essential.
- General and special education teachers with new job descriptions share responsibility for all students.
- Classes are heterogeneously grouped.
- Curriculum is thematic, performance oriented, constructivist, and based on high achievement standards for every student.

GUIDING QUESTIONS

Secondary school leaders are confronted with major issues in restructuring and inclusion as they lead their schools from a culture of isolation to one of community and collaborative relationships (Sergiovanni & Starratt, 1998). Relationships among staff members, students, parents, and administrators are critical in developing school communities. High schools that are struggling to become communities might use the questions offered by Sergiovanni (1994) to guide their planning efforts (see Table 5.1).

Regardless of the form that community takes in schools, it is the quality of the relationships among and between teachers, students, parents, and administrators that is the key to building an inclusive community. Allen (1994) pointed out that an essential ingredient in the development of a school community is the quality of the interpersonal relationships, and that these relationships need to be collegial, cooperative, and interdependent. The questions address issues regarding relationships and interdependent work between and among teachers, students, parents, and administrators. Each school will find its own answers to these relationship questions based on the needs, goals, and values of the staff, students, and parents involved.

EFFECT OF AN INCLUSIVE SCHOOL COMMUNITY

A strong sense of community in high schools has benefits for both teachers and students, and provides a necessary foundation for inclusive learning. A few of the outcomes or benefits are briefly discussed here.

Table 5.1.   Questions for planning a sense of community

1. What can be done to increase the sense of kinship, neighborliness, and collegiality among the faculty of a school?
2. How can the faculty become more of a professional community where everyone cares about each other and helps each other to grow, to learn together, and to lead together?
3. What kinds of relationships have to be cultivated with parents that will enable them to be included in this emerging community?
4. How can the web of relationships that exist among teachers and between teachers and students be defined so that they embody community?
5. How can teaching and learning settings be arranged so that they are more like a family?
6. How can the school, as a collection of families, be more like a neighborhood?
7. What are the shared values and commitments that enable the school to become a community of mind?
8. How will these values and commitments become practical standards that guide the lives of all members of the school community?
9. What are the patterns of mutual duties that emerge in the school as community is achieved?

Teachers and Staff Members

A strong sense of community can facilitate staff members' instructional efforts and enhance their personal well-being. Bryk and Driscoll (1988) found that schools that function as communities have high staff morale, low teacher absenteeism, and high teacher satisfaction related to their work. In addition, there is evidence that staff members who experience a strong sense of community are clearer about the expectations of others at school (Royal & Rossi, 1996). As community is fostered among staff members, appropriate behaviors and attitudes are modeled for students, helping them to mature in their own interpersonal relationships. Similar observations have been made with respect to the development of a collaborative school climate. Smith and Scott (1990) noted that schools where teachers actively and openly collaborate and cooperate with one another also have a high level of collaboration and cooperation among students.

Students

An inclusive school community may promote a variety of positive outcomes for all students. Bryk and Driscoll (1988) reported that schools that function as communities have fewer problems with student misbehavior (e.g., class cutting, student absenteeism) than do other schools. They also found that students in these schools showed more interest in academics and greater achievement gains and that they dropped out at lower rates. Royal and Rossi (1996) similarly suggested that students' sense of community is related to their engagement in school activities. Students with a sense of community are less likely to cut class and think about dropping out of school and are more likely to feel bad when unprepared for classes. They found that students having a high sense of community felt burned out less often at school.

Community improves schooling for all students, enhances their academic and social development, and provides them with experiences necessary to prepare them for full participation in a democratic society. A sense of community is an important component of educational programs targeted at students at risk of academic failure. Many students who are identified as having a disability drop out of school before graduating. This may be because they do not feel as if they belong or have membership in or the support of a school community. In his study of exemplary dropout-prevention programs, Wehlage (1989) observed that each program devoted major time and attention to overcoming the existing barriers that prevent students from connecting with the school and developing a sense of belonging, membership, and engagement.

School Leadership

Creating inclusive communities in secondary schools means change, and with that change come challenges. School leaders at the high school level have the tremendous responsibility of transforming rigidly structured school organizations into caring communities where the needs of students with varied abilities, experiences, and cultural and economic backgrounds are valued and respected.

Building community can be quite a task in high schools where traditional rules, roles, and relationships are deeply embedded in the school culture. Educational leaders at the secondary level are increasingly expected to display leadership in encouraging the empowerment of and collaboration among learners, staff, and parents. Many are having difficulty, however, providing the leadership needed to create collaborative school communities that support inclusive learning. Sergiovanni (1996) noted that the typical managerial role of administrators in many high schools requires that they, as primary decision makers, assume responsibility for the control of school activities and resources. He further noted that the principles utilized by secondary school leaders in their traditional role as managers are at odds with the principles of collegiality, empowerment, and reflection that are necessary for creating and building school communities.

Vision is an essential part of building community in inclusive high schools. The Working Forum on Inclusive Schools (1995), in its study of 12 schools, reported that if the school as a whole shares the vision that all children need to be a respected part of the school community, that vision alone brings its own sense of community. All students are greeted and talked to, all professionals are a part of the same staff, and all parents feel welcomed and encouraged to participate. In schools that effectively function as communities, the staff, administrators, students, and parents all share 1) common values related to school and education, 2) common activities that link school members to each other and to the school's traditions, and 3) an "ethos of caring" in interpersonal relationships (Bryk & Driscoll, 1988). This results in collaborative interactions and collegiality among and between the members of the school community.

Community is important in schools because of our basic need as humans to belong. However, when school leaders do not ensure that the basic need for community is met in schools, students and teachers will look elsewhere for substitutes and may begin to build dysfunctional communities among themselves. Historically, high schools have had isolated school cultures where collaboration and collegiality among the entire faculty has not been actively encouraged by the school leader or leaders. However, the literature suggests that a school culture that looks and acts like a community seems to be the type of environment necessary for inclusion at the high school level to be effective (e.g., Jorgensen, 1998; Lipsky & Gartner, 1997; Sergiovanni, 1994). Building high school communities that welcome everyone requires additional time, effort, and money, but the payoff is worth it (Van Dyke, 1995).

SUMMARY POINTS

- Successful inclusive high schools function as a community grounded in respect, care, trust, empowerment, and commitment.
- School communities function as community by kinship, place, mind, and memory.
- Schools that function as a community have strong interpersonal relationships that are collegial, cooperative, and interdependent.
- Schools that function as a community benefit teachers and students.

REFERENCES

Allen, J.M. (1994). *School counselors collaborating for student success.* Eugene, OR: ERIC Clearinghouse on Educational Management. (ERIC No. ED 377414)

Bellah, R.N. (1985). Creating a new framework for new realities. *Change, 17*(2), 35–39.

Bryk, A.S., & Driscoll, M.E. (1988). *The high school as community: Contextual influences and consequences for students and teachers.* Madison: National Center on Effective Secondary Schools, University of Wisconsin. (ERIC Document Reproduction Service No. ED 302539)

Ferguson, D.L. (1996). Is it inclusion yet? Bursting the bubbles. In M.S. Berres, D.L. Ferguson, P. Knoblock, & C. Woods (Eds.), *Creating tomorrow's schools today: Stories of inclusion, change, and renewal* (pp. 16–37). New York: Teachers College Press.

Fisher, D., Sax., C., & Jorgensen, C.M. (1998). Philosophical foundations of inclusive, restructuring schools. In C.M. Jorgensen (Ed.), *Restructuring high schools for all students: Taking inclusion to the next level* (pp. 29–47). Baltimore: Paul H. Brookes Publishing Co.

Irmsher, K. (1997). *Education reform and students at risk.* Eugene, OR: ERIC Clearinghouse on Educational Management. (ERIC No. ED 405642)

Jorgensen, C.M. (Ed.). (1998). *Restructuring high school for all students: Taking inclusion to the next level.* Baltimore: Paul H. Brookes Publishing Co.

Lipsky, D.K., & Gartner, A. (1997). *Inclusion and school reform: Transforming America's classrooms.* Baltimore: Paul H. Brookes Publishing Co.

Matusov, E. (1999). How does a community of learners maintain itself? Ecology of an innovative school. *Antrhopology and Education Quarterly, 30*(2), 161–186.

Raywid, M.A. (1993). *Community: An alternative school accomplishment in public schools that work: Creating community.* New York: Routledge.

Royal, M.A., & Rossi, R.J. (1996). Individual-level correlates of sense of community: Findings from workplace and school. *Journal of Community Psychology, 24*(4), 395–416.

Sailor, W., & Skrtic, T.M. (1996). School/community partnerships and educational reform: Introduction to the topical issue. *Remedial and Special Education, 17*(5), 267–270.

Salend, S.J. (1998). *Effective mainstreaming: Creating inclusive classrooms* (3rd ed.). Upper Saddle River, NJ: Merrill.

Sergiovanni, T.J. (1994). *Building community in schools.* San Francisco: Jossey-Bass.

Sergiovanni, T.J. (1996). *Leadership for the schoolhouse: How is it different? Why is it important?* San Francisco: Jossey-Bass.

Sergiovanni, T.J., & Starratt, R.J. (1998). *Supervision: A redefinition* (6th ed.). New York: McGraw-Hill.

Smith, S.C., & Scott, J.J. (1990). *The collaborative school: A work environment for effective instruction.* Eugene, OR: ERIC Clearinghouse on Educational Management. (ERIC No. ED 316918)

Thousand, J.S., Rosenberg, R.L., Bishop K.D., & Villa, R.A. (1997). The evolution of secondary inclusion. *Remedial and Special Education, 18*(5), 270–284.

Thurlow, M.L., Elliott, J.L., & Ysseldyke, J.E. (1998). *Testing students with disabilities: Practical strategies for complying with district and state requirements.* Thousand Oaks, CA: Corwin Press.

Van Dyke, R. (1995). How to build an inclusive school community: A success story. *Phi Delta Kappan, 76*(6), 475–479.

Wehlage, G.G. (1989). *Reducing the risk: Schools as communities of support.* New York: Falmer Press.

Working Forum on Inclusive Schools. (1994). *Creating schools for all our students: What 12 schools have to say.* Reston, VA: Council on Exceptional Children.

6

Designing Instruction
in an Inclusive Classroom

Anne M. Bauer

Teacher Contributors: Jason Haap, Richard Hague, Rick Hennegan,
Nicki Brainard, Lee Widmer

In the next several chapters, we reveal the nitty-gritty of teaching in an inclusive high school. We address, in this and subsequent chapters, designing instruction, managing the classroom, designing and evaluating accommodations and adaptations, and assessing learning and evaluating progress. Having these topics in separate chapters, however, may be a bit misleading. All of these components of teaching are integrated and interrelated in such a way that it is difficult to tell when one stops and another begins. In fact, as we worked with our teacher contributors on each of these chapters, we found it difficult to differentiate the areas. In order to try to address this essential information, however, we have broken it up into these separate units. After reading this chapter, you will be able to answer the following questions:

- How do you structure lessons to include all students?
- How do you address multiple intelligences in the classroom?
- What strategies can you use for cooperative learning?
- How can you stimulate critical thinking and open dialogue in classrooms consisting of students from diverse ethnic, cultural, linguistic, ability, and disability groups?

STRUCTURING LESSONS FOR ALL STUDENTS

Teachers may have some faulty assumptions about learning that can have a negative impact on their ability to structure lessons for all students. Berryman (1991) argued that many school learning situations are ineffective because they are based on mistaken assumptions. She contended that the following myths must be addressed:

MYTH: *Students predictably transfer learning from one situation to another.* Students do not transfer information from school to everyday practice, from everyday practice to school, or from one discipline to another within school without help and support.

MYTH: *Students are passive recipients of wisdom, vessels into which teachers pour knowledge.* Berryman (1991) argued that keeping control in the hands of the teacher undercuts the students' development of skills such as goal setting, strategic planning, monitoring, evaluating, and revising. Passive learning places a premium on correct answers to questions on tests, rather than on changes in behavior and knowledge.

MYTH: *Learning is strengthening the bond between stimuli and correct response.* This approach misses the point that humans are sense-making, problem-solving beings and doesn't capitalize on students' natural learning systems.

MYTH: *Students are blank slates on which knowledge is inscribed.* Students actually bring ideas and concepts that they have acquired elsewhere into every situation.

MYTH: *Skills and knowledge, to be transferable to new situations, should be acquired independent of their contexts of use.* Context gives meaning to learning.

Effective learning environments emphasize other assumptions. Berryman (1991) suggested that in effective environments, learning takes place in context. Parents and friends serve as models for imitative learning and provide structure to and connections between their experiences. Learning is functional, and concepts and skills are acquired as tools to solve problems. In addition, the need for and purpose of learning are explicitly stated for the student.

Johnson and Johnson (1991), pioneers in collaborative and cooperative classrooms, maintained that successful instruction depends on

- Specifying desired outcomes for the students and setting appropriate instructional goals
- Implementing the appropriate goal structure; goal structures can be cooperative, competitive, or individualistic
- Assembling the instructional materials and resources needed to facilitate the desired learning
- Creating an instructional climate that facilitates the type of interaction among students and between students and teachers needed to achieve the instructional goals
- Assessing and providing feedback on students' progress toward the desired outcomes while instruction is under way
- Assessing and providing feedback on the intended and unintended out-

comes of instruction; in addition to the sought-for outcomes, many times there are unanticipated outcomes. Teachers should be concerned with the actual consequences of an instructional program, irrespective of whether they are planned or expected.

The key to Johnson and Johnson's (1991) instructional ideas is the goal structure. A *goal structure* identifies the amount of interdependence among students. The three goal structures that they describe are cooperative, competitive, and individualistic. *Cooperative goal structures* are in place when the students perceive that in order to meet their own goal, the students with whom they are working must obtain the goal. In a *competitive goal structure,* students perceive that in order to obtain their goal, other students may need to fail. An *individualistic goal structure* exists when one student's obtaining his or her goal has no bearing on another student's meeting his or her goal. Although cooperation is essential, in their early work, Johnson and Johnson suggested that there are times when competition is enjoyable and provides an opportunity to apply one's abilities to compare oneself with other. Acting independently may provide the opportunity to apply one's competencies to compare oneself with others.

Our teacher contributors recognized the demands of structuring lessons for all students. Richard Hague, chair of the English department, described the need for instruction to be multichannelled, holistic, organic, and multilayered. Structuring a lesson, then, is a complex task. Our teacher collaborators provided several insights for structuring lessons for all students.

One strategy for structuring lessons is to use a consistent routine for the instructional period. Nicki Brainard, biology and environmental sciences teacher, indicated that she uses a consistent pattern for the instructional period. She begins with a presentation or a quiz, then moves to an activity, group work, or lab during which students are actively engaged in the material that was presented. The students then come back together for a "wrap up," which may include a review or a video to reinforce the concepts that were presented. During the presentation period, new terms are introduced in an effort to link past learning or experience to the content area. For example, when the new term *nucleus* is presented, students are asked to think about how they've heard the word used before applying it to cell structure. Rick Hennegan, religion and language arts teacher, also uses word study, pushing students to figure out what words mean and to derive definitions.

The use of routines often has been reported as the basis of lesson structure. The Clearinghouse on Handicapped and Gifted Education (1987) described the following routine grounded in research on instruction:

* *Gain the students' attention:* The teacher should monitor that students are paying attention.

- *Review relevant past learning:* The teacher forms a link between new information and what the student already knows.
- *Communicate the goal of the lesson:* The teacher describes what is being learned, why it is important, and how it relates to other learning.
- *Model the skill to be learned:* The teacher demonstrates the skill, exaggerating steps so students attend to critical features.
- *Prompt for correct response:* The teacher provides opportunities for guided practice, with prompts and feedback.
- *Check for skill mastery:* When students have demonstrated the skill, they should perform the behavior under supervision with no prompting.
- *Close the lesson:* The teacher should provide closure by reviewing the skill, discussing what will be covered next, or introducing independent work or homework.

Rick Hennegan utilized the K-W-L-H technique to link the learning in his classroom. This group instruction activity, developed by Ogle (1986), was initially used as a model for active thinking during reading. In using K-W-L-H, the teacher begins by listing in a column on a chalkboard or chart what the students indicate they know (K) about the subject. The teacher then helps the students determine what they want (W) to learn. As the students work through the lesson, the teacher helps them identify what they learn (L) as they read or listen. At the conclusion of the activity, the students identify how (H) they can learn more. The K-W-L-H chart helps the teacher gain an awareness of students' background knowledge and interests, and often are used at the beginning and end of a new unit of study (Tennenbaum, 1996).

Nicki Brainard also described the use of mnemonics to support student learning. Mnemonics have been demonstrated to be of great help to adolescents and adults with learning disabilities (Lowry, 1990). For example, students have developed mnemonics to remember the prefixes for the metric system—Kids (k = kilo) have (h = hecto) dropped (d = deco) over (o = the base unit) dead (d = deci) converting (c = centi) metrics (m = mili), and the taxonomy system—King (k = kingdom) Phillip (p = phylum) comes (c = class) over (o = order) for (f = family) green (g = genus) soup (s = species).

Our teacher collaborators emphasized the need to make the information real for the students, the need to relate to what they know. Richard Hague invited his students to go outside to write poetry—finding sunflowers growing by the dumpster, showing them that "poems can arise out of junk." Through recognizing their language and feelings, he suggested, students build trust, and when they feel safe, they express their emotions. Nicki Brainard described the structures of the cell using the metaphor of a local teen club. The cell wall is the bouncer, keeping out who doesn't belong; the nucleus is "the dude who runs the show;" the lysosome is the janitor, and the golgi apparatus is UPS, packaging and delivering supplies.

Graphic Organizers

Graphic organizers often are used to support students' learning. A *graphic organizer* is a visual way of depicting the relationships between pieces of information. Dye (2000) suggested that graphic organizers help students learn because they link new information to preexisting knowledge. By putting the information into a graphic structure, students move pertinent information into long-term memory. Graphic organizers serve as visual displays that help them learn.

Graphic organizers can help students in several ways (Larkin, 1997). They can help them locate and remember key facts and ideas. In addition, they may serve as a summary, allowing students to view information as a meaningful whole. A completed graphic organizer may serve as a study guide, giving the student both written and spatial arrangement of information. The information may serve as a summary of the unit or chapter. In using graphic organizers, Larkin suggested that a teacher should be explicit as to how the graphic organizer can be used and should provide examples. As the teacher works through a lesson, he or she can complete a graphic organizer and model its use. The teacher can summarize a lesson by placing a blank graphic organizer on the overhead projector and help students complete it. Students also may complete a blank graphic organizer individually or in small groups. Larkin also suggested giving students opportunities to create their own graphic organizers and design their own formats. The graphic organizers may be presented to the class to teach a mini-lesson, or to explain why the students chose a particular format. A wide range of graphic organizer formats are available (see Figure 6.1).

Graphic organizers also can be used to help students understand a unit of instruction. Boudah, Lenz, Bulgren, Schumaker, and Deshler (2000) proposed the use of a "Unit Organizer" as a strategic approach to planning for and teaching content to academically diverse groups of students. Use of the organizer focuses on how a teacher introduces, builds, and gains closure on critical ideas—a *unit* is any "chunk" of content. The Unit Organizer is presented to the students with blanks for them to fill in the following information:

- The current unit/experience
- The last unit/experience
- The next unit/experience
- The bigger picture (where the current unit fits into the quarter or semester)
- A "unit map," which captures the central point or meaning of the unit, and a graphic organizer for the unit
- Unit relationships, which are the names of relationships that might be important for the kinds of thinking required to learn the unit information
- Unit self-test questions

- A unit schedule
- An expanded unit map as a graphic organizer
- A new unit self-test as they explore the unit

Through the use of the unit organizer, students see the overall context of their current work.

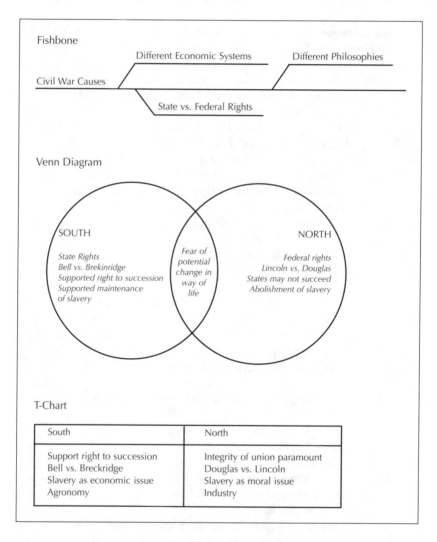

Figure 6.1.   Sample graphic organizer formats.

ADDRESSING MULTIPLE INTELLIGENCES

As we were developing this book, teachers frequently referred to addressing *multiple intelligences.* In *Frames of Mind: The Theory of Multiple Intelligences,* Howard Gardner (1983) proposed seven separate human intelligences. The first two, linguistic and logical-mathematical, are the ones most frequently demonstrated by *traditional* learners who respond to *traditional* instruction. Lee Widmer, a physics teacher, indicated that students who are entering inclusive settings for the first time may "mimic" traditional learners, assuming that linguistic and logical-mathematical intelligences will be rewarded. However, after a year or two of being challenged to use their "gifts," students begin to explore their more natural ways of learning and knowing. The intelligences Gardner proposed were

1. *Linguistic intelligence,* which involves a sensitivity to spoken and written language, an ability to learn language, and the capacity to use language to accomplish specific goals
2. *Logical-mathematical intelligence,* which involves the ability to analyze problems logically, carry out mathematical operations, and apply the scientific method
3. *Musical intelligence,* which involves the ability to perform, compose, and appreciate musical patterns
4. *Bodily kinesthetic intelligence,* which involves using one's body or parts of the body to solve problems or generate products
5. *Spatial intelligence,* which involves the ability to recognize and manipulate the patterns of wide space as well as patterns of more confined areas
6. *Interpersonal intelligence,* which involves a person's capacity to understand the intentions, motivations, and desires of other people and to work effectively with them
7. *Intrapersonal intelligence,* which involves the ability to understand oneself and to have knowledge of one's own desires, fears, and capacities, which are applied to regulate one's own life

In *Intelligence Reframed: Multiple Intelligences for the 21st Century,* Gardner (1999) described two additional intelligences: *naturalist intelligence,* the ability to recognize patterns and develop categories in nature, and *existential intelligence,* which involves the ability to locate oneself with respect to the further reaches of the cosmos and to relate to existential issues such as the significance of life, the meaning of death, and the fate of the world.

Gardner (1999) argued that these "intelligences" go beyond learning styles. He suggested that a *learning style* is a general approach that can be applied equally to an indefinite range of content. An *intelligence* is a capacity geared to a specific content. Schools that emphasize multiple intelligences, however, are characterized by several practices. First, there is an emphasis on faculty learning about multiple intelligences; faculty and staff view themselves as lifelong learners and address issues related to multiple intelligences in their own professional development. In addition, the culture is one of supporting diverse learning and encouraging steady, hard work. Collaboration is key in schools applying the multiple intelligences theory, and there are meaningful options in assessment of student growth and learning. High quality and meaningful work is demanded, and arts play an important part in the school. Gardner offered more specific information in terms of "entry points" for various students with the topic area:

- *Narrations,* which launches students who enjoy learning about topics through stories
- *Quantitative/numerical activities,* for students intrigued by numbers and the patterns they make, operations that can be performed, and insights into size, ration, and change
- *Logical activities,* which emphasize the ability to think logically
- *Foundational/existential activities,* for students who are attracted to fundamental kinds of questions
- *Aesthetics,* for students involved with art or with materials that are arranged in ways that feature balance, harmony, and composition
- *Hands-on work,* for students who learn more readily when they are fully engaged, including building and manipulating materials or experimenting
- *Social interactions,* for students who learn more effectively in group settings, assuming other roles, observing perspectives, and interacting regularly

Our teacher contributors remarked on the effect of addressing multiple intelligences in the classroom. Richard Hague indicated that students responded with deeper ownership and pride in their work—pride far greater than when the tasks involved only pencil and paper. Using *exhibitions,* in which students demonstrate their knowledge of a specific topic using various media, activities, props, and materials, students may utilize their intelligence to demonstrate what they know.

COOPERATIVE LEARNING

Throughout this book we talk about cooperative classrooms and a climate of collaboration rather than competition. Tinzmann et al. (1990) suggested that there are four characteristics of collaborative classrooms. First, there is shared knowledge among teachers and students. Collaborative teachers value and build upon the knowledge, personal experiences, language, and culture that students bring to the learning situation. Second, teachers share the authority of setting goals, designing learning tasks, and assessing what is learned. Students have opportunities to ask and investigate questions of personal interest, and they have a voice in the decision-making process. Third, teachers mediate learning. Teachers adjust the level of information and support to maximize the ability to take responsibility for learning. Finally, collaborative classrooms have heterogeneous groupings of students, which give students opportunities to learn from and with each other.

Roles in collaborative classrooms are different from those in traditional competitive classrooms. The teacher is a facilitator, model, and coach (Tinzmann et al., 1990). As a facilitator, the teacher creates rich environments, with multiple activities and projects. The teacher establishes diverse and flexible social structures that promote communication and collaboration among students. As a model, the teacher verbalizes his or her thinking process and shares thoughts about the various roles, rules, and relationships in the classroom. As a coach, the teacher gives hints or cues, provides feedback, and redirects students. Students' roles also shift, with students actively engaged in designing their own learning tasks, monitoring their learning, and assessing what they have learned.

Collaborative classrooms assume cooperative learning activities. Cooperative learning is not only a way to develop and maintain a supportive classroom climate; it is supported by child development and learning theory. Murray (1994) suggested that understanding the theoretical basis of cooperative learning can help teachers apply cooperative learning more successfully.

In terms of Piagetian child development, Murray (1994) contended that cooperative learning addresses *egocentrism*—the child's tendency to center on one aspect of a situation, usually his or her own perspective. Cooperative learning encourages children to attend to other dimensions and perspectives and to integrate these with his or her own prior views into a new, more inclusive view of the problem. Murray suggested that cooperative learning resonates with Vygotsky's view that our human functions and accomplishments have their origins in social relationships. The group's common perspectives and solutions, as they are debated, argued, negotiated, discussed, and compromised, are indispensable for cognitive growth. In terms of cognitive science theory, cooperative learning helps the student gradually develop a new conceptual model for the skill and couples it with specific strategies used by experts. Cooperative learning features expert–novice teaching to allow students to integrate multiple roles that the successful problem solver masters.

One of the primary reasons to use cooperative learning methods is to address the problems of competition. For most students who have to work harder than their peers to achieve, a competitive situation is a poor motivator; for some it is almost torture. It is essentially unfair that success is difficult for many students but comes easily for others; success is defined on a relative basis in the competitive classroom. Even if some children learn a great deal, they still may be at the bottom of the class. They may learn that academic success is not within their grasp (Slavin, 1995).

Sapon-Shevin, Ayres, and Duncan (1994) suggested that cooperative learning means establishing an ethic in the classroom grounded in cooperation. Through cooperative learning, a sense of community, cooperation, and connection is enhanced. In addition, cooperative learning facilitates teaching meaningful content: it serves a catalyst to thinking about what is important for students to learn and making things meaningful and functional for all students. Cooperative learning depends on supportive heterogeneous groups. It also requires structures that ensure the active participation of all students, including division of labor and materials, flexible interpretation of roles, and individualized student responsibilities. Cooperative learning provides opportunities for ongoing evaluation.

Johnson and Johnson (1994) have specific strategies for optimizing cooperative learning. They suggested that cooperative learning is most effective when there is clear positive interdependence, when each group member's efforts are required and indispensable for group success, and when each group member has a unique contribution to make. In addition, face-to-face interaction, with students encouraging and facilitating each others' efforts, enhances the experience. Each person in the group should do his or her own share, with individual accountability and personal responsibility. In cooperative learning, students can frequently use interpersonal and small-group skills in which students get to know and trust each other, communicate accurately, accept and support each other, and constructively resolve their conflicts. Frequent and regular group processing of current functioning improves the group's future effectiveness. Both the small group and the whole class should reflect on the process.

In describing complex instruction, Lotan (1997) described using a *multiple ability orientation* that begins by naming the different abilities necessary for successful completion of an activity. The teacher then points out the relevance of each ability to the task, creating a mixed set of expectations for competence. Each individual brings different abilities, an effective repertoire of problem-solving strategies, and valuable experiences to the task. All are needed to complete the task successfully. In addition, the teacher must assign competence to low-status students. In assigning competence, the teacher pays particular attention to low-status students and watches for those moments when they show how competent they are on some of the abilities previously identified in the orientation (Lotan, 1997).

The teacher has a specific role in designing cooperative learning lessons. Udvari-Solner (1994) indicated that the teacher is responsible for identifying academic and social objectives related to group and individual performance. The teacher determines the group size, membership, and how long the group will be assigned to work together. Groups may work together for a single activity or for a specific period of time such as a week, the duration of a unit, or a month. Arranging the learning environment is a key task; there must be sufficient space between groups to reduce distractions and allow easy access by the instructor. Udvari-Solner suggested that teachers establish a positive interdependence between group members. Through goal interdependence, the students will have resource interdependence, role interdependence, and incentive interdependence. The teacher should be explicit about the criteria for academic and social success and monitor student performance. At the end of the lesson, the teacher should provide closure to the lesson and evaluate the product and progress of the group work.

Putnam (1998) described four major approaches to cooperative learning. She indicated, however, that all of these approaches involve a common task or learning activity suitable for group work, small-group learning, cooperative behavior, positive interdependence, and individual accountability. The four approaches she described are 1) the conceptual approach, 2) the curricular approach, 3) the structural approach, and 4) the complex instruction approach.

The conceptual approach was developed by David and Roger Johnson. This approach is referred to as the *conceptual approach* because it is based on the assumption that teachers can become the "classroom manager" who structures effective learning activities that meet the needs of their students (Putnam, 1998). Johnson and Johnson (1991) emphasized the cooperative learning process and structures that can be used in any content area. They recommended using groups that are maintained throughout the academic year and that provide students with social interaction and support. Their structures include activities such as jigsaw learning or simultaneous explanation pairs. We describe several of these structures later in the chapter.

The curricular approach was developed by Slavin and his associates to teach mathematics (Slavin, Leavey, & Madden, 1984) and reading and writing (Slavin, 1990). In addition to these specific programs for curricular areas, Slavin has researched two general cooperative learning methods. In student teams achievement divisions (STAD) students work together in groups of four to master assigned material and then take individual quizzes. Students' quiz scores are compared with their past averages, and each student earns improvement points if the former average is exceeded. Individual students' improvement scores are totaled for team scores. If teams meet a predetermined criteria, they receive some type of reward. Students are encouraged to help each other in their group to learn the material. All students can contribute to their team's success by improving. Tournament group teams (TGT) replace the quizzes with weekly tournaments that involve individual competition between members of opposing teams (Slavin, 1995). The teams are heterogeneous, with students competing against their classmates who have similar records of performance.

The structural approach was developed by Spencer Kagan (1990) who contended that a *structure* is a content-independent way of organizing social interactions in the classroom. Structures that are content-independent can be used in a variety of academic areas. Kagan described a menu of structures that are appropriate for functions such as 1) mastery, 2) concept development, 3) team building, 4) class building, 5) communication building, and 6) multifunctional uses. Several of these structures are described later in this chapter.

The final approach Putnam (1998) presented is that of complex instruction. Elizabeth Cohen (1991) developed the complex instructional approach to involve students in activities that are challenging and intrinsically motivating. Complex tasks, which require a wide range of strengths, are assigned. Students work in groups, using one another to complete the assignments. Students are assigned roles such as materials manager, harmonizer, or resource person. Tasks are "multiple ability" and 1) have more than one correct solution; 2) are intrinsically interesting and rewarding; 3) permit different contributions from different students; 4) apply multimedia, sight, sound, and touch; 5) require a variety of skills or behaviors as well as reading and writing; and 6) are challenging (Cohen, 1994).

Kagan (1998) differentiated group work and cooperative learning. In *group work,* there is usually unequal participation, and students are not held individually accountable. Students "turn to their partner and talk it over" or "discuss in groups." In *cooperative learning structures,* there is positive interdependence, individual accountability, equal participation, and simultaneous interaction. Kagan used "Timed-Pair-Share" as an example of a true cooperative learning structure. In Timed-Pair-Share, students work in pairs, with one student labeled "a" and the other "b." In pairs, the "a" students share their thoughts with their "b" partners while the "b" students listen. Then the "b" students share their thoughts for 1 minute while the "a" students listen. Although teachers can implement this structure as easily as "talk it over with a partner," there is equal participation and equal accountability with this structure. Rather than being a separate activity that teachers conduct as a part of their traditional lesson, cooperative learning structures become part of the "fabric" of classroom life. Kagan also linked cooperative learning to Gardner's (1999) theory of multiple intelligences. He provided a "thumbnail sketch" of structures that relate to some of the various intelligences:

Verbal/linguistic intelligence–Telephone. One student from each team moves to where he or she cannot hear the teacher's instructions. The remaining students receive the instructions. When the instruction is over, the teams plan who will teach each portion of the instruction to the absent student. Team members instruct the teammate because the teammate will be quizzed on the information, and the score will be a reflection of how well the whole team has communicated the information.

Mathematical/logical intelligence–Find My Rule. The teacher places items in a graphic organizer, and the students try to discover what the rule is as to how items are placed. Teammates work together to discover the rule, then test it.

Visual/spatial intelligence–Team Mind Map. Each team works on a large sheet of chart paper. Each student works with a different colored marker. The team writes the main idea inside a rectangle in the center of the paper. The team then goes around adding core concepts around the main idea. When they are satisfied with the core concepts, team members add supporting elements and make bridges.

Bodily/kinesthetic intelligence—Formations. In formations, student try to create a bodily representation of a symbol, object, or system. For example, students may stand, holding hands, to create an addition equation or demonstrate the space between molecules in a solid, liquid, or gas by standing varying distances apart.

Musical/rhythmic intelligence—Songs and poems for two voices. Students alternate reciting or singing the words of a poem or song, then move to scripting existing poems and songs, finally creating their own original poems and songs for two voices.

Interpersonal/social intelligence—Team interview. The teacher introduces a topic, and for 1 minute a designated student responds to questions from teammates. When the time is up, the interviewed student sits down and another stands up and is interviewed by teammates. The team interview is over when all students have been interviewed.

Intrapersonal/introspective intelligence—Visualize share. Students shut their eyes as the teacher describes something for them to visualize. Through guided visualization, students can visit a historical scene, enter a novel, or become part of the human model.

Naturalist intelligence—Same/different. Students are in pairs and are presented with a picture of an animal. However, each picture varies in a number of ways. Without looking at each others' pictures, students try to discover what is the same and what is different between their pictures.

Cooperative, collaborative classrooms do present several challenges to the teacher (Tinzmann et al., 1990). These classrooms tend to be noisier, which is difficult for some teachers and administrators. Students should be taught the parameters for interaction. Preparation time also is significant, though Tinzmann and associates argued that there is a trade-off between the extra planning time needed and benefits, such as less time correcting papers, increased student motivation, and fewer attendance and discipline problems. Some teachers also have a conflict of values and simply do not feel comfortable allowing students to initiate dialogue, determine topics, or explore perspectives other than the teacher's.

Student Teams Achievement Divisions

Slavin (1995) suggested that STAD is one of the simplest cooperative learning methods, and one that can be used by teachers who are new to the cooperative approach. STAD has five major components:

- *Class presentations:* Material is initially presented
- *Teams:* Groups of four or five students representing a cross section of the class in terms of performance, gender, and race or ethnicity. The function of the team is to make sure all team members are learning and to prepare its members to do well on quizzes.
- *Quizzes:* Students take quizzes after one or two periods of teacher presentation and one or two periods of team practice. Students do not help each other during quizzes, so every student is individually responsible for knowing the material.
- *Individual improvement scores:* Students are given a performance goal that can be attained if he or she works harder and performs better than in the past. Any student is able to contribute maximum points to his or her team in this scoring system, but no student can do so without doing his or her best work. Students earn points for their teams based on the degree to which their quiz scores exceed their base scores.
- *Team recognition:* Teams earn certificates or other rewards if their average scores exceed a certain criterion.

An advantage of STAD is that it can be used with materials adapted from textbooks. In addition, students work together. Slavin (1995) suggested the following team rules:

- Students have a responsibility to make sure that their teammates have learned the material.
- No one is finished studying until all of the teammates have mastered the subject.
- "Ask three before me." Students should get information from their teammates before asking the teacher.
- Teammates should monitor their noise level.

Teams-Games-Tournaments

Teams-Games-Tournaments is the same as STAD except instead of using quizzes and individual improvement scoring system, Teams-Games-Tournaments uses academic tournaments in which students compete as representatives of their teams with members of other teams. The first two components of Teams-Games-Tournaments, class presentations and teams, are the same as STAD. However, games take the place of quizzes. Games are comprised of questions designed to test the knowledge students gain from class presentations and team practice. Games are played by teams comprised of three students, each of whom represents a different team, and a moderator. Most games include numbered questions on a ditto sheet. A student selects a numbered card and attempts to answer the question corresponding to the number. Students may challenge each others' answers for the points. Tournaments, held at the end of a week or a unit, are used as the structure for games. Students are assigned to tables with other students of similar ability. After the first tournament, students change tables depending on their performance. Winners, for example, move up to higher tables, and those who had lower scores move to lower tables. Team recognition remains the same as STAD.

KAGAN'S MASTERY STRUCTURES

Kagan (1990) presented a series of structures that assist students in practicing skills and reviewing information. These *mastery structures,* in addition to reviewing skills and information, support team building, communication building, and concept development. Traditional whole-class question-and-answer situations are not supportive of a collaborative, cooperative classroom climate. In traditional question and answer situations, the failure of one student increases the chances of success for another, and students may even hope their peers respond incorrectly so that they have a chance to shine. To avoid this negative interdependence, Kagan presented a series of activities that support mastery and review. Some of these activities include Numbered Heads Together, Pairs Check, Send a Problem, and Toss a Question.

Numbered Heads Together

In order to prepare for Numbered Heads Together, the teacher should have a set of questions or problems ready. To begin, the students form their teams or groups. Within each group, the students number off. The teacher then asks a question, and the students put their "heads together" to make sure everyone knows the answer of the question. The teacher may put a time frame on the question to quicken the pace ("You have 30 seconds to make sure everyone in your group knows the president of the Confederacy during the Civil War.") The teacher then calls a number at random and the student with that number who knows the answer raises his or her hand to be called on or to stand. If only one or two groups have the answer, the teacher may redirect the students to work together again. Otherwise, each of the students respond with the answer for their group.

Pairs Check

Pairs Check uses a traditional worksheet. Teams break into sets of pairs. One student works on the first problem on the worksheet, while the other student, serving as coach, watches and helps if necessary. The coach then checks the work to see if he or she agrees with the answer. If the partners don't agree on the answer, they may ask another pair on the team for help. If the team as a whole cannot agree on an answer, each teammate raises a hand. The teacher knows that when all hands are raised, it means a team question. If the partners agree on the answer, the coach congratulates his or her partner. For the next problem, the partners switch roles. The student who had been the coach now becomes the problem solver and the other student becomes the coach. The team then comes together and "pairs check." Again, if team members disagree and are unable to figure out why, all team members raise their hands. If the team agrees, the team congratulates themselves with a team handshake.

Send a Problem

Send a Problem involves students developing questions. Each student on a team develops a review problem or question. The author of the question asks it to his or her teammates. If there is consensus, the author writes the answer on the back of the card. If there is no consensus, the question is revised so that the group can come to consensus. The teams then pass their stack of review questions to another team. The new teams attempt to answer the problem or question. If they have consensus, they turn the card over to see if they agreed with the sending team. If not, they write their answer as an alternative. The stack of cards can them be sent to another team when they are completed. When the cards are returned to the senders, there is a discussion about the responses on the back of the cards.

Toss a Question

Toss a Question can provide a bit of activity and relief. In Toss a Question, students use a wad of paper and take turns tossing review questions. Each time the wad of paper is tossed to a student, he or she must answer a question and toss the paper to another individual on the team.

ISSUES IN GROUP WORK

Our teacher contributors remarked about the need for careful construction of groups for cooperative learning activities. Rick Hennegan indicated that he has utilized a wide range of ways to construct cooperative learning groups. He may number students off, construct the groups ahead of time, or construct the groups at the time of describing the activity based on students' response to the content.

Slavin (1995) presented a fairly formal way to assign students to teams, which may be helpful. On a sheet of paper, rank students from the highest to the lowest in past performance, using whatever information you have. Then decide on the number of teams and the size of teams. In assigning students to teams, balance out the teams so that each team includes students whose performance levels range from low to average to high and so that the average performance of all the teams in the class is about equal. A fairly easy way to do this is to use your ranked list, and going down the list, assign the students to teams.

Managing Teams

Several structures for managing teams are essential. Slavin (1995) suggested a "zero-noise signal" for students to stop talking, to give their full attention to the teacher, and to keep their hands and bodies still. Group praise occurs when the teacher goes to the group that is being most productive, gives the "zero-noise signal," and praises the group's work. Special recognition bulletins and special recognition ceremonies also can be used to recognize outstanding teams.

Our teacher contributors remarked about the need for explicitness related to group activities. Rick Hennegan suggested being explicit about the structure of the group, initially giving each individual a job with a complete description. By providing this structure early, students gradually learn to self-structure their groups. Jason Haap, English teacher, utilized *prework*–activities that the students complete before entering the group–so that everyone is confident that he or she has something to contribute.

CRITICAL THINKING, DIALOGUE, AND PROBLEM SOLVING

Critical thinking is an important aspect of collaborative classrooms. Instructional conversations, problem-based learning, and projects are all ways to enhance critical thinking among students.

Instructional Conversations

Classrooms often are driven by a "recitation script" (Goldenberg, 1991). Teachers usually ask a question, the student responds, and the teacher evaluates the response (Mehan, 1979). This results in teachers doing most of the talking in the classroom, not only preventing students from creating and manipulating language, but limiting the students' need to engage in critical thinking.

Goldenberg (1991) indicated that a good instructional conversation looks like an excellent discussion conducted by a teacher and a group of students. There is a high level of participation, without domination by any one person, including the teacher. The teacher draws out the students' ideas at some times, and at other times eases up, allowing thought and reflection to take over. In an instructional conversation, the students are expected to construct their own knowledge and understanding by making connections, building mental schemata, and developing new concepts from previous understandings. The teacher facilitates learning and encourages expression of students' own ideas, building on information students provide, and guiding students to higher levels of conversation.

Goldenberg (1991) described several elements of instructional conversations:

- The teacher selects a theme on which to focus discussion and has a general sense of how the theme will unfold.
- The teacher provides students with pertinent background knowledge and schemata necessary for understanding the information, weaving the new content into the discussion.
- When necessary, the teacher provides direct teaching of a skill or concept.
- The teacher elicits more extended student contributions by using a variety of elicitation techniques—invitations to expand, questions, restatements, and pauses.
- The teacher gently probes, asking questions such as, "What makes you think that?"
- Discussion focuses on questions for which there might be more than one correct answer.
- The teacher responds to students' statements and the opportunities that they provide.
- The teacher connects the comments so that the discussion is characterized by multiple, interactive, connected turns, where one conversation turn builds on and extends previous ones.
- The teacher creates a challenging atmosphere that is balanced by a positive climate; the teacher is more collaborator than evaluator, and students are challenged to negotiate and construct the meaning of the content.
- The teacher doesn't hold exclusive rights to determine who talks; students are encouraged to volunteer or influence the selection of speaking turns.

One of the keys to instructional conversations is the teacher's use of questions. Brualdi (1998) suggested that students may be hesitant to admit that they do not understand a concept, prompting teachers to assure them that their questions aren't stupid or bad. However, teachers must avoid some pitfalls in questioning during instructional conversations. Teachers should avoid vague questions (i.e., "What do you think about this book?"), trick or abstract questions (i.e., "What is friendship?"), and questions to which students may not be able to construct a response and that may decrease participation. Teachers' questions should have a clear purpose of guiding rather than determining what knowledge is known.

Problem-Based Learning

Problem-based learning was introduced by Barrows (1986) as an alternative to prepare medical students for real-world problems by letting them solve medical problems based on real-life cases, rather than having them learn through lectures. Students worked in teams and were assigned a medical practitioner who acted as a facilitator. Problem-based learning made the learning more applicable because students were encouraged to think and act as they would in the real world of medicine. Using problems can situate learning in the real world (Abdullah, 1998). Problem-based learning requires learners to explore resources other than the teacher, including reference materials and community members, and to draw on knowledge from various subject areas such as mathematics, geography, and science. During the inquiry process, students use language to obtain and communicate information, express options, and negotiate as they would in the real world. They document their discussions and decisions, consult reference materials, talk to others, and present findings while learning to listen, speak, read, and write effectively.

Duffy and Savery (1995) presented a model of the problem-based learning process. The process begins with the facilitator identifying or designing an ill-structured problem or task that is relevant to the students. The facilitator then presents the problem to the students. Students, in their own groups 1) generate working ideas as possible solutions, 2) identify available information related to the problem, 3) identify learning issues, 4) identify resources to look up or consult, 5) assign tasks to the various group members, 6) gather information, and 7) propose their solution.

The role of the teacher in problem-based learning is that of a facilitator who with well-timed, well-phased questions guides students in encountering the concepts and knowledge that are crucial for a good solution. Ask questions such as "How do you know?" "How can you find out?" "What are the consequences?" The teacher designs problems that naturally lead to the content and knowledge that students must encounter. In addition, the teacher creates a safe climate, and students express themselves free from judgment, enabling them to take risks and pursue blind alleys. If a misconception surfaces or a flawed argument is presented, the teacher does not jump in to set the record straight. Student misconceptions are identified by well-phrased questions. Students will become more comfortable with noting errors in each others' thinking, identifying errors in their own thinking, and seeing inconsistencies in the published materials and even errors in the teacher's thinking.

Problem-based learning is a strategy that develops problem-solving skills and content area knowledge and skills by placing students in the active role of problem solvers confronted with an ill-structured problem that resembles real-world problems (Finkel & Torp, 1995). The tasks involved in problem-based learning include 1) determining whether a problem exists, 2) creating an exact statement of the problem, 3) identifying resources to be used to gather information, 4) identifying resources needed to gather information, 5) generating possible solutions, 6) analyzing the solutions, and 7) presenting the solution. Stepien, Gallagher, and Workman (1993) presented the following steps in applying problem-based learning:

- The teacher presents the problem statement. The ill-structured problem or scenario should be one about which the students do not have adequate prior knowledge to develop a solution without gathering new information or learning new concepts.

- Each group develops a list under the heading "What do we know?"
- The group develops a problem statement.
- The group lists what is needed in order to fill in the missing information, preparing a second list labeled "What do we need to know?" This second list prompts in and out of class research.
- The group lists possible actions, recommendations, solutions, or hypotheses. After reviewing all of their information, the students generate a list of actions under the heading "What should we do?"
- The group presents and supports the solution. Teachers may require a presentation of the product including the problem statement, questions, data gathered, analysis of data, and support for solutions or recommendations.

Stepien et al. (1993) recognized that there are some issues in implementing problem-based learning. Students comfortable with the traditional lecture or book learning may feel less adapt in roles of conducting research, coordinating with peers, and generating unique products. Students who have been successful in performing discrete tasks or answering questions may be uneasy about how to "get a good grade" and the lack of concrete directions. It also is vital that the students take ownership of the problem.

Perhaps one of the most challenging aspects of problem-based learning for the teacher is the ill-structured problem. The Center for Problem-Based Learning (1998) indicated that ill-structured problems are complex, require inquiry, are changing and tentative, and have no right solution. The center presents several examples of these problems (see Table 6.1).

Projects

Project-based learning is a way to conceptualize learning by presenting students with problems to solve or products to develop (Moss & Van Duzer, 1998). Projects place students in situations that require authentic use of skills. Students work in pairs or teams, practicing skills in planning, organizing, negotiating, making a point, arriving at consensus, determining who will be responsible for each task, and designing how information will be researched and presented. Within the group, work integral to the projects and individuals' strengths and preferred ways of learning strengthen the work of the group (Lawrence, 1997). Moss and Van Duzer (1998) explained that project-based learning

- Builds on students' previous work
- Integrates reading, writing, speaking, and listening
- Utilizes collaborative teamwork, problem solving, negotiating, and other interpersonal skills
- Requires independent work

Table 6.1.   Ill-defined problems

Biology	You are working for the Department of Conservation. Urban sprawl has introduced subdivisions into areas that have traditionally been populated by small packs of coyotes. Homeowners are distraught. What action, if any, should be taken?
Literature	You are a member of a school board. Parents have expressed concern over students reading *Catcher in the Rye*. Prepare a report to the rest of the board regarding this text as to whether it should be censored in your district.
History	You are a member of President Kennedy's cabinet. The Russians have placed missiles on Cuba. What is your plan?
Mathematics	You are working at a local fast food restaurant making $5.75 an hour. You can no longer borrow your parents' car, so you need to buy your own car. What are your options?

Source: The Center for Problem-Based Learning, 1998.

- Challenges students to use their skills in new and different contexts outside of class
- Involves students in choosing the focus of the project and the planning process
- Engages students in learning information that is important to them
- Leads to clear outcomes
- Incorporates self-evaluation, peer evaluation, and teacher evaluation

Wrigley (1998) suggested that project-based learning follows a process of 1) selecting a topic, 2) planning, 3) researching, 4) developing products, and 5) sharing results. In the first phase, the project should reflect the interests and concerns of the students. Projects may address the objectives of one unit or they may span several units. The project may be the culminating event of a unit. The key is that students participate in decision making from the start of the project (Moss, 1998). As students continue with their topic, they work together to plan the project, conduct research, and develop their projects. Pre-project activities, such as working on problem-solving strategies or language for instruction, may be helpful. Projects may be shared in many ways, including through oral presentations, written products, or even the development of an entity. For example, students may develop a "salad bar" that they sell to teachers as a project.

Moss and Van Duzer (1998) presented several examples of project-based learning. In one project, a coloring and activity book of community information for families was developed. In another project, students taught a 30-minute lesson to another group.

The Foxfire Approach is an example of project learning. The Foxfire framework allows teachers to construct meaningful, experience-based educational environments (Starnes, Paris, & Stevens, 1999). The four core principles—student choice, teacher as facilitator, academic integrity, and community connections—are so interwoven that they become inseparable. The experiences and projects, which began as the student-produced *Foxfire Magazine* and a series of books on Appalachian life and folkways, are the projects developed by a program originally intended to teach basic English skills to freshmen in Appalachian Georgia (Starnes, 1999). The emphasis is on an audience beyond the classroom and a product that can be disseminated.

SUMMARY POINTS

- Structuring lessons to meet the needs of all students in the classroom demands the use of a consistent structure and recognition of the goal structures at work in the classroom.
- Graphic organizers can support students' learning through locating and remembering key facts and ideas, and the organizers serve as a study guide.
- Recognizing multiple intelligences may serve as a "entry point" for students in addressing a topic area.
- Cooperative learning approaches involve a common task or learning activity, and employ group work, cooperative behavior, positive interdependence, and individual accountability.
- Critical thinking can be enhanced through using instructional conversation, problem-based learning, and projects.

REFERENCES

Abdullah, M.H. (1998). *Problem-based learning in language instruction: A constructivist model.* Bloomington, IN: ERIC Clearinghouse on Reading, English, and Communication. (ERIC No. ED 423550)

Barrows, H.S. (1986). A taxonomy of problem-based learning methods. *Medical Education, 20,* 481–486.

Berryman, S.E. (1991). *Designing effective learning environments: Cognitive apprenticeship models.* New York: Institute on Education and the Economy, Teachers College, Columbia University. (ERIC No. ED 337689)

Boudah, D.J., Lenz, B.K., Bulgren, J.A., Schumaker, J.B., & Deshler, D.D. (2000). Enhance content learning through the unit organizer routine. *Teaching Exceptional Children, 32*(3), 48–57.

Brualdi, A.C. (1998). *Classroom questions.* College Park, MD: ERIC Clearinghouse on Assessment and Evaluation. (ERIC No. ED 422407)

Center for Problem-Based Learning. (1998). *An introduction to problem-based learning.* Illinois Math and Science Academy. (Available at http://www.imsa.edu/team/cpbl/problem.html.)

Clearinghouse on Handicapped and Gifted Education. (1987). *Lesson structure: Research to practice.* Reston, VA: Author. (ERIC No. ED 291206)

Cohen, E.G. (1991). Strategies for creating a multi-ability classroom. *Cooperative Learning, 12*(1), 4–8.

Cohen, E.G. (1994). *Designing groupwork: Strategies for the heterogeneous classroom* (2nd ed.). New York: Teachers College Press.

Duffy, T.M., & Savery, J.R. (1995). Problem based learning: An instructional model and its constructivist framework. *Educational Technology, 35*(5), 31–38.

Dye, G.A. (2000). Graphic organizers to the rescue! *Teaching Exceptional Children, 32*(3), 72–76.

Finkel, S.L., & Torp, L.L. (1995). *Introductory documents.* Aurora, IL: Center for Problem-Based Learning, Illinois Math and Science Academy.

Gardner, H. (1983). *Frames of mind: The theory of multiple intelligences.* New York: Basic Books.

Gardner, H. (1999). *Intelligence reframed: Multiple intelligences for the 21st century.* New York: Basic Books.

Goldenberg, C. (1991). *Instructional conversations and their classroom application* (Educational Practice Rep. No. 2). Washington, DC: National Center for Research on Cultural Diversity and Second Language Learning, Center for Applied Linguistics. (ERIC No. ED 341253)

Johnson, D.W., & Johnson, R.T. (1991). *Cooperative learning lesson structures.* Edina, MN: Interaction Book Co.

Johnson, R.T., & Johnson, D.W. (1994). An overview of cooperative learning. In J.S. Thousand, R.A. Villa, & A.I. Nevin (Eds.), *Creativity and collaborative learning: A practical guide to empowering students and teachers* (pp. 31–44). Baltimore: Paul H. Brookes Publishing Co.

Kagan, S. (1990). A structural approach to cooperative learning. *Educational Leadership, 47*(4), 12–15.

Kagan, S. (1998). New cooperative learning, multiple intelligences, and inclusion. In J.W. Putnam (Ed.), *Cooperative learning and strategies for inclusion: Celebrating diversity in the classroom* (2nd ed., pp. 105–136). Baltimore: Paul H. Brookes Publishing Co.

Larkin, M. (1997). Graphic organizers. *Collaborator, 5*(2), 2.

Lawrence, A. (1997). Expanding capacity in ESOL programs (EXCAP): Using projects to enhance instruction. *Literacy Harvest: The Journal of the Literacy Assistance Center, 6*(1), 1–9.

Lotan, R.A. (1997). Complex instruction: An overview. In E.G. Cohen & R.A. Lotan (Eds.), *Working for equity in heterogeneous classrooms: Sociological theory in practice* (pp. 15–27). New York: Teachers College Press.

Lowry, C.M. (1990). *Teaching adults with learning disabilities.* Columbus, OH: ERIC Clearinghouse on Adult, Career, and Vocational Education. (ERIC No. ED 321156)

Mehan, H. (1979). *Learning lessons: Social organization in the classroom.* Cambridge, MA: Harvard University Press.

Moss, D. (1998). *Project-based learning and assessment: A resource manual for teachers.* Arlington, VA: Arlington Education and Employment Program.

Moss, D., & Van Duzer, C. (1998). *Project-based learning for adult English language learners.* Washington, DC: National Clearinghouse for ESL Literacy Education. (ERIC No. ED 427556)

Murray, F.B. (1994). Why understanding the theoretical basis of cooperative learning enhances teaching success. In J.S. Thousand, R.A. Villa, & A.I. Nevin, (Eds.), *Creativity and collaborative learning: A practical guide to empowering students and teachers* (pp. 3–11). Baltimore: Paul H. Brookes Publishing Co.

Ogle, D.S. (1986). K-W-L group instructional strategy. In A.S. Palincsar, D.S. Ogle, B.F. Jones, & E.G. Carr (Eds.), *Teaching reading as thinking* (pp. 11–17). Alexandria, VA: Association for Supervision and Curriculum Development.

Putnam, J.W. (Ed.). (1998). *Cooperative learning and strategies for inclusion: Celebrating diversity in the classroom* (2nd ed.). Baltimore: Paul H. Brookes Publishing Co.

Sapon-Shevin, M., Ayres, B.J., & Duncan, J. (1994). Cooperative learning and inclusion. In J.S. Thousand, R.A. Villa, & A.I. Nevin (Eds.), *Creativity and collaborative learning: A practical guide to empowering students and teachers* (pp. 45–58). Baltimore: Paul H. Brookes Publishing Co.

Slavin, R.E. (1995). *Cooperative learning: Theory, research, and practice* (2nd ed.). Needham Heights, MA: Allyn & Bacon.

Slavin, R.E., Leavey, M.B., & Madden, N.A. (1984). Combining cooperative learning and individualized instruction: Effects on student mathematics achievement, attitudes, and behaviors. *Elementary School Journal, 84,* 409–422.

Starnes, B.A. (1999). *The Foxfire approach to teaching and learning: John Dewey, experiential learning, and the core practices.* Charleston, WV: ERIC Clearinghouse on Rural Education and Small Schools (CRESS). (ERIC No. ED 426826)

Starnes, B., Paris, C., & Stevens, C. (1999). *The Foxfire core practices: Discussions and implications.* Mountain City, GA: Foxfire.

Stepien, W.J., Gallagher, S.A., & Workman, D. (1993). Problem-based learning for traditional and interdisciplinary classrooms. *Journal for the Education of the Gifted, 16*(4), 338–357.

Tennenbaum, J.E. (1996). *Practical ideas on alternative assessment for ESL students.* Washington, DC: ERIC Clearinghouse on Languages and Linguistics. (ERIC No. ED 395500)

Tinzmann, M.B., Jones, B.F., Fennimore, T.F., Bakker, J., Fine, C., & Pierce, J. (1990). *What is the collaborative classroom?* Oak Brook, IL: North Central Regional Educational Laboratory.

Udvari-Solner, A. (1994). A decision-making model for curricular adaptations in cooperative groups. In J.S. Thousand, R.A. Villa, & A.I. Nevin (Eds.), *Creativity and collaborative learning: A practical guide to empowering students and teachers* (pp. 59–77). Baltimore: Paul H. Brookes Publishing Co.

Wrigley, H.S. (1998). Knowledge in action: The promise of project-based learning. *Focus on Basics, 2*(3), 13–18.

7

Enhancing the Development of Prosocial Behavior and Classroom Management

Anne M. Bauer
Kimberly Moore Hill

Teacher Contributors: Jason Haap, Rick Hennegan, Nicki Brainard, Randy Reeder

Supporting positive interactions and managing unproductive interactions are of great concern to teachers. As we try to build rapport and maintain a positive climate, we become intensely aware of the difficult lives many of our students live. Students may have experienced a breakdown in family and community support systems. They may have experienced violence themselves and have seen few if any consequences for aggression (in some settings, aggression is rewarded). Students have difficulty with the "proper behavior" demanded by school, which may actually put them at risk in the community in which they live. Students see increased violence in the streets and may have few positive role models in managing that violence. The majority of students involved in discipline incidents in high schools do not have disabilities (Council for Exceptional Children [CEC], 1998a).

In this chapter, we take a positive stance related to classroom management and discuss ways to enhance the development of prosocial interactions in the classroom. The legal issues related to classroom management are discussed, as well as schoolwide programs to manage behavior. Strategies for managing surface behaviors are discussed, and positive behavioral support is proposed as a way to manage more challenging behaviors. The chapter concludes with ways to enhance positive social interaction and friendships, crisis management, and the use of medication as a behavioral support. After reading this chapter, you will be able to do the following:

- Describe assumptions about students' behavior that are grounded in enhancing the development of prosocial behaviors
- Describe ways to enhance positive social interaction in your classroom
- Recognize legal issues related to classroom management and students with disabilities
- Discuss schoolwide programs to manage behavior
- Implement strategies for managing surface behaviors
- Describe and apply positive behavioral support
- Complete a functional assessment
- Identify ways to enhance positive social interaction and friendships
- Describe issues related to crisis management
- Be aware of the use of medication as a behavioral support

ASSUMPTIONS ABOUT BEHAVIOR

Classroom and behavior management traditionally has been grounded in defining the problem, selecting goals, deciding on an appropriate intervention, and defining cures (Hitzing, 1992). Hitzing suggested a communication/feedback cycle in which certain factors that precede the behavior affect the person (see Figure 7.1). Because people react based on how they feel, someone who is bored or confused may react in an erratic way. Behaviors that "work" in garnering attention, whether they are disruptive or even aggressive, change the interactions of surrounding people. Although the behavior "works," long-term problems may occur because the behaviors interfere with the student's independence in the school or community.

Behaviors have a purpose and are used to communicate. Carr et al. (1994) proposed the following assumptions related to working on undesirable behaviors:

- Problem behavior is purposeful. The student uses the behavior to communicate something or to achieve some goal.
- Assessments must be done to identify what purpose problem behavior serves. Unless you know the goal of the behavior and provide the student with more effective ways to meet that goal, the behavior will persist.
- Interventions for problem behaviors must focus on education, not simply behavior reduction. Simply reducing behaviors without providing the student with the way to meet his or her goals will not work.
- Problem behavior typically serves many purposes and therefore requires many interventions. Simple cause-and-effect relationships are rare. Behaviors may be linked to several factors in the environment—environmental factors that occurred previously or those that will occur in the future.

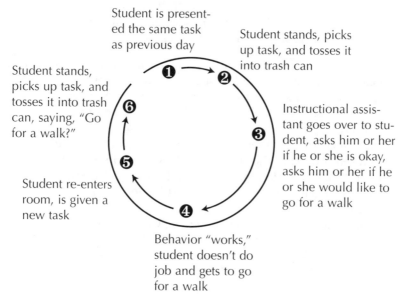

Student is present-
ed the same task
as previous day

Student stands, picks
up task, and tosses it
into trash can

Student stands,
picks up task, and
tosses it into trash
can, saying, "Go
for a walk?"

Instructional assis-
tant goes over to stu-
dent, asks him or her
if he or she is okay,
asks him or her if he
or she would like to
go for a walk

Student re-enters
room, is given a
new task

Behavior "works,"
student doesn't do
job and gets to go
for a walk

Figure 7.1.   Sample communication/feedback cycle.

- Lifestyle change rather than the elimination of problem behavior per se is the ultimate goal of intervention. Our goal should not be to make our lives easier as teachers, but to improve the students' quality of life.
- Intervention involves altering the way in which individuals with and with-out disabilities interact; therefore, intervention involves changing social systems. Classroom and behavior management involves changing what we do, and, as a result, changing what the student does.

It is natural for teachers to make assumptions about students' behavior. Don-nellan (1984), however, cautioned teachers to always make the "least danger-ous assumption." The *criterion of the least dangerous assumption* means that in the absence of reliable and valid data about students' capabilities or behavior, the assumption that does the least amount of harm should be made. For example, if a student is wearing a hat in class, the least dangerous assumption—the as-sumption that would do the least harm if it later is realized that the assump-tion was wrong—is that the student is unaware of a school rule against wear-ing hats. The teacher would approach the student and indicate that there is a rule against wearing hats and asks the student to please remove the hat. A far more dangerous assumption would be that the student is deliberately flaunting the rule; the teacher would immediately reprimand the student or give the student demerits. The teacher contributors for this chapter describe several assumptions about behavior and behavior management:

- By providing a structure in which every student understands the expectations, students can begin to "self-structure." (Rick Hennegan)
- The classroom has to be based on mutual respect. You demand the respect of the students, and they should demand respect from you. (Nicki Brainard)
- Clarity is key. Students should understand that rules have a rationale and are for their benefit. They may ask, "What's in it for me if I follow the rules?" Safety, better learning, and rewards. (Randy Reeder)
- Students should understand the expectations for their behavior. (Randy Reeder)
- What is "the same" when you're working with students and it isn't producing the same results for every student? What is "the same" is finding out where each student is at and bringing him or her forward—that's what's fair and equal. (Jason Haap)

WAYS TO ENHANCE POSITIVE SOCIAL INTERACTION IN THE CLASSROOM

Good teaching is the best form of classroom management. Good teaching enhances the positive social growth of students. Good and Brophy (1995) identified general attributes of teachers that contribute to their success in socializing students; such teachers

- Are cheerful, friendly, emotionally mature, and sincere
- Have an ego, strength, and self-confidence that allows them to be calm in a crisis
- Listen, avoid win/lose conflicts, and maintain a problem-solving orientation
- Have realistic perceptions of themselves and their students and are not clouded by romanticism, guilt, hostility, or anxiety
- Enjoy their students while maintaining their identity as teacher
- Are clear about their role as the teacher and are comfortable in that role
- Are patient and determined in working with students who persist in testing limits
- Accept the individual but perhaps not his or her behavior
- State and act on firm but flexible limits

Our teacher contributors communicate these attributes to their students through printed procedures or expectations at the beginning of the academic year (see Figure 7.2).

Ms. Brainard
Biology/Ecology
2001–2002 school year

Welcome back to another great year at Purcell Marian High School! I hope all of you had a fun and enjoyable summer. I also hope that you are all ready to get back to work. This class will hopefully be a little different from what you have probably come to expect in science classes . . . in other words, hopefully this biology/ecology class will not be boring! I will not give out any of my secret plans, but keep in mind that any and all activities we may do will depend on your behavior and work ethic as a class.

Now I think it is only fair that I let you in on a few important details:

Classroom expectations and policies:

Respect: Without respect we have nothing. This means respect of Ms. Brainard from all students at all time, but also from Ms. Brainard for all students.

Participation: A boring class is one where the teacher is the only one providing input. I am not the only one with ideas. Let me and others learn from your ideas. This not only means answering questions, but asking them. There is no such thing as a stupid question. Odds are, if you have a question, someone else in the class has the same one. I am getting paid to teach you . . . make me earn my salary.

Coming prepared to class every day: This means that each student comes with either a pen or pencil (one that works), paper to take notes (either a notebook or binder with loose leaf paper), and your textbook. If you do not come prepared, the "Brainard School Supply Store" will be open for sales every day prior to class. Paper will cost 1 cent, pens will cost 15 cents, and pencils will cost 10 cents. If you do not have any of these items, you must buy one. You may not borrow from anyone once class has started.

Homework policy: You will most likely have homework every evening. All assignments will be posted on the right hand side of the chalkboard with their due dates. Homework also can be found on my homework hotline (ext. 831) daily. My advice: Write each assignment in a homework notebook or on your calendar. Homework will not be accepted late without severe penalties.

Figure 7.2.   Sample procedure/expectation letter.

Figure 7.2.   *(continued)*

<u>Labs</u>: You are responsible for maintaining your equipment. This means cleaning all supplies, returning them to their proper places, pushing your lab stool back under the table, and making sure the lab area is in better condition than you found it (garbage free, etc.). If you cannot perform these small tasks, you will be required to do your labs after school. I am a teacher, not a maid.

<u>Grading</u>: I follow the grading policy in the Purcell Marian High School Handbook. A: 93–100, B: 85–92, C: 77–84, D: 70–76, F: 0–69.

<u>Projects</u>: There will be one project assigned per quarter. For the college prep biology classes, one project will be your science fair project. There will be class presentations involved as well as written portions. Ecology students will be expected to perform one service project per quarter to be announced.

<u>After-school study tables</u>: I will use demerits only if you force me to use them. I prefer to use the study tables. If you are misbehaving for any reason or disturbing the class, you will be invited to an after-school detention where you will volunteer for me or another teacher in need of your "services."

<u>Policy on sleeping in class</u>: You may not sleep in class. PERIOD. If you fall asleep in class, you will be asked to stand in the back of the classroom until you are more alert. This is not an optional exercise.

<u>Policy on classroom distractions (makeup, cologne, gadgets of any kind, etc.)</u>: You will be asked to put it away one time. After that, it is mine and you must "earn" its return (i.e., clean glassware). After the first time, the object is mine until the end of the quarter.

<u>Policy on tardiness</u>: Tardiness without a note is not acceptable. You may not enter the classroom if you are tardy without a note.

<u>Policy on food in class</u>: There is no food allowed in class. This includes chewing gum. You will be charged 25 cents each time I have to ask you to spit out any gum.

<u>Restroom policy</u>: You may leave the classroom to use the restroom or go to your locker once a week. If you do not leave the classroom for any reason all quarter, you will receive bonus points added onto your quarter point total.

<u>Garbage can usage</u>: You may only use the garbage can before or after class. Please do not leave your seat to dispose of garbage at any other time.

All school policies including dress code will be upheld.

Campbell and Olsen (1994) concurred that improving instruction in secondary schools may in itself improve behavior. They suggested careful classroom design with a few clear rules. Rules should be taught systematically, using a mnemonic strategy if necessary. Teachers should use their own actions as models. Consequences of behaviors should emphasize positives. One key is to help students manage their own behavior, assigning them individual responsibilities and holding them accountable. Students can sign off each day on how well they followed the rules, routines, and procedures in order to use time more efficiently. Most important, Campbell and Olsen suggested that classrooms should be pleasant, friendly places in which individual differences are accepted and supported through individual objectives and work rates.

Classroom teachers can usually manage the behavior of students with disabilities with the same tools that they use to manage the behavior of students without disabilities. The behaviors you would want to encourage or discourage often is similar among students with and without identified disabilities (Daniels, 1998). The information presented, then, can be used for all the learners in an inclusive classroom.

The CEC (1998a) suggested that the three Cs—curriculum, conditions, and consequences—are key in managing classrooms. In terms of conditions, the students must be physically comfortable and feel valued. The curriculum should be appropriate, that is, stimulating yet attainable. Problem-solving skills should be a part of the curriculum. Students need to feel safe and should be taught to effectively communicate with each other and authority figures. Teachers can help students practice problem solving on simple, real-life situations. Teachers support the students as they develop alternative solutions and help them evaluate their options.

Good teachers also use guidance techniques. Through these techniques, students are provided with more positive than negative feedback. Even in the middle of misbehaving, students should be rewarded for doing something well. Teachers should make sure their goals are realistic for the student. Determining why the interactions are occurring is key in helping the student develop an alternative (CEC, 1998b).

ASSESSING MANAGEMENT PROBLEMS

When the behaviors that are occurring in your classroom are annoying or somewhat disruptive, some self-directed questions may be helpful. Daniels (1998) suggested that teachers ask themselves the following:

- Could this behavior be a result of using the wrong curriculum or teaching strategies? Some behaviors can arise from the teacher's inability to meet the students' needs. Variables that contribute to disruptive behaviors include group size, group composition, cultural and linguistic barriers, or lack of access to equipment, materials, and resources. Sometimes adapting content and instructional delivery can reduce the occurrence of undesirable behavior.

- Could this behavior be a result of the students' inability to understand what is being taught? Students may demonstrate undesirable behaviors when the activity has no meaning to them or they do not have the readiness or prerequisite skills to join in the class. As discussed previously, the curriculum may have an impact on students' behavior.
- Could this behavior be related to the student's disability? A student may, as a result of his or her disability, avoid reading aloud, hesitate to participate, or appear to daydream. Ask about the student and ways to address the impact of the disability on the student's ability to access teaching and learning in the classroom.
- Could this behavior be a result of other factors such as the physical arrangement of the room, boredom, frustration, transition, or a lack of awareness of what is going on? Sitting in desks may be difficult for adolescents. If your room's windows open out to the courtyard in which the dumpsters are located, students' attention (and yours) may be challenged when the garbage trucks arrive.
- Could the behavior be related to things you cannot control? Are you teaching at a time that it is difficult for the student to pay attention (i.e., right before lunch, the last bell of the day)? Are there issues in other classes that distress the student and carry over into your classroom?
- Could the behavior be classroom based? You may need to self-evaluate your teaching and instructional practices. Identify events, variables, and circumstances that could contribute to the problem. If you give a quiz or test during the last part of the class, students may be distracted by anxiety or studying rather than attending to the class until the test is completed.

More detailed information about assessment is discussed later in this chapter in the section on functional assessment.

LEGAL ISSUES RELATED TO CLASSROOM MANAGEMENT AND STUDENTS WITH DISABILITIES

The Individuals with Disabilities Education Act (IDEA) Amendments of 1997 (PL 105-17) have increased the attention given to assisting students in developing productive behaviors. Some of the requirements of IDEA '97 refer to rights and responsibilities related to students whose behavior exceeds that of the school expectations. Other requirements describe the ways behavior management should be addressed in the student's individualized education program (IEP).

Students Whose Behavior Exceeds the Expectations of the School

Students with disabilities have the right to a free, appropriate public education. IDEA '97 indicates that even students who have been suspended or expelled from school must receive a free, appropriate public education. The right to a free, appropriate, public education is triggered when the student has been suspended for more than 10 days in a school year (20 U.S.C. §§ 1412[a][1]). Students with identified disabilities may only be suspended from school for more than 10 days in a given year, or expelled to the same extent as students without identified disabilities, if the behavior for which they are being suspended or expelled is not a manifestation of their disability. If a suspension of 11 days or more in a given year is being considered, there must be a manifestation determination hearing (20 U.S.C. §§ 1415[k][4], [5]).

A manifestation determination is made by the student's IEP team, which must include the parents. The team must find that the behavior was a manifestation of the student's disability in any of four ways: 1) if the student's IEP or placement was inappropriate in view of the behavior, 2) if special education services, supplementary aids and services, and behavior intervention strategies were not implemented in a manner consistent with the student's IEP or placement, 3) if the student's disability impaired his or her ability to understand the impact and consequences of the behavior, or 4) the student's disability impaired his or her ability to control the behavior. Many school districts broadly interpret manifestation determination by seeing if the behavior is on the IEP. All four considerations must be studied before determining if the behavior is a manifestation of the disability.

If a student's behavior is interfering with his or her learning or that of others, strategies and supports to address that behavior must be a part of the student's IEP. IDEA '97 requires a functional assessment of the student's behaviors (discussed later in this chapter), the determination and implementation of intervention strategies, and their evaluation (CEC, 1998b).

IDEA '97 requires that the functional behavior assessment be used with the behaviors of students with disabilities in public school settings who exhibit behaviors leading to a change in school placement or whose challenging behavior constitutes a pattern. The regulations pertaining to alternative school placement say the following:

(A) School personnel under this section may order a change in the placement of a child with a disability—(i) to an appropriate interim alternative educational setting, another setting, or suspension, for not more than 10 school days (to the extent such alternative would be applied to children without disabilities); and (ii) to an appropriate interim alternative educational setting for the same amount of time that a child without a disability would be subject to discipline, but not for more than 45 days if (I) if the child carries a weapon to school or to a school function under the jurisdiction of a state or a local educational agency; or (II) the child

knowingly possesses or uses illegal drugs or sells or solicits the sale of a controlled substance while at a school function under the jurisdiction of a state or
local educational agency.

(B) Either before or not later than 10 days after taking a disciplinary action described in subparagraph (a)(i) if the local educational agency did not conduct a
functional behavioral assessment and implement a behavioral intervention plan
for such a child before the behavior that resulted in the suspension described in
subparagraph (A), the agency shall convene an IEP meeting to develop an assessment plan to address that behavior; or (ii) if the child already has a behavioral intervention plan, the IEP Team shall review the plan and modify it, as necessary, to address the behavior.

Alternative placements vary widely from district to district. Your school
may use an in-school suspension room, or may place students on homebound
instruction. The alternative placement may be a separate facility for individuals with challenging behavior.

WHAT ARE SOME FEATURES OF
SCHOOLWIDE PROGRAMS TO MANAGE BEHAVIOR?

Discipline is "the steps or actions that teachers, administrators, parents, and students follow to enhance student academic and social behavior success" (Office
of Special Education Programs [OSEP], 1999b, p. 1). Schools that have been
successful in building schoolwide systems develop procedures in which behavioral interventions are defined as a small number of clearly identified rules and
behavioral expectations that are taught in real contexts. In successful schools,
appropriate behaviors are acknowledged. Schools' interactions with students
should be positive four times as often as they are negative. Successful schoolwide systems provide ways to proactively correct behavior incidents. Clear procedures are needed to provide information to the student that the behavior was
unacceptable and to prevent the unacceptable behavior. Program evaluations
and adaptations are made by a team, and the administration is active and supportive. In addition, individual student support systems are integrated with a
schoolwide discipline system (OSEP, 1999b). Effective school discipline systems have six major components (Colvin, Kameenui, & Sugai, 1993):

1. An agreed-upon and common approach to discipline
2. Positively stated statement of purpose
3. A small number of positively stated expectations for all students and staff
4. Procedures for teaching these expectations to all students
5. A continuum of procedures for encouraging displays and maintenance of
   these expectations
6. A continuum of procedures for discouraging displays of rule-violating behavior

7. Procedures for monitoring and evaluating the effectiveness of the discipline systems on a regular and frequent basis

Schoolwide systems of discipline or positive behavioral interventions create environments in which 1) learning and teaching are valued, and aggressive, unsafe behaviors are discouraged; 2) respect, responsibility, cooperation, and other highly valued character traits are taught and encouraged; 3) individual differences are valued rather than criticized; 4) students with disabilities can be supported to be more effective and efficient; and 5) teaching fundamental skills can be maximized (OSEP, 1999b). At Purcell Marian High School, expectations related to student behaviors are described in the mission statement, which indicates that "faculty and staff strive to be an example in the classroom of what we want our graduates to be: respectful of others, thirsting for knowledge, and equipped with tools and a foundation necessary for a life of learning and service" (Purcell Marian High School, 1995). In the handbook, rules are clearly stated and exemplified.

Randy Reeder, Dean of Students, describes several ways that expectations can be clearly communicated to students. Every student should have a handbook that specifies the school rules and contingencies. In an annual assembly, expectations for behaviors should be clearly communicated to the students. As the rules are presented, however, a rationale and the potential benefit of the rules should be described. Throughout the discussion, the benefits of safety, increased learning, and positive consequences should be emphasized.

Several of our teacher contributors emphasized the role of mutual respect. In addition to respecting students as individuals, differences must be respected. Randy Reeder suggested that when behavior incidents occur, each situation must be reviewed independently. Each student's history, ability, and needs must be recognized. The most "unequal thing," he suggested, is to "treat unequals equally." In a climate of respect, students understand that not all students are the same and that consequences may vary.

WHAT STRATEGIES CAN BE USED TO MANAGE SURFACE BEHAVIORS?

Clearly communicating expectations can be helpful in establishing the climate in a classroom. Minor violations of those expectations, however, may not require immediate, direct intervention. Redl (1959) suggested that teachers may permit, tolerate, interfere, or prevent behaviors from occurring. For example, students may be slouching down in the chairs during a discussion. The teacher may permit the behavior, recognizing that adolescents are still getting used to their larger bodies and may be more comfortable working in less rigid positions. The teacher would continue the discussion, actively involving the sprawling students, communicating that their posture is fine. As an alternative, the teacher may tolerate the behavior, providing nonverbal cues such as "teacher looks" to communicate that he or she would prefer that the students sit up. In terms of interference, the teacher could make a specific response to the slouching students, telling them to "sit up" and "look like they are ready to work." As a preventive action, the teacher may use a seating chart and assign students who typically slouch in the back of the room to the front row.

When interfering, teachers may not necessarily be applying specific individualized interventions. Rather, they may be employing what Long, Morse, and Newman (1996) referred to as *surface management techniques*. These techniques do not solve any deep-rooted behavioral issue but are useful to teachers. Their techniques include

- Planned ignoring, in which the teacher simply ignores the student's inappropriate behavior
- Signal interference, in which the teacher provides the student with a nonverbal gesture or cue that the behavior is inappropriate. Teachers often use signals such as "teacher looks," finger tapping, or shifting position.
- Proximity control, in which the teacher moves toward or stands near the student who is engaged in the problem behavior
- Interest boosting, in which the teacher encourages students to continue an activity by exhibiting a personal interest in their efforts
- Humor, in which the teacher interjects humor during a tense or anxious situation (recognizing that humor is never directed at a particular child or group)
- Restructuring activities when students become more disruptive
- Support from a routine to provide structure and security
- Direct appeal to value areas, in which the teacher appeals to students' understanding of fairness, authority, and the consequences of their behavior on themselves or others
- Removing seductive objects, in which the teacher removes an object that is distracting or disturbing the student with the understanding that it will be returned at an appropriate time
- Antiseptic bouncing, in which the teacher provides the student with an alternative activity when he or she needs to re-organize him- or herself. The teacher may ask the student if he or she needs to get a drink, could carry a note, or do some other activity which would cause a brief absence from the room or activity.

When behavior problems are deeper or more serious, specific interventions should be identified. IDEA '97 indicates that in these cases positive behavioral support should be used.

WHAT IS POSITIVE BEHAVIORAL SUPPORT AND HOW IS IT APPLIED?

Positive behavioral support is not new. Rather, it is an application of a behaviorally based systems approach of enhancing the capacity of schools, families, and communities to design effective environments that improve the fit or link between research-validated practices and the environments in which teaching and learning occurs (OSEP, 1999c). Positive behavioral support goes beyond one approach—reducing challenging or impeding behavior. Rather, it uses multiple approaches, such as changing systems, altering environments, teaching skills, and focusing on positive behavior. IDEA '97 specifically addresses positive behavioral support and functional behavioral assessment. It indicates that in the case of a child whose behavior impedes his or her learning or the learning of others, the IEP team must "consider, if appropriate, strategies, including positive behavioral interventions, strategies, and supports to address that behavior" (Section 1414[d][3][B][i]; 34 C.F.R. §§ 300.346[a][2][i]).

Functional behavioral assessment is a systematic process for describing problem behavior, identifying environmental factors and setting events that predict the problem behavior, and guiding the development of effective and efficient behavioral support plans. It is the foundation of positive behavioral support. Many states have created laws or regulations stipulating the need for a functional behavioral assessment before permitting the development of significant behavioral interventions (e.g., the Hughes Bill in California; OSEP, 1999a). Conducting a functional assessment is discussed later in this chapter.

Positive behavioral support is not only about reducing challenging behavior, but includes multiple approaches of changing systems, altering environments, teaching skills, and appropriating positive behavior. Positive behavioral support expands the focus of behavior management beyond the behavior itself to lifestyle concerns such as happiness, independence, and social interaction. Weigle (1997) presented several basic tenets of positive behavioral support:

- Considers long-term goals and outcomes over years
- Determines the function of the behavior rather than just the topography
- Bases interventions in individual needs and effectiveness rather than hierarchies of intervention
- Teaches useful, functionally equivalent skills to replace excess behaviors
- Uses reinforcement procedures whenever possible
- Focuses on antecedent procedures to prevent the occurrence of excess behaviors
- Includes a wide range of procedures

Outcomes can be accomplished by selecting an appropriate functional replacement behavior, directly teaching that behavior, and facilitating access to the same functional outcome when the student displays the desirable replacement behavior. In other words, if you find out what purpose the behavior is serving for the student, you should help the student serve the same purpose through a different, productive behavior. The goal is to develop a proactive (positive and preventive) individualized behavioral support plan.

In positive behavioral support, interventions 1) consider the contexts within which the behavior occurs, 2) address the function of the behavior, 3) are justified by their outcomes, and 4) strive for outcomes that are acceptable to the individual, the family, and the community (Haring & De Vault, 1996). The outcomes of positive behavioral support are greater independence and an improved quality of life (OSEP, 1999c).

Providing students with choices can have a significant impact on behavior. Umbreit and Blair (1996) reported that with one student, hitting, throwing, running away, biting, spitting, and screaming were eliminated through providing the student with more preferred activities, choices, and positive attention. Choice provides the student with shared control of the learning environment (Carr et al., 1994). Ruef, Higgins, Glaeser, and Patnode (1998) suggested that teachers respond to students by altering the classroom environment, increasing predictability and scheduling, increasing choice making, developing curricular adaptations, and appreciating positive behavior.

CONDUCTING A FUNCTIONAL BEHAVIORAL ASSESSMENT

There are several definitions of functional assessment—a process also called *functional behavioral assessment* in IDEA '97. Regardless of the title, *functional assessment* is "a systematic process of identifying problem behaviors and the events that a) reliably predict occurrences and nonoccurrences of those behaviors and b) maintain the behaviors across time" (Sugai, Sprague, & Horner, 1999, p. 254). There are several models for functional assessment; following is one developed by O'Neill et al. (1997).

One of the primary goals of functional behavioral assessment is to bring clarity to a problem situation that may be dangerous, chaotic, and frustrating. It is a process of redesigning the environment so that it works for people with disabilities. It also is a process of understanding physiological and environmental factors that may impact and influence problem situations (O'Neill et al., 1997).

Underlying Assumptions

Larson and Maag (1998) described two specific behavioral assumptions that are fundamental to understanding one's functional assessment results. One must understand that behavior is purposeful and has contextual meaning. For instance, a student may yell out loudly during class to get a peer's attention, which may work well in a classroom. However, that same yelling may not be as efficient or effective in gaining peer attention in the hall when classes are changing.

Neel and Cessna (as cited in Larson & Maag, 1998) referred to *behavior intent* as a way to describe the relationship between a student's behavior and the outcome of that behavior. When a student engages in some sort of behavior, he or she does so for a specific result, for example, getting out of doing a difficult assignment, obtaining a rest period, or possibly avoiding ridicule from classmates. This desired outcome is the purpose, function, or intent of the behavior. In many cases, the function of the behavior is appropriate; it is only the form of the behavior that is inappropriate. Therefore, the goal of a functional behavioral assessment may be to provide the student with an alternative behavior to fulfill the same function.

Larson and Maag (1998) used performing a certain emergency medical procedure to illustrate a behavior's contextual meaning. It is completely inappropriate to cut a person's throat with a knife during a robbery or a mugging. However, if that same person was suffocating due to an allergic reaction, cutting his or her throat to perform an emergency tracheotomy to help him or her breathe may be perfectly acceptable. The context in which the behavior occurs is what causes a behavior to be perceived as either inappropriate or socially acceptable.

Value Statements

O'Neill and colleagues (1997) provided additional assumptions that are vital to conducting a meaningful functional assessment. First, the assessment must be conducted without damaging the student's dignity. It is important to remember that a person engages in these inappropriate behaviors because these patterns of behavior have worked for them in the past and continue to do so. They are not engaging in behaviors simply because they have mental retardation or some other disability. There is a specific logic to their behavior patterns.

Second, the objective of the assessment is not only to eliminate the problematic behavior but also to teach new skills or appropriate behaviors that fulfill the same function. The previous section about the purposefulness of behavior also touched on this concept. A functional assessment should enable classroom teachers and other school personnel to 1) avoid unnecessary situations that prompt the problem behaviors; 2) identify new or more appropriate skills to teach, making the inappropriate ones unnecessary; and 3) determine effective staff responses when the problem behaviors do arise.

Third, a functional assessment is a review of the student's behavior in relation to the environment. It should not lead to blaming the student for engaging in the behaviors. Rather, it should be an analysis of the environment (i.e., schedules, routines, staff-to-student ratios) as well as an analysis of the behavior itself.

WHY CONDUCT A FUNCTIONAL BEHAVIORAL ASSESSMENT?

There are two main reasons for conducting a functional behavioral assessment. First, the information gathered during the assessment is necessary for developing effective interventions and positive behavioral support plans. It is impossible to develop ways to support the student without first determining when, where, and why a behavior is occurring. Interventions and support plans developed without this information are likely to be ineffective or make the behavior worse (O'Neill et al., 1997).

Second, federal law mandates conducting a functional behavior assessment. IDEA '97 states that if the school did not conduct a functional assessment and implement a plan before a behavior resulted in suspension, then they should convene an IEP meeting to develop an assessment and intervention plan.

IDEA '97 states that a team of professionals must conduct this assessment. It logically follows that everyone on the team must have an understanding of what a functional behavior analysis entails, especially the general and special education teachers. Teachers have one of the biggest responsibilities in this assessment. Their classrooms are usually the primary setting for the assessment and provide the main source of assessment information.

OUTCOMES OF A FUNCTIONAL BEHAVIORAL ASSESSMENT

O'Neill et al. (1997) offered five main outcomes of the functional assessment process. First, the team will have a clear description of the problem behavior and any typical patterns and sequences of those patterns. Second, the key stakeholders involved in supporting a particular child will be able to predict what events, times of day, and situations will cause the behavior to occur and which do not lead to the behavior. Third, the team will understand what functions the behavior serves and what consequences are maintaining the behavior. Fourth, the team will have summary statements about the behavior, which include hypotheses about specific behaviors, specific situations, and outcomes or reinforcements for the behavior in that situation, for example, "When Ryan is confronted with work demands that he is unable to complete independently, he slumps in his chair, sleeps, or asks the teacher a series of off-topic questions to avoid the task." Finally, the team will have direct observation data that support their summary statements, which can be useful for that student's future teachers as well.

Functional assessments require a team of people working together. In order to gather the needed information about the problem(s), the team has three specific strategies at its disposal: informant methods, direct observations, and functional analysis manipulations. Each of these strategies has a specific purpose, and it is common to use one or more in combination.

The informant method involves talking with the person with the problematic behavior, if possible, and those involved in educating or caring for that student. This method is especially useful for narrowing a wide range of behaviors into a smaller list. It also is good for determining a link between typical routines and events in a student's environment and the problem behavior. The interview or informant method also is useful for pointing out which components of these routines are salient for the student. There are several examples of specific functional assessment interview formats in the literature, which typically ask questions such as 1) What are the problem behaviors? 2) What events or physical conditions occur earlier in time that may signal the behavior? 3) What happens just prior to the behavior occurring? 4) What are the consequences of the behavior? 5) What are alternate behaviors that will fulfill the same purpose? and 6) What successful strategies have been done to address the problem behaviors in the past?

The second strategy is that of directly observing students in their natural environments. These observations should be done repeatedly and over a specified time period. These observations should be conducted with little disruption in the natural occurrences of the environment. Teachers, direct support personnel, and family members are all appropriate observers, depending on the particular situation. Direct observation information gives the team insight into patterns, as well as when, where, and with whom the behaviors are occurring.

The last method of gathering information is the most rigorous or controlled method of assessment. In the literature, the terms *functional assessment* and *functional analysis* often are used interchangeably. However, this is not quite accurate. Functional assessment is the whole process, while functional analysis is the one method that can be used in the process.

Functional analysis can be conducted by either manipulating the consequences that maintain a behavior or by manipulating structural variables (e.g., task difficulty level, level of attention given during an activity, choice making during the activity). Functional analysis involves creating situations that will provoke the problem situation, then studying the relationship between the altered variable and the problem behavior. This allows the team to either confirm or disconfirm their hypotheses about the behavior (O'Neill et al., 1997).

Informative, functional analysis can be the most costly in terms of time and needed resources; however, in some cases it may be the only way to gather accurate information to develop effective support plans. Functional analysis should only be used when the team has difficulty establishing hypotheses or when the behavior is particularly resistant to intervention. This method also requires direct involvement of a professional trained in behavior analysis, specific informed consent of the family, and specific procedures for monitoring the behavior and accurate implementation of the analysis procedures.

Before beginning the assessment, O'Neill et al. (1997) suggested gathering three additional types of information that often are useful in developing comprehensive behavioral support plans. The first is person-centered planning. This process involves developing a vision for the student being assessed, with the intent of gathering assessment information that would relate to that vision. The support plans would involve making sure the student has the skills needed to meet his or her goals and vision.

The next source of additional information is that of the student's social activities and patterns—the variety of activity that a student performs, community integration, and the extent to which he or she is able to make choices and express preferences have a significant effect on the student's behavior. Examining these aspects of a student's life are subtle nuances that can make support plans more effective.

Finally, the team should consider any medical and physical conditions that may be influencing the student's behavior. It is important to determine whether a student has any low-incidence syndromes that could typically be associated with certain problematic behavior patterns. In addition, the team needs to consider any side effects from medications.

ASSESSMENT STEPS

A functional assessment may be completed by following six steps. The first step involves gathering information on setting events, antecedents of the behavior, consequences of the behavior, and the topography of the behavior. O'Neill et al. (1997) defined a *setting event* as any aspect of a student's environment or routine that does not necessarily occur immediately before the undesired behavior but still affects whether the behavior occurs (e.g., medication, sleep patterns, diet). The tools and procedures typically used to gather this information include record reviews, interventions, and direct observations with specific emphasis on daily routines. Outcomes of this step usually include descriptions of setting events, triggering situations, and response classes of the behavior.

In the second step, the team will propose testable explanations of the student's behavior; a hypothesis that may explain the relationship between a problem behavior and stimuli in the environment that appear to predict and maintain its occurrences. A complete testable explanation includes descriptions of the problem behavior, possible triggering antecedents, possible maintaining consequences, and possible setting events. For example, when she has a conflict with a peer in the hallway before class (setting event) and the teacher presents her with a difficult task that requires a written response (triggering antecedents), Cleo uses profanity, destroys her materials, and threatens teachers and peers (problem behaviors). The teacher then sends Cleo into the hallway to calm her down (maintaining consequences). As a result of these behaviors, she effectively avoids having to respond to the difficult task (function).

The goal of the third step is to document specific variables that are present or absent during occurrences and nonoccurrences of the behaviors. The tool used in this step is direct observation and the outcome is data to support or conform the team's hypotheses. Multiple observations should occur across several settings. Functional analysis also would occur at this step (if needed) to better understand the behavior, with careful adherence to the guidelines and cautions detailed previously.

The fourth step of the program involves transforming the information from the first three steps into a behavioral support plan. This plan should include 1) desired acceptable alternative behaviors, 2) ideas for adapting or changing antecedents, 3) plans for changing consequences that are maintaining the behavior, 4) plans for teaching the student the appropriate replacement behavior, and 5) plans for altering setting events and daily operations that are maintaining the behaviors. These behavior plans should be preventive in nature, instructionally focused, and environmentally based (Sugai et al., 1999).

The purpose of the fifth step is to develop scripts that would guide the implementation of the intervention support plan. The scripts are simple checklists written in the language of those responsible for implementing the intervention procedures. It should be collaboratively developed so that it fits within the context of the classroom and its normal daily routines. The scripts should specify the who, what, when, where, and how of the intervention as well as the procedures for any crises. This step also involves developing a plan for monitoring intervention progress.

The final step is designed to collect information on the efficacy of the intervention. The team examines the progress monitoring information gathered in the fifth step to make decisions about effectiveness. If the plan is effective, the team makes plans to update or fade procedures as necessary. At this point, the team may decide to redesign the plan if it isn't working effectively.

CONTINUUM OF BEHAVIORAL SUPPORT

One of the main purposes of this book is to describe a school in which inclusion is successful and to define what is enabling that success. One characteristic that enables this and other schools to successfully support students with severe behavior problems is that these schools provide their students with a continuum of behavioral support. These schools utilize strategies like those described in the crisis intervention section. Classroom teachers effectively utilize surface management techniques, and they adequately prepare for crises. These schools take a systems approach to positive behavioral support (Sugai et al., 1999). This systems approach frames behavioral support in terms of prevention. Four elements characterize the systems approach to positive behavioral support: 1) a change in systems (e.g., new policies and routines); 2) a change in the environment; 3) a change in student, parent, and teacher behavior; and 4) a change in the value of appropriate replacement behaviors.

The functional assessment process described previously is informative but too time consuming to use on all students. Therefore, Sugai and associates (1999) suggested that functional assessment is the most intensive on a continuum of behavioral support. Far more students will be involved in specialized group interventions and schoolwide programs. In most cases, functional assessment is designed to be used with severe and chronic behaviors.

CRISIS MANAGEMENT

The environment of educational institutions changed drastically throughout the 20th century. The extent of these changes is extremely obvious when one examines a portion of information collected by the Fullerton Police Department in Canada (as cited in Pitcher & Poland, 1992). In the 1940s, a majority of the classroom teachers reported discipline infractions that included behaviors such as talking in class, chewing gum, making noises, getting out of line, and not putting paper in the trash can. In contrast, classroom teachers in the 1980s reported discipline infractions that included instances of drug and alcohol abuse, rape, robbery, suicide, assault, bombings, arson, murder, extortion, and gang warfare.

It is obvious that knowledge about crises and crisis management are indispensable to classroom teachers and all other personnel. The goal of this section is to answer the following questions: What is a crisis? Why does the number of crises in schools appear to be growing? What does crisis management have to do with inclusive practices? What can I do to prevent crises in my classroom and the school building?

Definition

The term *crisis* tends to invoke images ranging from large-scale disasters that devastate entire communities to a flat tire that disrupts your day. The reason for this large range is that identifying an event as a crisis depends on the person experiencing it. Pitcher and Poland noted, "It is the perception of the individual that defines a crisis, not the event itself" (1992, p. 9). Auerbach and Kilmann (1977) conducted a review of research on crisis intervention and found that most formal definitions of crisis describe a *crisis* as a "response state characterized by high levels of subjective discomfort at which the individual is at least temporarily unable to emit the overt or covert behaviors required to modify the stressfulness of his environment" (p. 1189). In other words, a person experiencing a crisis is faced with an extremely stressful situation in which the accompanying stress cannot be alleviated by that person's typical problem-solving skills or defense mechanisms, and therefore the person views the situation as hopeless. A crisis is defined by the response to events, not the event itself. Examples of responses may be physical (e.g., crying, hyperventilating) and unpredictable behaviors (e.g., aggression).

Kinds of Crises

Baldwin (cited in Pitcher & Poland, 1992) developed a useful taxonomy of the different types of crises that people are likely to experience. The first type is a dispositional crisis. In this situation, a person needs reassurance or additional information to confront the problem. The second type is a crisis caused by an anticipated life transition. This type of crisis is categorized by changes in lifestyle (e.g., moving, birth of a sibling). The third type is a maturational/developmental crisis, which deals with attempts to solve major interpersonal problems. Determining one's sexual identity and developing emotional intimacy are two examples of this type of crises. The fourth type are the crises that are the result of traumatic stress. Events such as divorce, death, or physical abuse fall into this category. Crises in schools today are typically of this type (Pitcher & Poland, 1992). The fifth type are the crises reflecting psychopathology. In these instances, one's ability to problem solve is impaired by some sort of psychopathology or mental illness. Finally, there are psychiatric emergencies. The individuals are dangerous to themselves and others in these situations. The person is often "rendered incompetent or unable to assume personal responsibility" (Pitcher & Poland, 1992, p. 34). None of these situations is exclusive to adults in our society. Children are just as likely to experience these types of crises. No one is immune to a crisis.

Reasons for the Increase in Crises at School

Teachers and other school personnel often ponder why there is an increased occurrence of crises in schools and attempt to find reasons as to why children today are more aggressive and violent than in previous years. Simpson, Myles, Walker, Ormsbee, and Downing (1991) offered three hypotheses: 1) increased violence in society, 2) decreased educational and treatment options outside of school, and 3) increased preferences for the general education classroom for students with aggressive behaviors.

A survey conducted by the Office of Juvenile Justice and Delinquency Prevention (1989) gave startling testimony to the increasing prevalence of aggression and violence in society. They reported that 3 million attempted or completed assaults, rapes, robberies, or thefts occurred within school buildings or on school property. These statistics included 76,000 aggravated assaults and 350,000 simple assaults. Information on the prevalence of guns in schools was one specific statistic that was included in this report. For example, 64% of the students surveyed in Baltimore knew someone who carried a gun to school, 60% of them knew someone who had been held at gunpoint at school, and 50% of the male respondents occasionally carried a gun to school themselves.

Many children see aggression as an accepted form of behavior. Violent role models (more so than positive nonviolent ones) bombard their lives due to issues such as drug abuse, gangs, and child abuse (Myles & Simpson, 1994). As a result, when students enter school they must learn a new set of rules for dealing with problems and stressful situations. These new rules may be difficult for many students to learn and implement, especially because they are contradictory to what they are expected to do at home. Navigating through these different sets of rules could be challenging to these children. Rappaport (1962) found a challenge, a loss of some sort, or even the threat of a loss could trigger a crisis.

There also have been changes in the delivery of mental health services. Treatment options have begun to focus on community-based services. Many children are now placed in less restrictive halfway houses or back into their homes for treatment and once again attend their respective public schools (Pitcher & Poland, 1992). There are still some children who receive part of their education in more restrictive environments. However, their stay in these facilities is greatly reduced, so they re-enter school, still likely to engage in aggressive behaviors (Myles & Simpson, 1994). Private facilities also are becoming more expensive due to changes in health care policy. Many families do not have affordable treatment alternatives available to them. Finally, there also is a shortage of professionals to meet the mental health needs of children (Pitcher & Poland, 1992).

Stages of a Crisis

To effectively prevent or address a crisis it is useful to know the stages through which a crisis typically progresses. Caplan (1964) described four stages of a crisis. The first stage is an initial rise in anxiety caused by a traumatic event. The second stage involves continued exposure to the stressful event, and additional attempts to use problem-solving skills continue to be ineffective. The third stage is characterized by an increase in anxiety, and additional resources are utilized to resolve the stressful event. If these additional resources continue to be ineffective, a crisis enters the fourth stage. This stage is characterized by "severe emotional disorganization" (Poland, Pitcher, & Lazarus, 1995, p. 446). Individuals in this stage have exhausted their internal strength as well as their social supports.

Managing a Crisis as a Teacher

Students often follow a predictable pattern of behaviors, enabling teachers to determine whether a crisis is pending (Myles & Simpson, 1994). The first stage is frustration. Students at this stage tend to exhibit behaviors such as nail biting, tensing muscles, or grimacing. Teachers often can utilize the same surface behavior management strategies that were mentioned previously (e.g., proximity control, interest boosting, planned ignoring). There also are teacher responses that are likely to escalate this type of situation. For example, raising one's voice, using sarcasm, backing the student into a corner, or insisting on having the last word can all cause this situation to advance to the defensiveness stage.

The defensiveness stage involves behaviors such as withdrawing emotionally or physically from others or threatening the teacher or other students. A power struggle between the teacher and student is typical at this stage. Interventions at this stage involve restating or reminding the student of the rules and consequences. Using the student's name to personalize the rule, making direct eye contact, and closing the distance between you and the student when speaking, intensify the message that the teacher is the one in control. It is important not to get into a lengthy discussion about what is right or wrong.

The third stage is one of aggression. Aggression can be either verbal or physical. It is critical that teachers have plans for obtaining assistance from another adult, getting the rest of the students out of the area, or using physical restraint until the agitated student calms down. It is important to keep all students and personnel safe as well as preserve the dignity of the student in crisis.

The final stage is the self-control stage. This stage happens once the student has calmed down. This is the time that is most crucial to new skill development. It is here that a teacher can offer strategies that teach self-control. An example of this would be teaching a specific way to communicate frustration. This also is the time when supportive efforts or punishments are delivered in response to the aggressive behavior.

Teachers also should train others to respond to aggression and violence. Students who are particularly prone to aggression or violence need to have specific written plans that staff and personnel consistently follow when they interact with that student. These plans should include intervention procedures as well as specific steps to take when their behavior intensifies.

Students and faculty should practice for a crisis in a manner similar to the way in which they practice for a fire or tornado. Teachers and administrators should predetermine things such as exits, who to contact, and staff roles during a crisis situation. Teachers also should dress for possible aggressive or violent acts. Myles and Simpson (1994) found that teachers who regularly interact with violent or aggressive students should modify their dress so that their clothing or accessories will not interfere with their ability to intervene with a student. Examples of dress modifications include low-heeled shoes; small, nondangling earrings; loose-fitting clothing; and shorter hairstyles.

Teachers also should remove items of monetary and sentimental value from easy reach. Throwing objects that are within an arm's reach is a common reaction when a student is extremely upset. As a precautionary measure, it may prove helpful to keep important objects in a safe place within the classroom or avoid bringing them at all.

Myles and Simpson suggested consistently modeling "positive human values and attitudes toward students" (1994, p. 379). This would include showing respect for their ideas, opinions, and values. It also is important to model appropriate ways to deal with frustration and anger.

Carr and associates (1994) suggested that crisis management strategies should be implemented when the problem behavior is likely to increase to a serious level, or when the behavior has reached a level that poses a danger to the person with disabilities or to others around him or her. The key to crisis intervention is having rapport with the student. Carr and associates described this as making yourself signify positive interaction, for approach and for simple communication. In addition, the teacher should teach communication forms that serve the same purpose as a problem behavior.

Teachers should carefully define expectations. It is important to explicitly explain what behaviors are and are not acceptable in the classroom. However, one key is that rules and expectations should be taught as well as stated so that there is no confusion as to whether students understand.

It is important that teachers follow through with consequences consistently. It has been well documented that a good way to decrease or prevent aggressive behaviors is to consistently enforce rules and deliver consequences. Students tend to respond better in structured situations in which they know the consequences for their actions. It logically follows that if a student can predict the consequence for his or her actions, then a crisis situation may be averted. For example, a student prone to violence will know what to expect at all times. It is only when the consequences are changed that one may have to exhaust his or her problem-solving skills to get out of a stressful situation.

Remaining calm can be difficult when faced with a crisis; however, there are several actions that can allow a classroom teacher to remain in control. It is important to acknowledge a student's feelings and ignore any accusations that he or she may make. Tell him or her that it is okay to be angry as long as he or she expresses his or her anger in a socially acceptable way. It also is crucial to communicate to the agitated student that you and the rest of the staff are there to help him or her. However, even in a crisis situation, the student should be reminded of the rules and consequences. A key way for teachers to maintain control is to avoid arguing with the student because this will usually escalate the situation. Finally, focus on what the student is doing, not why he or she is doing it, keeping yourself, the student, and the rest of the class as safe as possible. There is time for the "why" once the student is calm.

The teacher also should maintain a therapeutic attitude. This involves considering a student's unique circumstances when dealing with aggression or crises. A therapeutic attitude involves a great deal of empathy for one's students, striving to maintain a student's dignity and self-esteem. Not belittling or humiliating a student for inappropriate behavior may help students maintain dignity even when they are upset or in crisis.

HOW CAN POSITIVE SOCIAL
INTERACTIONS AND FRIENDSHIPS BE ENCOURAGED?

Van der Klift and Kunc (1994) stated that this is the first generation of students with and without identified disabilities to grow up being educated together. They argued that in our classrooms we are working toward a time when asking for and receiving help is not considered an admission of inferiority. However, students may need help in approaching friendships with students with more severe disabilities. Hunt, Farron-Davis, Wrenn, Hirose-Hatae, and Goetz (1997) suggested that teachers provide information to classmates about the communication systems individuals with disabilities use and the adapted curriculum and materials the students with disabilities use during natural opportunities. In addition, teachers could identify and use various media that could serve as the basis for interactive exchanges between the focus students and others. In addition, social exchanges can be planned through partnering systems, arranging interactive activities across the day, and prompting and interpreting communicative exchanges when necessary.

There are several conditions that are essential for supporting the development of friendships in inclusive high schools. Martin, Jorgensen, and Klein (1998) contended that first there should be real inclusion in all aspects of the school community. In addition, students with disabilities should have access to their means of communication all of the time and to their classmates who understand and know how to use the system. If a student is using sign language, for example, the interpreter should be present outside of class, when students typically interact informally. If a student communicates using a book, words, or pictures, the book should always be with the student and others should know how to use it. Martin et al. also contended that supports should be provided in such a way that independence, interdependence, self-determination, and natural interactions are emphasized. Students should all be involved in creative problem solving related to including everyone in social activities. Parents and staff members should make sure that students with disabilities use age-appropriate and respectful materials, language, expectations, and modifications. In addition, family members may need to be involved in facilitating and supporting friendships and social activities. Martin and associates also contended that there must be a schoolwide climate of acceptance and celebration of diversity.

The very organization of secondary schools, with individual schedules and changing classes, can hinder the development of friendships (Schnorr, 1997). Hughes and colleagues (1999) suggested the use of an innovative *peer buddy* program. In this program, a credit-bearing course was created that allows peer buddies to spend at least one period each day with a student partner who has a disability. In this course, students were screened and matched. Training was provided that established expectations for interactions. Activities were developed including a "lunch bunch" and a "peer buddy club" to further encourage interactions. At Purcell Marian High School, students also may register for a credit-bearing work study course in which they may provide natural supports to students with identified disabilities. Students with disabilities also may register for the course; in one situation, Karen Matuszek reported that a student with a disability was assigned the role of "helper" for probably the first time in her life.

Randy Reeder described another program to enhance social support. Seniors who themselves could use positive support may serve as "student ambassadors" to freshman homerooms. In this role, these students are cast in a positive role, explaining rules and activities to other students. In addition, the students who are in classes with students with disabilities and are acting as natural supports become friends with the students with disabilities.

WHAT MEDICATIONS ARE USED AS BEHAVIORAL SUPPORTS?

Even though it remains controversial, use of medication to manage students' behavior significantly increased in the 1990s (Campbell & Cueva, 1995). Between 2% and 3% of all school-age children and adolescents may be on one or more medications at any given time. Among students with disabilities, 15%–20% may be on one or more medications (Sweeney, Forness, Kavale, & Levitt, 1997). Our purpose of discussing medication in this chapter is not to promote its use but to inform you of issues involved in the use of medication to manage behavior and your role as a teacher related to medication.

It is important to remember that medication does not cure a disability; it targets specific symptoms. Although medication may be effective, there are several logistical issues that must be considered when medication is prescribed. A major problem is ensuring that the individual is taking the medication as prescribed (Brown, Dingle, & Landau, 1994). Following medication schedules may be complicated. In addition, medication may be prescribed for long periods of time, and parents and/or students may become ambivalent about its use. When medication is to be administered at school, the responsibility to give the appropriate medication at the appropriate time may be affected by school staff and faculty attitudes toward medication and their availability to administer it. In addition, the way the community accepts the use of medication may impact the parents' decision making about medication.

The frequent misadministration of medication is one reason why the decision to use medication should be made after attempts at other interventions and consultation with a psychiatrist (School Mental Health Project, 1997). Direct communication must be established and a plan must be developed for the person who will administer the medication, as well as how and when it will be administered. Teachers should emphasize to the student that he or she remains responsible for his or her behavior. Students may need help explaining the use of medication as well as reminders to take the medication. Teachers, the student, and the student's parents should develop an evaluation plan to determine if the medication is having the desired effect. Forness, Sweeney, and Toy (1996) suggested that a professional who is knowledgeable about medication and its effects should be present at the student's IEP meeting.

Stimulants are the most commonly prescribed medications related to behavior. The two most frequently prescribed are Ritalin and Dexedrine. Dexedrine is usually used with children who have not responded to Ritalin. Stimulants are prescribed to increase control of physical activity, goal-directedness, attention, performance, and cooperation. They also are prescribed to decrease impulsivity, disruptiveness, distractibility, and negative behavior. Side effects of stimulants are insomnia, decreased appetite, gastrointestinal pain, irritability, and a worsening of symptoms (Sweeney et al., 1997). These side effects can be managed by administering the medication early in the day, after meals, and planning the time for other doses. An advantage of stimulants is that they are short-term (time) acting drugs, so they may be administered during the times when behavior is most problematic (Brown et al., 1994).

Antidepressants or mood stabilizers are becoming the second most frequently prescribed medications for children and youth (Sweeney et al., 1997). They are administered for depression, attention-deficit/hyperactivity disorder, obsessive-compulsive disorder, and school phobia. Antidepressants are administered primarily to treat behaviors such as appetite and sleep problems, fatigue, lack of energy, and problems in attention and concentration. If the individual with attention-deficit/hyperactivity disorder has severe side effects then the antidepressant is prescribed with stimulants (Brown et al., 1994).

There are several other medications that are used less frequently with students to address behavior. Antihistamines are sometimes prescribed for children and youth with insomnia. Antianxiety agents are rarely used because few data on the efficacy and safety of using these drugs with children are available. These medications are reserved for times and occasions when other interventions are insufficient or inadequate (Brown et al., 1994). Anticonvulsants may be used for students with seizure disorders.

The teacher plays a supportive role in the use of medication with students. This supportive role includes 1) collaborating with and reporting of observations, 2) modifying classroom structure and curricular content, 3) obtaining permission to administer medication, and 4) safeguarding and administering medication in the school (Shea & Bauer, 1987). Teachers are not qualified to refer a child directly to a physician or to suggest the prescribing of medication.

Teachers provide current and objective feedback to the physician on the observable effects of medication on the child's behavior and learning. This information can help the prescribing physician know how to maximize the positive effects and minimize the side effects of medication. Because teachers are trained observers and are with the child throughout the day, they are in an excellent position to observe the effects of the medication and report, through proper channels, to the physician.

Professional school personnel must obtain permission to dispense medication in the school when medical personnel (a physician or nurse) are not available during the school day. Schools need to develop a policy with regard to medication in an effort to improve services and minimize personnel liability (Courtnage, Stainback, & Stainback, 1982). When medication is dispensed in the school, the following guidelines should be followed:

- Permission forms should be obtained and filed in the child's permanent record.
- Medication should be stored in a central location in a locked cabinet. A refrigerator may be needed for some medications.
- Medication must be properly labeled with the child's and physician's names. The label should include directions for use.
- Medications should be logged in and out of the school. Medication should be inventoried daily. One professional member of the school's staff, preferably a nurse, should be appointed to inventory medication and function as a contact person in all communications with parents, physicians, pharmacists, and other medical personnel related to medication.
- A responsible adult must be present when the child takes his or her medication.
- A log, to be completed each time a child takes medication, should be maintained in the medication area or the child's record file.

SUMMARY POINTS

- Students' behaviors are purposeful and communicative.
- Good teaching is the best form of classroom management.
- Teachers usually manage the behavior of students with disabilities in the same way as those without identified disabilities.
- IDEA '97 ensures students with disabilities a free, appropriate public education, and this must be considered in discipline policies.
- In positive behavioral support, teachers consider changing systems, altering environments, teaching skills, and affirming desired behaviors.
- Teachers serve as a support role in the use of medication with students.

REFERENCES

Auerbach, S.M., & Kilmann, P.R. (1977). Crisis intervention: A review of outcome research. *Psychological Bulletin, 84,* 1189–1217.

Brown, R.T., Dingle, A., & Landau, S. (1994). Overview of psychopharmacology in children and adolescents. *School Psychology Quarter, 9,* 4–25.

Campbell, M., & Cueva, J.E. (1995). Psychopharmacology in child and adolescent psychiatry: A review of the past seven years. Part II. *Journal of the American Academy of Child and Adolescent Psychiatry, 34*(10), 1262–1272.

Campbell, P., & Olsen, G.R. (1994). Improving instruction in secondary schools. *Teaching Exceptional Children, 26*(3), 51–54.

Caplan, G. (1964). *Principles of preventive psychiatry*. New York: Basic Books.

Carr, E.G., Levin, L., McConnachie, G., Carlson, J.I., Kemp, D.C., & Smith, C.E. (1994). *Communication-based intervention for problem behavior: A user's guide for producing positive change*. Baltimore: Paul H. Brookes Publishing Co.

Colvin, G., Kameenui, D.J., & Sugai, G. (1993). School-wide and classroom management: Reconceptualizing the integration and the management of students with behavior problems in general education. *Education and Treatment of Children, 16*, 361–381.

Council for Exceptional Children (CEC). (1998a). The discipline problem—and ways to deal with it. *CEC Today, 3*(4), 1–4.

Council for Exceptional Children (CEC). (1998b). Strategies to meet IDEA 1997's discipline requirements. *CEC Today, 4*(5), 1–6.

Courtnage, L., Stainback, W., & Stainback, S. (1982). Managing prescription drugs in school. *Teaching Exceptional Children, 15*(1), 5–9.

Daniels, V.I. (1998). How to manage disruptive behavior in inclusive classrooms. *Teaching Exceptional Children, 30*(4), 26–31.

Donnellan, A.M. (1984). The criterion of the least dangerous assumption. *Behavioral Disorders, 9*, 141–150.

Forness, S.R., Sweeney, D.P., & Toy, K.I. (1996). Psychopharmacologic medications: What teachers need to know. *Beyond Behavior, 7*(2), 4–11.

Good, T.L., & Brophy, J. (1995). *Contemporary educational psychology* (5th ed.). Reading, MA: Addison Wesley Longman.

Haring, N.G., & De Vault, G. (1996). Discussion. In L.K. Koegel, R.L. Koegel, & G. Dunlap (Eds.), *Positive behavioral support: Including people with difficult behavior in the community* (pp. 115–120). Baltimore: Paul H. Brookes Publishing Co.

Hitzing, W. (1992). Support and positive teaching strategies. In S. Stainback & W. Stainback (Eds.), *Curriculum considerations in inclusive classrooms. Facilitating learning for all students* (pp. 143–158). Baltimore: Paul H. Brookes Publishing Co.

Hughes, C., Guth, C., Hall, S., Presley, J., Dye, M., & Byers, C. (1999). "These are my best friends": Peer buddies promote inclusion in high school. *Teaching Exceptional Children, 31*(5), 32–37.

Hunt, P., Farron-Davis, F., Wrenn, M., Hirose-Hatae, A., & Goetz, L. (1997). Promoting interactive partnerships in inclusive educational settings. *Journal of The Association for Persons with Severe Handicaps, 22*, 127–137.

Individuals with Disabilities Education Act (IDEA) Amendments of 1997, PL 105-17, 20 U.S.C. §§ 1400 *et seq.*

Larson, P.J., & Maag, J.W. (1998). Applying functional assessment in general education classrooms: Issues and recommendations. *Remedial and Special Education, 19*(6), 338–349.

Long, N.J., Morse, W.C., & Newman, R.G. (Eds.). (1996). *Conflict in the classroom: The education of at-risk and troubled students* (5th ed.). Austin, TX: PRO-ED.

Martin, J., Jorgensen, C.M., & Klein, J. (1998). The promise of friendship for students with disabilities. In C.M. Jorgensen (Ed.), *Restructuring high schools for all students: Taking inclusion to the next level* (pp. 145–181). Baltimore: Paul H. Brookes Publishing Co.

Myles, P.S., & Simpson, R.L. (1994). Prevention and management considerations for aggressive and violent children and youth. *Education and Treatment of Children, 17*(3), 330–384.

Office of Juvenile Justice and Delinquency Prevention. (1989). *Report of acts of aggression and violence*. Washington, DC: Author.

O'Neill, R.E., Horner, R.H., Albin, R.W., Sprague, J.R., Storey, K., & Newton, J.S. (1997). *Functional assessment and program development for problem behavior: A practical handbook* (2nd ed.). Pacific Grove, CA: Brooks/Cole.

138   Bauer and Hill

Pitcher, G.D., & Poland, S. (1992). *Crisis intervention in the schools.* New York: The Guilford Press.

Poland, S., Pitcher, G., & Lazarus, P.J. (1995). Best practices in crisis intervention. In A. Thomas & J. Grimes (Eds.), *Best practices in school psychology–III* (pp. 445–458). Bethesda, MD: National Association of School Psychologists.

Purcell Marian High School. (1995). *Student handbook.* Cincinnati, OH: Author.

Rappaport, L. (1962). The state of crisis: Some theoretical considerations. *Social Service Review, 36*(2), 211–217.

Redl, F. (1959). The concept of the life space interview. *American Journal of Orthopsychiatry, 29,* 1–18.

Ruef, M.B., Higgins, C., Glaeser, B.J.C., & Patnode, M. (1998). Positive behavioral support: Strategies for teachers. *Intervention in School and Clinic, 34*(1), 21–32.

Schnorr, R.F. (1997). From enrollment to membership: "Belonging" in middle and high school classes. *Journal of The Association for Persons with Severe Handicaps, 22,* 1–15.

School Mental Health Project. (1997). *Students and psychotropic medication: A resources aid packet.* Los Angeles: Author.

Shea, T.M., & Bauer, A.M. (1987). *Teaching children and youth with behavior disorders* (2nd ed.). Upper Saddle River, NJ: Prentice-Hall.

Simpson, R.L., Myles, B.S., Walker, B.L., Ormsbee, C.K., & Downing, J.A. (1991). *Programming for aggressive and violent students.* Reston, VA: Council for Exceptional Children.

Sugai, G., Sprague, J.R., & Horner, R.H. (1999). Functional assessment–Behavioral support planning: Research to practice to research. *Research on Behavioral Disorders, 24*(3), 253–257.

Sweeney, D.P., Forness, S.R., Kavale, K.A., & Levitt, J.G. (1997). An update on psychopharmacologic medication: What teachers, clinicians, and parents need to know. *Intervention in School and Clinic, 33*(1), 4–21.

Umbreit, J., & Blair, K.-S. (1996). The effects of preference, choice, and attention on problem behavior at school. *Education and Training in Mental Retardation and Developmental Disabilities, 3*(2), 151–161.

U.S. Department of Education, Office of Special Education Programs (OSEP), Technical Assistance Center on Positive Behavioral Interventions and Supports (PBIS). (1999a). *Functional behavioral assessment.* (Available http://www.ideapractices.org/docs/OSEPdocs/fba.htm.)

U.S. Department of Education, Office of Special Education Programs (OSEP), Technical Assistance Center on Positive Behavioral Interventions and Supports (PBIS). (1999b). *School-wide positive behavioral interventions and supports.* (Available http://www.pbis.org/english/main.php3?name=School-wide_PBIS.)

U.S. Department of Education, Office of Special Education Programs (OSEP), Technical Assistance Center on Positive Behavioral Interventions and Supports (PBIS). (1999c). *What is PBIS?* (Available http://www.pbis.org/english/main.php3?name=What_is_PBIS?)

Van der Klift, E., & Kunc, N. (1994). Beyond benevolence: Friendships and the politics of help. In J.S. Thousand, R.A. Villa, & A.I. Nevin (Eds.), *Creativity and collaborative learning: A practical guide to empowering students and teachers* (pp. 391–401). Baltimore: Paul H. Brookes Publishing Co.

Weigle, K.L. (1997) Positive behavior support as a model for promoting educational inclusion. *Journal of The Association for Persons with Severe Handicaps, 22,* 36–48.

8

Designing and Evaluating Accommodations and Adaptations

Anne M. Bauer
Karen Matuszek

After reading this chapter, you will be able to answer the following questions:

- What are general accommodations and adaptations that will increase the learning of students in your classroom?
- How do you identify individual student needs and design accommodations and adaptations?
- What are some specific areas that may require accommodations and adaptations in secondary schools?
- What are natural supports?
- How do you know that accommodations are working?

GENERAL ACCOMMODATIONS AND ADAPTATIONS TO INCREASE LEARNING

General educators and special educators often refer to accommodations and adaptations as if they are the same thing. Janney and Snell (1997), however, clearly differentiated between accommodations and adaptations. *Accommodations,* they suggested, are modifications that are documented on the student's individualized education program (IEP) or on a student's 504 plan, which is in accordance with the Rehabilitation Act of 1973 (PL 93–112). The 504 plan identifies accommodations that the student requires in order to fully participate in classes or activities. Janney and Snell defined *adaptations* as changes to learning task requirements, such as changes to the instructional content, teaching methods, materials, or the physical environment. These adaptations may be temporary and may be faded as the students succeed in the classroom. Yet, in their synthesis of 20 studies of the perceptions of students with disabilities in general education classrooms, Klingner and Vaughn (1999) reported that across the studies, students with disabilities want the same activities, books, homework, grading criteria, and group practices as students without disabilities. Students with and without disabilities value teachers who slow down instruction when needed and clearly explain concepts and assignments. All students reported preferring teachers who taught learning strategies and covered the same material in various ways so that everyone could learn.

When teachers typically plan, they first plan content and tasks, and then plan adaptations to meet the needs of their students (Janney & Snell, 1997). Although a great deal of emphasis in past research on inclusive classrooms has been placed on significant restructuring of curriculum and instruction for specific students, Janney and Snell found that teachers tend to address inclusion of students with disabilities in the same manner that they address other diversity issues. The teachers they studied described an *assimilationist approach* to diversity, in which inclusion was understood to require downplaying the differences between students with disabilities and their classmates without disabilities. Modifications and adaptations, then, were contained within the content. Rather than significantly redesign what they did, teachers tended to make modifications specific to students, and designed their lessons to incorporate accommodations within the existing instructional structure and process. Without knowing it, these teachers may have been applying principles of universal design.

Principles of Universal Design

Students must have access to the curriculum. *Access,* used in this way, means that students are able to interact with the curriculum in order to learn. Yet, in inclusive classrooms there are many students who, to a greater or lesser degree, may not be learning from the general curriculum when it is presented in a traditional way. In addition to the students with identified disabilities, there are many students who may understand part of the subject yet may not be competent. In order to provide access to the curriculum to all of these students, there must be flexibility built in. This flexibility is the premise for universal design for learning (Center for Assistive Supportive Technology [CAST], 1999).

Universal design is the design of objects, environments, and activities so that they are able to be used by all individuals, to the greatest extent possible, without the need for adaptations or modifications (Center for Universal Design, 1997). Universal design leads to increased usability for everyone (CAST, 1999). For example, curb cuts, originally designed so that individuals using wheelchairs can negotiate curbs, ease travel for people pushing carriages, riding skateboards, using canes, and, in fact, for anyone walking. The Center for Universal Design described several principles and guidelines that, though originally described for architects, product designers, engineers, and environmental designers, may apply to teachers and classrooms. These principles each have related guidelines.

The first principle of universal design is equitable use. *Equitable use* means that the design is useful to people with diverse abilities. The guidelines for applying this principle suggest that the design should have an identical means of use for all people whenever possible, or an equivalent means when it is not possible. No users should be segregated or stigmatized by the design. In addition to making the design appealing to all users, the designer should make provisions for privacy, security, and safety equally available.

The second principle of universal design is *flexibility in use,* ensuring that the design accommodates a wide range of abilities and preferences. The design should provide choice, accommodate right- or left-handed access, and facilitate accuracy and precision.

The third principle is *simple and intuitive use,* which suggests that the design should be easy to understand regardless of the user's experience, knowledge, language skills, or attention. Unnecessary complexity should be eliminated, and the design should be consistent with user expectations and intuition. A wide range of literacy and language skills should be accommodated. Information should be arranged consistent with its importance, and prompting and feedback should be provided during and after task completion.

The fourth principle of universal design is *perceptible information.* This principle suggests that the design communicates necessary information effectively to the user, regardless of the environment or the user's sensory abilities. Different modes for redundant presentation of essential information should be used. Essential information should be as legible as possible, and individual elements should be differentiated in clear ways so that directions are not confusing.

In the fifth principle, universal design provides a *tolerance for error,* minimizing hazards and the adverse consequences of accidental or unintended actions. In following this feature, fail-safe features are provided, and unconscious actions in tasks that require vigilance are discouraged. The sixth principle, *low physical effort,* suggests that the design can be used efficiently and comfortably with a minimum of fatigue, allowing the user to maintain a neutral body position, minimizing repetitive actions, and minimizing physical efforts.

The seventh principle is *size and space for approach and use,* which suggests that appropriate size and space is provided for approach, reach, manipulation, and use regardless of the user's body size, posture, or mobility. This guideline suggests that a clear line of sight to important elements is available for any seated or standing user. All components should be comfortable for the user, and variations in hand and grip size should be available. Adequate space should be available for the use of assistive devices or personal assistance.

CAST (1999) argued that universal design is an economical, legal, and ethical way to provide equitable educational opportunities for diverse learners. Economically, the development, storage, and distribution of separate forms of curriculum are not as feasible as one accessible curriculum. Universal designs, serving a broader audience, save money in terms of development, storage, and distribution. Legally, universal design is a viable way to comply with the Americans with Disabilities Act (ADA) of 1990 (PL 101-336) and the Individuals with

Disabilities Education Act (IDEA) of 1990 (PL 101-476). Ethically, universal design provides scaffolds so that students with disabilities can participate in general education learning contexts, responding to the ethical need to adjust curriculum tools and materials for equal educational opportunity. In terms of efficacy, educational curricula and materials that meet the needs of the most challenging consumers better meet the needs of all consumers.

Universal design for learning is achieved by using flexible curricular materials and activities that provide alternatives for students with various abilities and backgrounds. These alternatives are built into the way lessons and activities are designed and operated. Accommodations are built in, not added later. However, universal design for learning varies from universal design for other purposes. Curriculum also must offer challenges to a wide range of students. Universal design for learning does not mean "dumbing down" or simplifying curricular material; rather, it means presenting a challenging, engaging curriculum to all students. Universal design applies not only to the content of curriculum, but also to its goals, methods, and manner of assessment (ERIC/OSEP, 1998).

CAST (1999) presented three principles of universal design for learning. The first principle is *providing multiple representations of content to learners*. Universally designed materials provide alternative representations of key information, allowing students with different learning styles and needs to select the medium most suited for them. In some cases, a direct translation, such as a text-to-speech or a speech-to-text caption is possible. Some content, however, such as music, is difficult to translate across media, and multiple representations are needed.

The second principle involves *providing multiple options for expression*. It follows that if no single mode of presentation meets everyone's needs, no single mode of expression may meet everyone's needs. In view of multiple intelligences, more options are needed for greater numbers of students to successfully communicate the knowledge that they have gained and their talents. Students demonstrate differences in their abilities to use different tools. Universally designed materials offer students multiple options to select media, supports, and options that enable them to demonstrate their knowledge.

The third principle of universal design for learning is *providing multiple options for engagement*. Engaging and motivating students may be the most challenging aspect of teaching in an inclusive learning community. Nurturing students' enthusiasm and interests is critically important. This is a multifaceted problem. For any given student, teachers need to provide content that interacts, challenges, includes supports and scaffolds that can be withdrawn as skill improves, is timely, provides feedback, and communicates a clear purpose for learning.

CAST (1999) recognized that universal design for learning requires new curricula. They contended that the new curriculum will provide alternate routes for students and increase engagement by allowing students to work from their areas of strength and interest. The new curriculum will allow customization to learning goals and instructional approaches and will provide a viable and continuous updating and revision process. In addition, the new curriculum will take advantage of technology, providing current, relevant, and real-life learning experiences.

There are several cognitive supports that increase learning and support content for all students (ERIC/OSEP, 1998):

- Summarizing the big ideas
- Providing scaffolding for learning and generalization
- Building fluency through practice
- Providing assessment for background knowledge
- Including explicit strategies to clarify the goals and methods of instruction

Orkwis (1999) also presented a framework for universal design in curriculum development. The first aspect of the framework is to provide flexible means of representation, recognizing that no single method for the presentation of information provides access for all learners. Alternatives may reduce perceptual barriers. For example, audio, image, and graphic materials may be used to support or take the place of textual materials. In addition, alternatives can be used that reduce cognitive barriers, such as emphasizing the "big ideas" and providing for various levels of background knowledge. The second aspect of the framework is to provide flexible means of expression. Alternative means of expression may reduce the motor barriers to expression, including writing, speaking, or drawing. Alternatives also may reduce cognitive barriers to expression when explicit strategies and scaffolds are employed. The third aspect of the framework is to provide flexible means of engagement. Materials must support a wide range of students and challenge them. Include a variety of materials, both novel and familiar, to increase interest and opportunities for success. Materials would recognize the students' developmental levels and culture, as well as be flexible enough to increase access to learners.

Unit and lesson planning can demonstrate the use of universal design. In designing units and lessons for all students, Onosko and Jorgensen (1998) suggested that teachers attend to eight elements:

1. There should be a central unit issue or problem.
2. The unit should begin with an opening "grabber" or motivator.
3. Lessons should be linked to the central issue or problem.
4. Source material for the unit should be richly detailed and varied.
5. Students should participate in culminating projects.
6. Lesson formats should vary.
7. Multiple assessments should be used.
8. Students should be allowed varied modes of expression.

Onosko and Jorgensen (1998) continued describing supports and accommodations. They suggested that "people supports," ranging from classmates to adult volunteers, be used. In addition, materials can be modified or made accessible through technology. Key to meeting the needs of all students is individualized performance standards and expectations, as well as personalized instruction. Finally, evaluation and grading plans can be designed to meet the needs of the students.

IDENTIFYING AND PLANNING ACCOMMODATIONS

Universal design does not eliminate the need for individual accommodations. However, CAST (1999) argued that emphasizing adaptations places the burden on the learner rather than the curriculum. Inaccessible aspects of curricula could be viewed as inadequacies, and the idea that students must procure special individual tools or adaptations to learn in the classroom undermines learning for everyone. Grigal (1998) argued that teachers should approach accommodations for children with disabilities the same way they would approach adjusting their teaching for typical students.

When identifying and planning accommodations, the teacher maintains his or her role in designing lessons. The teacher is responsible for identifying academic and social objectives related to group and individual performance. The teacher determines group size, membership, and duration of affiliation within the group. The teacher arranges the learning environment and establishes positive interdependence among the students. The teacher is responsible for explaining the criteria for academic and social success, monitoring student performance, providing closure to the lesson, and evaluating students' progress and products (Udvari-Solner, 1994).

What accommodations can the teacher make within these responsibilities? First, the teacher can select alternatives to instructional arrangements. Although as students ourselves we often have been subjected to whole-group lecture and participation, there are many other instructional arrangements available to teachers (see Table 8.1).

There also is a series of questions the teacher can ask him- or herself in planning general accommodations, for example, "Will the students' participation and understanding be increased if I change . . ."

- The lesson format?
- The delivery of instruction or teaching style?
- Curricular goals?
- The way in which the activity is evaluated?
- The classroom environment or lesson location?
- Instructional materials?
- Personal assistance?

Table 8.1.   Alternatives to whole-group instructional arrangements

Teacher-directed small-group instruction
Small-group learning
Partner learning, peer tutors, cross-age tutors
One-to-one teacher–student instruction
Independent or individual seat work
Cooperative learning groups

Flexibility is the key to designing and implementing interventions in inclusive classrooms. The teacher should remain flexible in adapting his or her expectations and teaching style. Grigal (1998) suggested that flexibility is a support for teachers and students. Teachers may be flexible by making curricular changes, altering the format of the content, or changing the time and space for lessons. Flexibility also may mean adjusting the time for completion of assignments and texts, and anticipating and planning for conflicts that occur when scheduling classes.

In *Choosing Outcomes and Accommodations for Children (COACH): A Guide to Educational Planning for Students with Disabilities* (2nd ed.), Giangreco, Cloninger, and Iverson (1998) made several suggestions that are appropriate for high school students. They suggested that collaborative teamwork is essential to quality education, and that teachers should work together to choose and develop accommodations. This planning, they argued, is dependent on shared, discipline-free goals. Problem solving is necessary, grounded in the belief that special education is a service, not a place.

The Circles of Inclusion (1998) project reinforced the role of the IEP team in developing appropriate accommodations. It suggested that an environmental assessment should be conducted as the student enters the classroom, and periodically once the student is participating. Through the environmental assessment, performance discrepancies or potential problem areas are compared to typically developing students. Several components can then be considered:

- What strategies are necessary for accommodating the student's physical needs (e.g., seating, positioning, physical handling)?
- What adaptive equipment is needed in the setting? Would technology further support the student?
- Are classroom routes for participation and transitions within the classroom accessible to the student?
- What strategies are necessary for including the students' objectives and needs into the existing classroom objectives and activities?
- Are there any special health care routines and procedures?

- Are special behavioral supports needed?
- What is the overall level of ongoing support needed by the student to be a full participant in the classroom in the most natural manner?

In view of the IDEA Amendments of 1997 (PL 105-17), Etscheidt and Bartlett (1999) suggested a four-step approach for determining supplementary aids and services for students with disabilities. They suggested beginning with a review of the IEP that lists a general description of the services and aids that will be provided to support the student in the general education classroom. In the second step, they suggested several dimensions for discussing supplemental aids and services. In the physical dimension, aids or services related to mobility, room arrangement, acoustics, lighting, or seating are discussed. In the instructional dimension, issues of lesson planning and delivery, methodology, and assessment are described. In the social-behavioral dimension, factors related to the student's behavior are described. The collaborative dimension pertains to personnel resources and how time for collaboration will be managed. The final dimension, referred to as the "other" dimension, allows the team to ask "What else?" in the identification of other aids and services that may be appropriate for the student. In the third step, the IEP team discusses and documents the decision-making process for the supplemental aids and services and a rationale for their selection. In the final step, the data collection procedure is determined.

These general descriptions of supplemental aids and services may, however, be lacking in the specifics the teacher needs to successfully deal with the students. In order to develop more specific ways of supporting the students' successful learning, the teacher may engage in ecological assessment and collaborative problem solving.

Ecological Assessment

Ecological assessment is grounded in observation of the learning environment. Ecobehavioral observation helps the teacher identify classroom variables that correlate with student achievement and eliminate classroom practices that are likely to trigger problem behaviors (Hendrikson & Gable, 1997). Hendrikson and Gable suggested using a matrix or scatterplot that allows teachers to record student behavior that is associated with various classroom contexts and instructional activities. Analyzing the data derived from the observation helps the teacher critically evaluate the relationship between the subject areas or activities and instructional methods and materials. In addition, ecobehavioral assessment helps teachers document the relationship of ecological variables and student behavior.

Hendrikson and Gable (1997) suggested the use of a matrix to identify ecological variables. Teachers may apply their structure to develop a matrix specific for their classes (see Figure 8.1). The teacher would list materials and tasks utilized during the class down the left side of the matrix. Potential aca-

	Task/Materials	Homeroom	History	Fine arts	Consumer math	Family living	General science	English
Attention								
Length of tasks								
Manipulative/ concrete representations								
Reading level								
Writing								
Oral language								
Transitions								
Activity level								
Independent work								
Media captioning								
Computer access								
Physical requirements								
Assistive technology								
Behavior								
Social interactions								

Student: _____ Date: _____ Teacher: _____ Class: _____

Number of students: _____ Location: _____ Start time: _____ End time: _____

Adolescents and Inclusion: Transforming Secondary Schools © 2001 Paul H. Brookes Publishing Co., Inc.

Figure 8.1. Sample matrix used by teachers.

demic responses would be listed across the top. The data for this matrix is re-corded by hand. By studying the cluster of requirements for each of the classes and activities, teachers have information regarding areas that require accom-modations and adaptations. This information is brought to the problem-solving session.

Collaborative Problem Solving

Collaborative problem solving is a systematic way to create solutions to barriers for student success in inclusive classrooms (Hobbs & Westing, 1997). They reported that when professionals used collaborative problem solving, more problems, antecedents, objectives, and plans were identified than when teachers worked alone. Collaboration, however, is not easy. Friend and Cook (1991) suggested that collaboration should be voluntary, and should be based on mutual goals. There should be variety among participants, and responsibility and resources must be shared. Finally, team members must be collectively responsible for the outcomes of their decision.

Hobbs & Westing (1998) described a structured problem-solving process for identifying accommodations for successful inclusion. These closely re-semble the generic components of most educational or consultative processes:

- *Define the problem.* Ecobehavioral assessment, as described previously, pro-vides insights into the specifics of the problems.
- *Define the causes.* Any possible setting events that may be contributing to the problem should be identified. For example, if a student has a hearing loss, scheduling an English class as the last period of the day, when he or she may already be tired from the attention and challenges of using hearing aids or an interpreter, may be contributing to his or her difficulty under-standing the language of the class.
- *Setting objectives.* The team asks, "What are the desired outcomes for these issues?" The objectives of the students' participation in the class should be clearly identified.
- *Identifying solution activities.* With objectives that are grounded in the team's desired outcomes, and clear ecobehavioral assessment information, the type of accommodations and adaptations that will be required can be clearly identified. Teacher creativity is key to developing these accommodations. It also is important to keep in mind that the accommodations should be the simplest and most natural possible. Contrived, complex accommodations are unlikely to be consistently implemented.
- *Monitoring for success.* Monitoring activities also must be agreed on collabo-ratively. These simple yes-or-no checklists as to whether the accommoda-tion is in place, whether papers are collected, or whether data are kept on a graph are maintained by the teacher. Again, the simplest system that gives you the information that you need is best.

Regardless of the accommodations or adaptations selected, ongoing communication is essential. Our teacher contributors have utilized a variety of strategies to communicate with teachers regarding accommodations. These communications may be general, related to all students, or specific to individual students. In regard to general accommodations, periodic communications provide additional information and support for general education teachers (see Figure 8.2).

To: Homeroom teachers of students with disabilities

Thanks for everything you have already done to help these students in your homeroom! Many of our students tell us how much they enjoy homeroom and you specifically.

At conference time, a few of our parents asked for additional support during homeroom:

- Notes in plan book (they all have them) if something special is happening for that class (i.e., Junior Ring Ceremony, picture request, retreats, testing)
- A "buddy" assigned if the homeroom is going someplace as a homeroom group (i.e., pep rally, assembly)
- Reminders to students if they are acting inappropriately or need extra help with personal hygiene (i.e., nose blowing)

The good news is that many of our students don't need this extra support. The following students would definitely benefit:

Thanks in advance!
Karen Matuszek
Director of Student Support Services

Figure 8.2.   Sample communication letter for general education teachers.

In an effort to collaborate with you, we would appreciate the following information at the beginning of each chapter or unit of study:

Class: _Physical Science_   Teacher: _Mr. Malone_

Subject of chapter or unit: _State of Matter_

Textbook pages to be covered: _1–33_

I anticipate that this chapter or unit will be covered

from _9/6_ to _9/23_ (approximate dates).
Please attach a copy of any worksheets or tests.

List 5–10 facts that you feel are important
for this student to learn during this chapter or unit:

1. _Substances may be solids, liquids, or gases._

2. _In gases molecules are far apart._

3. _Ice is solid water._

4. _Steam is water as a gas._

5. _When molecules are warm, they move faster._

6. _Water freezes at 0° C._

7. _Water boils at 100° C._

8. _____

9. _____

10. _____

Is there any additional information
that you feel will be helpful for us to know?
We'll be doing a matter "scavenger hunt" on 9/15 and could use help.

Thank you for your cooperation!

Figure 8.3. Sample communication form for a chapter or unit of study.

In terms of support for specific students, more detailed information often is needed. Our teacher contributors have developed a communication form for general education teachers to complete at the beginning of each chapter or unit of study (see Figure 8.3). Through this communication form, general education teachers can provide support for teachers with the information necessary to provide additional supports and consultation with the teachers.

An additional consideration regarding general adaptations or accommodations for students with disabilities in secondary schools is communication with parents regarding accommodations. By receiving information not typically given to parents of students in secondary schools, parents can provide essential support to students. Without such communication, students with disabilities, particularly those with limited conventional language, may have a difficult time interacting with their parents about school structures or requirements. Our teacher contributors provided information to parents regarding the beginning of school and accommodations made for all students with disabilities (see Figure 8.4). In this letter, several accommodations are presented:

• Students who have difficulty with combination locks on their lockers use padlocks, which are easier to manipulate.
• Students who have difficulty managing all of their materials and supplies in a locker are provided with a desk in a classroom in which to store belongings.
• Student handbooks, which include space for daily assignments, are supplemented by plan books with larger areas in which to note assignments.
• "A Day" and "B Day" classes are organized in separate dividers.
• Students may be provided assistance at arrival and dismissal times.

SPECIFIC AREAS THAT MAY REQUIRE ACCOMMODATIONS AND ADAPTATIONS IN SECONDARY SCHOOLS

There are several areas related to accommodations and adaptations in secondary schools that require greater attention. These issues include notetaking, reading, homework, and the use of assistive technology.

Notetaking

A great deal of classroom learning in secondary school depends on understanding and retaining information presented in lectures, discussions, or group work (Potts, 1993). Potts suggested that notetaking serves two purposes for students. First, it is a way of encoding the incoming information in a way that is meaningful for the student, which in itself makes the material more memorable. Second, notes are a way of storing the information until the time of review. Potts argued that students on the whole need help with their notetaking. Even successful students generally fail to note many of the important

Dear Parents/Guardians:

Welcome to the 2001–2002 school year at Purcell Marian High School! Today was just as chaotic as we expected for the first day of school, but the students seemed to fare well, and we are slowly taking care of any problem areas.

In the morning your son/daughter should stop at his/her locker and drop off any hats, jackets, and so forth. His/her locker is outside room _____. Combination locks must be bought from the Spirit room. If your son/daughter uses a key lock, we would like to have a duplicate key in case of an emergency.

Some students also are assigned a desk to use for books and supplies. His/her desk is in Room _____.

In homeroom this morning, the following forms were given to each student: information forms, emergency health forms, and picture envelopes. The information forms and emergency health forms should be completed (if your son/daughter brought them home) and returned to school immediately. Student pictures will be taken on Monday, August 27. The students may wear uniforms or dress clothes—no jeans, T-shirts, and so forth.

Bus cards also were distributed. If your son/daughter did not receive one, please contact the main office.

Student handbooks are very important. We suggest that you keep them at home as they contain pertinent information for parents and the school calendar for early dismissals, off days, and student activities. Please do not allow your son/daughter to use them as plan books as they do not have sufficient space to record all assignments.

Pizza from Larosa's is sold at lunch every Friday beginning next Friday. It costs $1 a slice. Make-your-own tacos are sold every other Wednesday beginning in September. They cost $1.25. Drinks in the cafeteria vending machines cost 60 cents.

Students will need the following supplies:
  Red 2" binder with dividers for A day classes
  Blue 2" binder with dividers for B day classes
  Daily plan book—purchased from Spirit room
  Looseleaf paper inserted in binders
  Blue or black pens for assignments and notes
  Red correcting pens or markers

Figure 8.4. Sample information letter to parents regarding the beginning of the school year.

Yellow highlighters
Additional supplies may be needed for other classes

For safety reasons, we would like to know how your son or daughter gets to school (bus, carpool), where they are dropped off, and where they meet their ride after school. If he or she needs extra assistance, please let us know.

We know that you will have some questions, especially during these first few weeks. Please feel free to stop in before school, or call us for an appointment.

We look forward to working with you and your son/daughter this year!

Karen Matuszek

ideas presented in the classroom (Kiewra, 1985). Strangely enough, students who did not attend class but reviewed instructor's notes scored higher on tests than students who attended lectures and took and reviewed their own notes (Kiewra, 1985). The pattern changes, however, when tests involve analysis or synthesis of ideas. In those cases, students who simply use the instructor's notes do not do better.

Various formats for taking notes have been used with students. Kiewra (1995) reported that a flexible outline framework in which the order of sub-topics corresponds to the order of lecture presentation produced more note-taking among students. Katayama (1997), who contrasted the use of partial notes, complete notes, and graphic organizers, found that when teachers were interested in students, transfer and application of knowledge, graphic organizers and partial notes were more effective than providing students with full notes. We'll provide two examples of notetaking systems that may be helpful to your students with and without identified disabilities.

Cornell Notetaking System   The Cornell Notetaking System (Pauk, 2000) was developed more than 40 years ago to support students in taking better notes. To begin, the student prepares note paper (see Figure 8.5). Using a typical 8 1/2″ by 11″ piece of loose-leaf paper, the student draws a line down the sheet 2 inches from the left-hand edge. This line ends 2 inches from the

The Events that Led Up to the Civil War (1854–1861)	

Relations between north and south in Congress deteriorate	Increased tension in Congress
	• Fugitive Slave Law
	   • Made it more difficult for slaves to run away
	• Abolitionist Charles Sumner beaten by a cane by representative
	• Tariff of 1857
	   • North blamed Panic of 1857 on low tariff pushed through by south

Popular literature criticizes slavery	Literature
	• Uncle Tom's Cabin
	   • Harriet Beecher Stowe aimed to show people horror of slavery
	• Impending crisis of the south
	   • Hinton Helper claimed slavery hurt nonslaveowning whites

Buchanan, a weak president, elected in 1856	Election of 1856
	• Election of weak president
	   • James Buchanan was weak
	   • American "know-nothing" party put forward
	   • Millard Fillmore cut into the Republican strength
	   • Making election of Buchanan happen

The increased tension in Congress made it apparent that something was going to happen. With public sentiment in the north becoming more and more antislavery, and the election of a weak president, nothing was going to be resolved.

Figure 8.5. Sample notes made using the Cornell Notetaking System.

bottom of the paper. The student then draws a line that is 2 inches from the bottom of the page. This system is based on six steps:

1. *Record:* During this step the student writes as many facts and ideas as possible in the 6-inch column. Headings should be underlined, main ideas indented slightly under the headings, and details indented even further. Students should try to ensure that their notes will make sense when they review them later. This is the only "in-class" step of using the system.
2. *Reduce (or question):* As the student reads through his or her notes, key words or phrases and questions are written in the narrow column. The words and phrases act as memory cues during review, and questions help clarify meaning.
3. *Recite:* During recitation, the student states out loud in his or her own words the facts and ideas to be learned. The student covers the notes in the 6-inch column, leaving cue words and questions uncovered. The student reads each key word or question, then recites the information. If the information is correct, the student continues to review the material by reciting aloud.
4. *Reflect:* During the reflection step, the student reinforces deeper learning by trying to relate facts and ideas to other learning and knowledge.
5. *Review:* Notes should be reviewed nightly or several times during the week by reciting, not rereading.
6. *Recapitulate:* The recapitulation or summary goes at the bottom of the note page. After the student has reduced, recited, and reflected, the summary can be written. Summaries can be written at the bottom of each page or at the end of the day's material.

The Cornell Notetaking System links notetaking to preparing for evaluation. Main ideas and important details are available for writing, thinking, and preparing for evaluation.

Mind Maps The linear organization of the Cornell Notetaking System (Pauk, 1990) may not meet the needs of all students. On the other end of the spectrum, Buzan (1991) introduced mind maps. *Mind maps* are diagrammatic ways of organizing key ideas from lecture and texts that emphasize the interconnection of concepts and show the hierarchy of ideas from titles, to main ideas, to supporting information (see Figure 8.6). Mind maps can capture a great deal of information on a single page. Similar to the Cornell Notetaking System, an emphasis is on key words and phrases.

In a mind map, the central topic is usually placed in the center of the page and the main ideas are placed on branches connected to the central topic. Details are then linked to the main idea. Mind maps may be difficult to develop during a discussion or presentation because the structure may be unclear. Mind maps can be used to summarize a great deal of information in one place in a way that emphasizes the relationships among ideas.

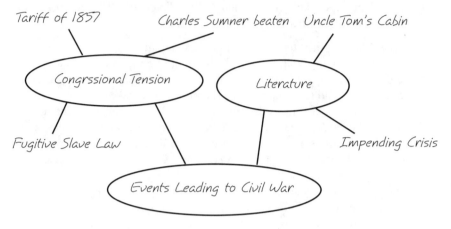

Figure 8.6.   Sample mind map.

Reading

The fundamental task of reading is getting meaning from the text (Collins, 1994). Yet, Armbruster and Anderson (1988) identified several "unfriendly" aspects of textbooks that make it difficult for students to learn. Not only are organizers, such as introductory statements, advance organizers, summaries, and textual highlighting neglected, but most information is presented in list-like fashion with little transition between concepts.

Our teacher contributors have identified several ways in which reading materials can be more accessible to students with disabilities. Teachers tape record the text and provide accompanying study guides or worksheets. Not only have these strategies also been identified in the literature, but Bergerud, Lovitt, and Horton (1988) reported that adding graphics to these study guides can further enhance students' learning. In addition, teachers report reading portions of the material aloud, modeling what they thought about when they read the material, and highlighting specific points. When studying novels that have been filmed, teachers often use the movie in the classroom, which also provides an additional area for discussion related to the differences between film and book.

Meese (1992) presented three general areas in which textbooks may be adapted. First, she suggested that the textbook itself can be modified by high-lighting information, tape recording text segments, or using an alternative version of the book. Second, she suggested that teachers alter instructional procedures by teaching students how to use the textbook's structure; helping them preview the chapter or section; providing advance organizers; and teaching key words, phrases, or other critical vocabulary. Finally, Meese contended that teachers should teach textbook reading strategies such as self-questioning about the main idea, summaries, and themes; developing a reading activity; and making study cards for the students.

Our teacher contributors report using KWL (Ogle, 1986) in helping students work through textbooks. This strategy is an acronym for "What I **K**now, What I **W**ant to Know, and What I **L**earned." This strategy can be used for both pre- and postreading. Before reading, students are directed to think about their prior knowledge and predict what information they will read about. After reading, students are directed to determine if their questions were answered and what further research they may need to do.

Prentice and Cousin (1993) suggested "moving beyond the textbook"– incorporating art, literature, and drama to help students acquire content area concepts and skills. They suggested that the teacher begin with student experiences and ideas about a topic, eliciting current responses and brainstorming ideas. Following this opening exercise, the students seek out the experts, reading the content area text and defining the main point of the text. The topics from the text are analyzed, and the main concepts are described. The class determines how the concepts could be best represented, whether it be through written expression (e.g., essay, poetry, fiction), visual arts (e.g., clay, painting, drawing, collage, model building), dramatic arts (e.g., scriptwriting, reader's theater, puppets), or trade books. After completing their projects, the students review their initial ideas about the topic. Finally, the students complete a self-evaluation.

Homework

Just as notetaking is an issue for all students in secondary schools, homework completion is a challenge. In their study with students with learning disabilities, Sawyer, Nelson, Jayanthi, Bursuck, and Epstein (1996) reported that students found homework easier when the teacher

- Explained the homework toward the beginning of class
- Explained how to do the homework and provided examples
- Gave students time to begin homework in class
- Assigned homework in small amounts
- Provided assistance when it was needed
- Related homework to classwork
- Checked homework after students completed it and gave feedback
- Established a routine at the beginning of the year of how homework would be assigned

Issues of clarity and expectations also are present in Paulu and Darby's (1998) work on homework completion. They argued that homework should challenge students to think and to integrate, making learning personal. Assignments should be tied to the present and should match the skills, interests, and needs of students. The success of homework depends on students' skills and their understanding of assignments, as well as parental expectations and participation (Nuzum, 1998). Nuzum suggested that homework assignments should be balanced among the seven purposes of 1) practice, 2) preview, 3) review, 4) discovery, 5) application, 6) problem solving, and 7) creativity. Teachers should allow sufficient time to give assignments and use the assignment as part of the learning process. Efforts should be made to help students organize their homework.

Technology

With the federal mandate that assistive technology be considered for every student with disabilities, technology is being recommended more to help students achieve in general education classrooms (McLane, Burnette, & Orkwis, 1998). *Assistive technology* is, according to the Technology-Related Assistance for Individuals with Disabilities Act of 1988 (PL 100-407), any item, piece of equipment, or product system that is used to increase, maintain, or improve functional capabilities of people with disabilities. Behrmann (1995) suggested that this includes a wide range of "low-tech" materials, ranging from notetaking audiocassette recorders to pencil grips, to carbon-free copying paper or copy machines, to switches, to head pointers, to picture boards, to taped instructions, to workbooks. There also are "high-tech" devices such as calculators, talking clocks, word processors with spelling and grammar checking, word prediction and voice recognition software, speech synthesizers, augmentative communication devices, and alternative keyboards.

The rationale for using technology is to reduce barriers. Lewis (1998) suggested that technology can reduce barriers to learning in these ways:

- The print barrier may be reduced by presenting information through senses other than vision.
- The communication barrier (poor handwriting, spelling, organization skills, and writing production) may be reduced through word processing, spelling, grammar tools, and programs to organize writing.
- The learning barrier may be reduced by providing alternatives to traditional approaches such as lecture and textbook through audiotapes, videotapes, and computers.

Assistive technology can support students in general education classes in many ways. Lahm and Nickles (1999) suggested that assistive technology can assist students with

- Organization, through the use of graphic organizers or the outline function of word processing software

- Notetaking, with the teacher providing copies of notes using either carbonless copy paper or a copy machine, microcassette recorders, videotapes of class sessions or demonstrations or with the student using laptop or notebook computers
- Writing assistance, using word processing, grammar/spell checkers, thesaurus programs, or the editing capabilities of word processing
- Productivity, enabling students to work on math or other subjects using spreadsheets, databases, or graphics software; small "personal digital assistants" can translate words printed with a pen input device to computer-readable text
- Access to reference materials, using the Internet or multimedia tools
- Cognitive assistance, through application software that provides tutorials, drill and practice, problem solving, and simulations
- Materials modifications, in which teachers can develop and modify computer-based instructional materials for students with mild disabilities

Sax, Pumpian, and Fisher (1997) suggested that technology must be considered from a variety of perspectives. First, the student must be involved in the process; one of the main reasons that students don't use technological devices is because they were not involved in the selection of the devices. In addition, Sax et al. suggested targeting a specific activity. Finally, they urged teachers to look for people with technical expertise beyond the educational realm.

NATURAL SUPPORTS

When including students in secondary schools, Ryan and Paterna (1997) suggested that teachers start with the general education curriculum. Once students have access then adaptations and modifications can be used to assist when necessary. These supports, Ryan and Paterna contended, should be a natural and ongoing part of the school, classroom, and community. *Natural supports* are "based on the understanding that relying on typical people and environments enhances the potential for inclusion more effectively than relying on specialized services and personnel" (Nisbet, 1992, p. 5). Stainback, Stainback, and Stefanich (1996) described several basic principles of support:

- Supports are based on the assumption that everyone has abilities and gifts, and is able to provide some form of support and assistance to others.
- Supportive relationships are reciprocal; students who are helpers will, at another time, be helped.
- Supportive relationships are equal, and individuals support each other as peers, friends, or colleagues.
- Supports will change over time.
- A diverse community increases the likelihood that everyone will have ways to support each other and become interdependent with each other.

- The focus of support is on what the person receiving support wants and needs.
- Supports focus on empowering a person to assist him- or herself and others.
- Administrators empower and encourage people to provide support to each other.
- Supports are a natural part of the school and classroom community.
- School supports are managed by those directly involved in the school community.
- Supports exist for everyone.
- Supports are grounded in the social interactions that naturally operate in classrooms and schools.
- The goal of support is to provide individuals with what is needed to empower people to assist and support themselves and others.

York, Giangreco, Vandercook, and Macdonald (1992) suggested that real supports occur when the recipient of support perceives that he or she has been helped, and when the responsibility for achieving desired student outcomes is shared among team members. Real supports increase the ability to meet diverse educational needs. In addition, in real supports the effort required is worth the outcomes, and priority outcomes for students at home, school, and in the community are achieved.

Instructional Assistants and Other Personnel Supports

Although it seems like an easy way to provide students with extra help, extra personnel can be an unknowing barrier to a student's successful integration into a classroom (Grigal, 1998). When instructional assistants are provided to several students in a classroom, teachers should avoid clumping together the students with disabilities. Instead, they should assign students places close to students who are helpful rather than having the "special education group" in the back.

Giangreco, Edelman, Luiselli, and MacFarland (1997), analyzing extensive observations and interviews, identified a series of concerns regarding the use of instructional assistants. They found that instructional assistants interfered with ownership and responsibility of general educators; teachers did not plan accommodations and depended on the instructional assistant to involve the student. The instructional assistant also separated the students with disabilities from their classmates without disabilities for ease of physical management (e.g., waiting until the halls were clear to take a student using a wheelchair to his or her next class). Students with disabilities tended to become dependent on the instructional assistance and lost some of their personal control in where to eat or with whom to interact. Peer interactions also changed due to having an adult "shadow." Instructional assistants took over the instruction for the child, at times limiting the competent instruction the student received and interfering with the instruction of other students. Giangreco and associates suggested that instructional assistants be assigned to classrooms rather than individual students and that the role of the adult be clarified. Planning and implementation of instruction is clearly outside of the realm of the instructional assistant; teachers plan, manage, and evaluate, using the instructional assistant as a support, not as another teacher.

In a study based on intensive interviews with 20 instructional assistants, Marks, Schrader, and Levine (1999) identified concerns similar to those identified by Giangreco and associates (1997). Instructional assistants indicated that they felt responsible for the success of the teacher and the student, to the extent of feeling that it was up to them to ensure that the student with disabilities was successful. Many instructional assistants felt that they were the only ones who truly understood the student with a disability and that teachers relied on them to be the expert in adapting for the student. Marks and associates questioned the use of instructional assistants to support the inclusion of students.

PARTIAL PARTICIPATION

What if universal design and accommodations are inadequate in allowing full access to the curriculum? Should students with disabilities still be included in those classes? Stainback et al. (1996) argued that including students in general education classrooms is essential so that we avoid separating a subgroup of students in a way that they share few common experiences and understandings with the people with whom they will live and work. They suggested that

> While not everyone can always learn the same things in these academic areas, whatever knowledge can be gained is of value and is worthwhile. There is more to life for anyone than learning only to make a sandwich or sweep a floor. It is also worthwhile, for any of us, regardless of individual characteristics, to have a sense of who we are, an indication of who our ancestors were, and an appreciation of the environment and world around us. It is a serious mistake to underestimate or place limitations on some students by assuming that the only things they can learn that are useful to them are how to tie their shoes or ride a bus. (1996, p. 15)

For these students, partial participation may be the key. *Partial participation* is "performing a quality skill within an age appropriate, meaningful, and functional activity" (Utah's Project for Inclusion, 1993, p. 3). It may include help from an adult or peer, team grouping, or other modifications that do not require the student to complete the activity or participate independently.

Any application of partial participation should maintain the focus of the students' class members. The degree of participation will naturally vary, though topical connections with class learning activities must be maintained. Janney and Snell (1997), in their discussion of students with moderate and severe disabilities, suggested that participation may be at one of three levels. The student may participate with academic adaptations, participating in the same activity as peers, using modified methods, input or response models, objectives, criteria, or materials. The second level, social participation, suggests that the student participate in the same activity as his or her peers, with social rather than academic goals. The third level of participation includes involving the student in a similar lesson topic while utilizing a completely different activity.

MONITORING ACCOMMODATIONS AND ADAPTATIONS

Rick Hennegan summarized his feelings about monitoring accommodations and adaptations to his teaching in this way: "If they're all getting 90s, I figure what we're doing is working." Monitoring accommodations does not need to be a complex process. In many situations, the student could be involved in monitoring. For example, if accommodations are made to assist the student in paying attention in class, the student may carry a set of "business cards" that are presented to the teacher at the conclusion of the class, so that he or she may indicate the extent of the student's attention and work (see Figure 8.7).

Janney and Snell (2000) used another form of a yes-or-no checklist to evaluate student evaluations. In their checklist, teachers include items about the team process, as well as information as to whether the student

- Receives adequate and appropriate support in the class
- Uses accommodations that are as nonintrusive as possible
- Uses accommodations that allow for active participation in class activities
- Receives adequate instruction and practice in IEP goals and objectives
- Is making satisfactory progress
- Is not prevented from being a full member of the class
- Has a variety of positive relationships with peers

Brad's daily report   Date: _____

Today, Brad
Wore his hearing aids	Yes	No
Used his plan book	Yes	No
Turned in his homework	Yes	No
Has a written assignment	Yes	No

Teacher's initials: _____

Figure 8.7.   Sample "business card" for teachers to indicate the extent of a student's attention and work.

Observer:_____ Date:_____

Student:_____ Teacher:_____

Class:_____ Bell/Time:_____

Observations:

Recommendations:

Figure 8.8.   Sample student observation form.

Student observation is probably one of the most effective ways to monitor what is happening in classrooms. To organize their observation notes, our teacher contributors use a student observation form (see Figure 8.8). The key to this form is the area that is marked "Recommendations."

SUMMARY POINTS

- When applying universal design, teachers design their interactions, activities, and lessons with students, to be used by all students to the greatest extent possible, without need for adaptations or modifications.
- The application of universal design in teaching is achieved by providing 1) multiple representations of content, 2) multiple options for expression, and 3) multiple options for engagement.
- Flexibility is key in designing and implementing interventions in inclusive classrooms.
- Ecological assessment helps teachers identify classroom variables that correlate with student achievement and manage classroom practices that seem to trigger problem behaviors.
- Ongoing communication regarding accommodations is essential.
- Notetaking and homework completion are two areas that may require specific accommodations in high school.
- Modifications and accommodations should be carefully monitored and evaluated.

REFERENCES

Americans with Disabilities Act (ADA) of 1990, PL 101-336, 42 U.S.C. §§ 12101 *et seq.*
Armbruster, B.B., & Anderson, T.H. (1988). On selecting "considerate" content area textbooks. *Remedial and Special Education, 9,* 47–52.
Behrmann, M.M. (1995). *Assistive technology for students with mild disabilities.* Reston, VA: ERIC Clearinghouse on Disabilities and Gifted Education. (ERIC No. ED 378755)
Bergerud, D., Lovitt, T., & Horton, S. (1988). The effectiveness of textbook adaptations in life science for high school students with learning disabilities. *Journal of Learning Disabilities, 21*(2), 70–76.
Buzan, T. (1991). *Use both sides of your brain: New mind-mapping techniques to help you raise all levels of your intelligence and creativity, based on the latest discoveries about the human brain* (3rd ed.). New York: Dutton.
Center for Assistive Supportive Technology (CAST). (1999). *Universal design for learning.* Peabody, MA: Author. (Available http://www.cast.org/concepts/concepts_three_p. htm.)
Center for Universal Design. (1997). *The principles of universal design, version 2.0.* Raleigh: North Carolina State University.
Circles of Inclusion. (1998). *Determining supports needed for an inclusive preschool program.* Parsons: University of Kansas.
Collins, N.D. (1994). *Metacognition and reading to learn.* Bloomington, IN: ERIC Clearinghouse on Reading, English, and Communication. (ERIC No. ED 376427)

ERIC/OSEP. (1998). *A curriculum every student can use: Design principles for student access.* Reston, VA: ERIC Clearinghouse on Disabilities and Gifted Education.

Etscheidt, S.K., & Bartlett, L. (1999). The IDEA Amendments: A four-step approach for determining supplementary aids and services. *Exceptional Children, 65,* 163–174.

Friend, M., & Cook, L. (1991). Principles for the practice of collaboration in schools. *Preventing School Failure, 35*(4), 6–9.

Giangreco, M.F., Cloninger, C.J., & Iverson, V.S. (1998). *Choosing outcomes and accommodations for children (COACH): A guide to educational planning for students with disabilities* (2nd ed.). Baltimore: Paul H. Brookes Publishing Co.

Giangreco, M.F., Edelman, S.W., Luiselli, T.E., & MacFarland, S.Z.C. (1997). Helping or hovering? Effects of instructional assistant proximity on students with disabilities. *Exceptional Children, 64,* 7–18.

Grigal, M. (1998). The time–space continuum: Using natural supports in inclusive classrooms. *Teaching Exceptional Children, 30*(6), 44–51.

Hendrikson, J., & Gable, R. (1997). Collaborative assessment of students with diverse needs. *Preventing School Failure, 41*(4), 159–163.

Hobbs, T., & Westing, D. (1998). Promoting successful inclusion through collaborative problem solving. *Teaching Exceptional Children, 31*(2), 12–19.

Individuals with Disabilities Education Act (IDEA) of 1990, PL 101-476, 20 U.S.C. §§ 1400 *et seq.*

Individuals with Disabilities Education Act Amendments of 1997, PL 105-17, 20 U.S.C. §§ 1400 *et seq.*

Janney, R.E., & Snell, M.E. (1997). How teachers include students with moderate and severe disabilities in elementary classes: The means and meaning of inclusion. *Journal of The Association for Persons with Severe Handicaps, 22,* 159–169.

Janney, R., & Snell, M.E. (2000). *Teachers' guides to inclusive practices: Modifying schoolwork.* Baltimore: Paul H. Brookes Publishing Co.

Katayama, A.D. (1997, November). *Getting students involved in note taking: Why partial notes benefit learners more than complete notes.* Memphis, TN: Paper presented at the annual meeting of the Mid-South Educational Research Association. (ERIC No. ED 415270)

Kiewra, K.A. (1985). Providing the instructor's notes: An effective addition to student notetaking. *Educational Psychologist, 20,* 33–39.

Kiewra, K.A. (1995). Effects of note-taking format and study technique on recall and relational performance. *Contemporary Educational Psychology, 20*(2), 172–187.

Klingner, J.K., & Vaughn, S. (1999). Students' perceptions of instruction in inclusion classrooms: Implications for students with learning disabilities. *Exceptional Children, 66*(1), 23–37.

Lahm, E., & Nickles, B. (1999). What do you know? Assistive technology competencies for special educators. *Teaching Exceptional Children, 32*(1), 56–65.

Lewis, R.B. (1998). Assistive technology and learning disabilities: Today's realities and tomorrow's promises. *Journal of Learning Disabilities, 31*(1), 16–26; 54.

Marks, S.U., Schrader, C., & Levine, M. (1999). Paraeducator experiences in inclusive settings: Helping, hovering, or holding their own? *Exceptional Children, 65*(3), 351–328.

McLane, K., Burnette, J., & Orkwis, R. (1998). Integrating technology into the standard curriculum. *Research Connections in Special Education, 3,* 1–4. (ERIC No. ED 421850)

Meese, R.L. (1992). Adapting textbooks for children with learning disabilities in mainstreamed classrooms. *Teaching Exceptional Children, 24*(3), 49–51.

Nisbet, J. (1992). Introduction. In J. Nisbet (Ed.), *Natural supports in school, at work, and in the community for people with severe disabilities* (pp. 1–10). Baltimore: Paul H. Brookes Publishing Co.

Nuzum, M. (1998). Creating success. *Instructor, 108*(3), 86–91.

Ogle, D.M. (1986). K-W-L: A teaching model that develops active reading of expository text. *Reading Teacher, 39,* 564–570.

Onosko, J.J., & Jorgensen, C.M. (1998). Unit and lesson planning in the inclusive classroom: Maximizing learning opportunities for all students. In C.M. Jorgensen, (Ed.) *Restructuring high schools for all students: Taking inclusion to the next level* (pp. 71–106). Baltimore: Paul H. Brookes Publishing Co.

Orkwis, R. (1999). *Curriculum access and universal design for learning.* Washington, DC: ERIC Clearinghouse on Disabilities and Gifted Education.

Pauk, W. (2000). *How to study in college* (7th ed.). Boston: Houghton Mifflin.

Paulu, N., & Darby, L.B. (1998). *Helping your students with homework: A guide for teachers.* Washington, DC: U.S. Government Printing Office. (ERIC No. ED 416037)

Potts, B. (1993). *Improving the quality of student notes.* Washington, DC: ERIC Clearinghouse on Assessment and Evaluation. (ERIC No. ED 366645)

Prentice, L., & Cousin, P.T. (1993). Moving beyond the textbook to teach students with learning disabilities. *Teaching Exceptional Children, 26*(1), 14–17.

Ryan, S., & Paterna, L. (1997). Junior high can be inclusive: Using natural supports and cooperative learning. *Teaching Exceptional Children, 30*(2), 36–41.

Sawyer, W., Nelson, J.S., Jayanthi, M., Bursuck, W.D., & Epstein, M.H. (1996). Views of students with learning disabilities of their homework in general education classes: Student interviews. *Learning Disability Quarterly, 19,* 70–85.

Sax, C., Pumpian, I., & Fisher, D. (1997). *Assistive technology and inclusion.* Pittsburgh, PA: Allegheny University of the Health Sciences, Child and Family Studies Program. (ERIC No. ED 408738)

Stainback, W., Stainback, S., & Stefanich, G. (1996). Learning together in inclusive classrooms: What about the curriculum? *Teaching Exceptional Children, 28*(3), 14–19.

Technology-Related Assistance for Individuals with Disabilities Act of 1988, PL 100-407, 20 U.S.C. §§ 2201 *et seq.*

Udvari-Solner, A. (1994). A decision-making model for curricular adaptations in cooperative groups. In J.S. Thousand, R.A. Villa, & A.I. Nevin (Eds.), *Creativity and collaborative learning: A practical guide to empowering students and teachers* (pp. 59–77). Baltimore: Paul H. Brookes Publishing Co.

Utah's Project for Inclusion. (1993). *Supporting students in general education classrooms.* Salt Lake City: Author.

York, J., Giangreco, M.F., Vandercook, T., & Macdonald, C. (1992). Integrating support personnel in the inclusive classroom. In S. Stainback & W. Stainback (Eds.), *Curriculum considerations in inclusive classrooms: Facilitating learning for all students* (pp. 101–116). Baltimore: Paul H. Brookes Publishing Co.

9

Assessing Learning and Evaluating Progress

The Grade's Not the Thing

Anne M. Bauer

Teacher Contributors: Jason Haap, Kathy Heekin, Margaret Jenkins, Sister Kristin Matthes, Cliff Pope, Karen Willig, Christine Bredestege

In this chapter, we explore issues related to assessing learning and evaluating progress in inclusive high schools. In addition to answering the question, "Why test?" we describe authentic ways to evaluate your students' progress and, thus, the effectiveness of your instruction. We also discuss issues related to grading students with disabilities and their participation in state- and districtwide assessments. After reading this chapter, you will

- Begin to formulate your rationale for evaluating learning and instruction in your classroom
- Recognize issues of fairness in evaluation
- Describe ways to integrate instruction and assessment
- Identify ways to measure student progress and learning
- Identify accommodations and modifications useful in testing situations
- Recognize issues related to grading in inclusive settings
- Describe issues related to state- or districtwide proficiency testing and students with disabilities

WHY TEST? A RATIONALE
FOR EVALUATING LEARNING AND INSTRUCTION

The teacher contributors for this chapter described several reasons for testing and evaluation:

- It is important for students to have to articulate about classwork and how it applies to their life; then, when the rubber hits the road, they can do it. (Sister Kristin Matthes, religion teacher)
- There are things students need to know, principles of which they must be aware; some things are not opinion but are reality. (Kathy Heekin)
- Frequent assessment provides students with ways to accumulate points as a basis of grades; quizzes aren't so much a measure of what they've mastered, but a measure of whether they're with me. (Christine Bredestege, math teacher)
- Students need to keep track of their learning and show how they've learned and changed. They should use their knowledge to produce something. (Jason Haap)
- Students need to reflect on their learning and classroom activities. (Margaret Jenkins, consumer and family science teacher)
- Testing is a learning experience for students—a way to help them think about and organize information. (Karen Willig, language arts and resource teacher)
- Testing is my way of knowing where the students are; it also gives them closure—a review of what we've done. (Cliff Pope, religion teacher)

Cullen and Pratt (1992) suggested that in inclusive environments, assessment can help determine if objectives were achieved and assist in the development and implementation of individualized education programs (IEPs). In addition, through evaluation, teachers can determine the direction of future instruction and develop a basis for extra help where needed.

The overriding purpose for all assessment is to gather information to facilitate decision making (Witt, Elliott, Kramer, & Gresham, 1998). These may be global decisions, such as how well the student does when compared with the rest of his or her class, or local decisions, such as the material that the individual student has mastered and the material that he or she needs to review. If we think about assessment as *assessment for intervention,* the basic purpose is to identify changes that are needed in behaviors or environments and to decide how to accomplish the goals of the needed changes (Barnett et al., 1997). In this chapter we consider both global and general assessment.

WHAT ARE ISSUES OF FAIRNESS AND EQUITY?

As Cliff Pope so succinctly put it, "If kids learn in different ways, then it just follows that you have to evaluate them in different ways." Lam (1995) suggested that assessment is unfair if students are 1) not provided an equal opportunity to demonstrate what they know, 2) judged on abilities and needs using biased assessments, and 3) limited in their educational opportunities because of assessment information. Although some teachers may insist that equality means that all students use the same test that is scored the same way, bias results from characteristics such as gender, ethnicity, race, linguistic background, socioeconomic status, or disability (Lam, 1995). It is unlikely that any group of students would have all of these characteristics. Therefore, administering the same tests to all students and scoring those tests the same way for all children is inherently unfair. As one of our teacher contributors stated, "We need to redefine what *same* means. *Same* is finding out where each student is and pulling him or her forward—that's what is fair and equal" (Jason Haap).

The National Center for Research on Evaluation, Standards, and Student Testing (CRESST) (1996) defined *equity* as the concern for fairness (i.e., that assessments are free from bias or favoritism). An assessment that is fair enables every student to demonstrate what they can do. At the minimum, teachers should review their assessments to make sure that the assessment is free from 1) stereotypes, 2) situations that may favor one culture over another, 3) language demands that prevent some students from showing their knowledge, and 4) form or content that exclude students with disabilities or limited English proficiency. Biases may occur because of unfamiliar language or format, not because the student does not grasp the concept (Nickell, 1993).

Fair assessment is adapted to the individual student's instructional context and background. It recognizes variations in prior knowledge, cultural experience, language proficiency, cognitive style, and interests (Lam, 1995). Using assessment methods and administration procedures appropriate to the student reduces bias because factors that could inhibit the student's performance are reduced. The student's performance is a truer measure of what he or she knows or can do.

What does fair assessment mean for teachers? For our teacher contributors, it meant that they frequently designed four or five forms of a test that covered the same content. Tests may be read to the student with responses recorded by a scribe, additional time may be given to take the tests, the tests may be taken in a different environment, or one sentence may be written instead of three. Most of all, it means that assessment is a daily part of the teaching process, and that instruction and assessment are integrated.

Stainback, Stainback, and Stefanich (1996) argued that one set of objectives cannot be expected to meet the unique learning abilities of all students in inclusive classrooms. They stated that although not everyone will achieve the same objectives, whatever knowledge can be gained is valuable and worthwhile. Jason Haap, however, suggested that alternative forms of assessment can cater to an inherent accommodation. For example, the same structure for a performance-based project can be used for various learners, but the expectations of outcomes based on individual student ability can be altered. The project is the same but the participants are different.

HOW CAN I INTEGRATE INSTRUCTION AND ASSESSMENT?

Teaching in an inclusive learning environment has made our teacher contributors attentive to the relationship of instruction and assessment. Assessment is seen as part of the learning process (Margaret Jenkins) and is in itself a learning experience (Karen Willig). Assessing learning is grounded in learning. Cullen and Pratt (1992) contended that continual evaluation of student learning is an integral part of the teaching and learning process, and forms the basis for immediate action.

To ground assessment in student learning, we need to describe the relationship between learning and assessment. Herman, Aschbacher, and Winters (1992) used cognitive learning theory as a basis for a discussion of instruction and assessment. If we recognize the role of learning theory, traditional tests such as true and false, multiple choice, and fill in the blank have to be evaluated. For example, cognitive learning theory tells us that knowledge is constructed, and that when we learn we create personal meaning from new information and prior knowledge. This implies that discussion of new ideas and encouragement of divergent thinking with multiple correct responses must be emphasized. Critical thinking skills of analysis, comparisons, generalization, prediction, and formation of hypotheses must be used to relate new information to personal experience. All information should be applied to a new situation. Table 9.1 shows additional implications of cognitive learning theory for aligning instruction and assessment.

One way to look at the relationship between instruction and assessment is described by Herman (1998) who uses the acronym WYTIWYG: What you test is what you get. Rudner (1991) contended that testing has traditionally focused on whether students get the right answers; how they arrive at their answers has been considered only during the development of the test. Yet, two primary reasons for testing are discovering how students think or determining where they are having problems (Ascher, 1990). Tests administered to groups emphasize the acquisition of simple facts, low-level skills, superficial memorization, and isolated evidence of achievement (Meisels, 1993).

To show the integration of instruction and assessment, we use an example from one of our teacher collaborators. During senior year, all students participate in a class called *life philosophy,* in which *Siddhartha* by Hermann Hesse is read. Although this is a complex book, multiple supports are provided for all students, and the theme of searching is one that resonates with the seniors (Sister Kristin Matthes). To begin the unit, the teacher presents background information on Hermann Hesse. Some students take notes; some listen and receive copies of the overheard transparencies later; and some follow along, highlighting copies of the overhead transparencies depending on their needs and learning style (see Figure 9.1).

Table 9.1. Implications of cognitive learning theory for assessment

If cognitive learning theory contends that . . .	Then, assessment should . . .
Knowledge is constructive, and learning that occurs as personal meaning is created from new information and prior knowledge	Encourage divergent thinking and multiple correct responses Encourage various ways of self-expression Emphasize critical thinking
Learning is not a linear progression of discrete skills	Engage students in problem solving and critical thinking
Students vary in learning style, attention span, memory, learning rate, and strengths	Provide choices in tasks Provide choices in how to show mastery Provide opportunities to reflect, revise, and rethink Include concrete experiences
Students learn better when the goal and criteria for evaluation are clear	Engage students in defining goals Provide a range of models for students Provide students with opportunities for self-evaluation and peer review, with input on criteria
Students should know how and when to use knowledge, adapt it, and manage their own learning	Provide real world opportunities Engage students in self-evaluation
Motivation, effort, and self-esteem affect learning	Encourage students to see the connection between effort and results
Learning has social components	Provide group work in heterogeneous groups. Consider group products and processes

As the students begin their study of the book, several supports are provided. Audiotaped recordings of the book are available. In addition to the reading of the book, these audiotapes contain explanations interjected in the reading. At the conclusion of the chapters, the tapes provide supports for the students to complete the group work related to the chapter. In addition, students with disabilities (and those who need additional help) have the option to work in a small group with the teacher. In the small group, the teacher reads chapter by chapter with the student and completes a study chart with them (see Table 9.2). As the small group continues its work, the teacher relies more on the students to complete the chart according to the model or earlier chapters.

Background on Hermann Hesse
A. Biographical information
    1. Born in Germany in 1877
    2. His parents were missionaries in India
- It was assumed Hermann also would study for the ministry
- Hermann experienced a religious crisis and ran away from the seminary in 1892
- He was later expelled from high school and began to work in bookshops

    3. During World War I Hermann became a pacifist and was active in the antiwar movement
    4. Hermann studied the works of Freud and underwent analysis with Carl Jung
    5. Hermann visited Switzerland in 1914, and in 1919 moved there permanently
    6. Later he tried to move back to Germany but was unable to identify with the rising patriotism
    7. Hesse won the Nobel Prize for literature in 1946 for his novel *Magister Ludi*
    8. He lived in seclusion in Switzerland until his death in 1962
B. Ideas background
    1. Antinationalism: He believed Europe should be one unity instead of separate, warring countries
    2. Existentialist: He reacted to the chaos of his time; similar to the U.S. and Vietnam in the 1960s
    3. Environmentalist: He opposed war and technocracy
C. Literary themes
    1. He wrote about the polarities of human nature
- Reason versus intuition
- Reflection versus spontaneity
- Discipline versus instinct
- Flesh versus spirit

    2. He concluded that success and happiness in life come from balancing the polarities
    3. He believed that what happens inside of a person is as real as what happens outside of a person
D. *Siddhartha*
    1. Hesse wrote it in 1922 at the age of 45
    2. Siddhartha's life parallels the Buddha's. This was a technique used to convey Hesse's message.
    3. Siddhartha lives the extremes. He eventually finds salvation in the resolution of these.
    4. Characters are symbolic in *Siddhartha*
- Siddhartha: Searcher
- Govinda: Friend, loyal one
- Kamala: Love

Figure 9.1.   Background information notes on Hermann Hesse.

The test concerning *Siddhartha* is specifically linked to the material presented to the students or gleaned through their group work. However, alternative forms of the test are presented to students depending on their individual needs. For example, a short-answer question on the test asks, "What was Siddhartha like at the beginning of the book?" The information for this question is one of the items entered into the study chart (characters in the chapter and two words to describe them). Through his or her study guides, instruction, and group work, the teacher has operationalized "What you test is what you get."

The test concerning *Siddhartha,* which uses alternative forms and rubrics for evaluation, is a fairly traditional test using true and false, matching, short answer, and essay questions. There are alternative ways of assessing progress, which we discuss in the next section.

WHAT ARE WAYS TO MEASURE
STUDENT LEARNING AND PROGRESS?

Salvia and Ysseldyke (1998) described four basic approaches used to gather information about students. The first is observation, which can provide highly accurate, detailed, and verifiable information. Observation may be systematic, in which the observer gathers data on one or more precisely defined behaviors, or nonsystematic, in which the observer watches an individual in his or her environment and takes notes on the behaviors, characteristics, and personal interactions that seem significant. As one of our contributors stated, "I watch their interactions with each other and what they do in class, as well as my interactions with them" (Kathy Heekin). Another teacher uses dry-erase boards in mathematics class to observe the students working through the problems. The second approach Salvia and Ysseldyke described is recollection via interview or rating scales. In recollection, people familiar with a student can be asked to recall observations and interpretations of behavior and events and complete an interview or Likert format rating scale. A third approach includes record review. In record review, information can be gathered from school cumulative records, school databases, student products accumulated in portfolios, anecdotal records, and nonschool records. Finally, testing–the most common approach–is the process of measuring student competencies, attitudes, and behaviors by presenting a challenge or problem and having the student generate a response.

Although it is used most often in high schools, fixed-response testing cannot gain access to the student's ability to function as a competent participant in society. As Nickell (1993) indicated, if we really expect students to be able to examine an issue, make a decision, research an idea and synthesize that research to make a presentation, initiate a project and see it through, or even evaluate an idea, we must use assessment instruments. Because of the

Table 9.2. Reading and study chart for *Siddhartha*

Chapter title	Characters in the chapter (fill in two words to describe them)	Setting of the chapter	Main events of the chapter	Symbolic people or things in the chapter
"The Brahmin's Son" pages 3–12	Siddhartha: Govinda: Samanas: Siddhartha's father:	Siddhartha's home village	We meet Siddhartha and Govinda Siddhartha is not happy Siddhartha and Govinda go to meditate Siddhartha decides to join the Samanas Siddhartha's father at first refuses but finally gives in and lets Siddhartha go Govinda goes with Siddhartha to follow the Samanas	Govinda: friendship, loyalty The river: life, rebirth
"With the Samanas" pages 13–24	Gotama:	Traveling with the Samanas	Siddhartha and Govinda were accepted into the Samanas	

"Gotama"
pages 25–42

Gotama:

The town of Savanthi, in the grove of Jetavana

Siddhartha sought to empty himself by depriving himself of things and by meditating

Siddartha does not find what he is looking for

They decide to follow the Buddha

They find Gotama, the Buddha

They listen to Gotama preach

Govinda decides to follow Gotama

Siddhartha questions and challenges Gotama; Gotama respects Siddhartha's questions

Siddhartha leaves Gotama but Govinda stays

Gotama: wisdom, enlightenment

need to assess students on these more complex skills, alternative forms of evaluating student progress are changing testing (Nickell, 1993). The familiar multiple-choice test is giving way to expanded generative formats in which students are called upon to demonstrate what they know. Traditional fixed-response testing does not provide a clear or accurate picture of what students can do with their knowledge. These tests only show that students can recall; comprehend; or in some cases, interpret, but they do not measure students' ability to use knowledge (Nickell, 1993).

Although she wrote about social studies, Nickell (1993) provided insight into the potential impact of ways to assess students. First, the curriculum will need to be re-examined and re-organized to ensure mastery of knowledge, ways of thinking, and specific behaviors. Instruction also must change; learning must change to doing when activities connect classroom-based learning with the real world. A significant implication also is the integration of assessment with instruction. Expected outcomes should be specified and the criteria for judging success must be clear.

The direct examination of student performance on real world tasks is referred to as *authentic assessment*. Authentic assessments do the following (Wiggins, 1989):

- Require students to be effective performers with the acquired knowledge
- Present students with the full array of tasks found in the best instructional activities, including conducting research; writing, revising and discussing papers; providing an engaging oral analysis; and collaborating with others
- Attend to whether students can craft polished, thorough, and justifiable answers, performances, or products
- Emphasize and standardize the criteria for scoring such varied products
- Involve challenges and roles that help students rehearse for the complex ambiguities of life

Authentic assessments often take the form of performance-based assessments. *Performance assessments* were defined by the U.S. Congress, Office of Technology Assessment (1992) as testing methods that require students to create an answer or product that demonstrates their knowledge and skills. Performance assessments share three common features: 1) students construct rather than select a response, 2) students are observed completing tasks that resemble those in the real world, and 3) students reveal their learning and thinking processes along with their answers (U.S. Congress, Office of Technology Assessment, 1992). Elliott (1994) suggested that two terms are key to performance assessment. First, it is a *performance*. The student actively generates a response that is directly or indirectly observable through a product. Second, it is *authentic*. The nature of the task and context in which the assessment occurs is relevant and represents real world problems or issues. A key feature of performance assessments is that students are active participants (Rudner, 1991). Rather than choosing from presented options, as in traditional multiple-choice tests, students are responsible for creating or constructing their responses.

Performance assessment has several advantages. Students are assessed in real and complex situations, considering both process and product (Maker, 1993). In addition, the gap between testing and instruction is reduced (Frechtling, 1991). There is a concern, however, that performance-based assessment relies on the teacher's observations or judgments, increasing subjectivity over other measurement strategies (Frechtling, 1991). In performance assessment, judgments are made about student knowledge and skills based on observation of student behavior or examination of student products (Lam, 1995). Although the instructional advantages of performance assessment when teachers focus on higher-order thinking skills are obvious, there is no evidence that assessment bias vanishes with performance assessment (Linn, Baker, & Dunbar, 1991). Performance assessment may generate its own potential sources of bias, including students' ability to use higher-order thinking skills; metacognitive skills; cultural problem-solving patterns; shyness; inadequate communication skills in presenting, discussing, arguing, or debating; inadequate or undue help; lack of resources inside and outside of school; incompatibility in language and culture between assessors and students; and subjectivity in rating (Lam, 1995).

In performance assessment, items directly reflect intended outcomes. They have the potential for measuring skills that traditionally have not been measured in large groups of students such as integrating knowledge across disciplines, contributing to the work of a group, and developing a plan of action when confronted with a novel situation (Rudner, 1991).

One aspect of a performance assessment is making an assessment of a curriculum event. In this way, the assessment is a series of theoretically and practically coherent learning activities structured in a way that they lead to a single predetermined end (Elliott, 1994). When planning a performance assessment as a curriculum event, teachers should consider

- The content of the instrument
- The length of activities required to complete the assessment
- The type of activities required to complete the assessment
- The number of items in the assessment instrument
- The scoring rubric

An example of a performance assessment that is in itself a curriculum event is provided by one of our teacher contributors (Margaret Jenkins). In her parenting class, the students participate in a simulation using a 5-pound bag of flour as a "baby." Each day's activities are described, providing a format for the simulation, including work to be completed in and out of class, and the evaluation of these activities. As they learn about parenting and child development, each student completes a baby book that includes a birth certificate that they generate, a description of their baby's daily schedule, and reflective journal entries. In addition, students are evaluated on their participation in the simulation. The materials used in this performance assessment are provided in Figures 9.2 and 9.3.

Performance assessments can take other forms as well. Ascher (1990), for example, described station activities as one way to employ performance assessment. In station activities, students proceed through a series of discrete tasks, either individually or in teams, in a given amount of time. Ascher gave the example of a science laboratory in which a variety of tasks, such as inferring the characteristics of objects sealed in boxes, measuring electrical currents, and sorting seeds are set in various places around the lab. Students may participate in individual or group projects, which serve as comprehensive demonstrations of skills or knowledge. Interviews or oral presentations allow students to verbalize their knowledge (Rudner, 1991).

More traditional formats also can serve as performance assessments. For example, Rudner (1991) required students to produce their own answers rather than select from an array of possible answers. Assessment questions can vary from filling in a blank or writing a short answer to drawing a graph or diagram or writing all the steps of a geometry proof. Essays have long been used by teachers so that students employ critical thinking, analysis, and synthesis. Experiments test how well a student understands scientific concepts and can carry out scientific processes.

Portfolios

A *portfolio* is a purposeful collection of student work that tells the story of achievement or growth (Arter, Spandel, & Culham, 1995). Portfolios benefit instruction by developing student skills in self-reflection, critical thinking, responsibility for learning, and content area skills and knowledge (Arter et al., 1995). They benefit assessment because collecting multiple samples of student work over time enables educators to 1) develop an in-depth look at what students know and can do, 2) base assessment on authentic work, 3) supplement standardized tests, and 4) communicate student progress (Arter et al., 1995). For example, portfolios are used in California as a certification of competence to demonstrate student mastery in science (California State Department of Education, 1994). They can track growth over time, presenting a chronological collection that shows how students have changed by contrasting early work to later work. Arter and associates (1995) cautioned, however, that the use of portfolios for assessment is not without controversy. They posed a series of questions that elucidate these issues:

- To what extent does the portfolio process, content, and performance criteria need to be standardized so that results are comparable?
- Is the use of portfolios feasible and affordable?
- Will teachers cooperate?
- Will the conclusions drawn from portfolios be valid?

Flour babies
Parenting simulations

Parenting a "newborn" often looks easy and fun. This action project is designed to help you experience not only what it is like to tote around an infant, but also what it takes to care for someone else 24 hours a day.

1. The simulation will last 3 weeks, 24 hours a day.
2. Treat your baby as a real baby; you wouldn't stuff a baby in a locker, drop it on the floor, or leave it in the car.
3. You are the parent and are responsible for the constant care of your baby. Bring your baby to school every day and to each parenting class. You may arrange for a baby sitter if you work. Agree on a fee with your baby sitter. On that day, the baby sitter must sign your journal entry in the baby book stating the number of hours he or she took care of the baby.

    If it is inappropriate for your baby to go with you during an activity, then arrange for a baby sitter. The infant's time away from you in the care of a baby sitter is not to exceed _____ hours a day. Again, the baby sitter must sign the daily journal entry in the baby book.
4. Your baby should receive the care it needs to develop appropriately.
5. Your baby needs to be clothed appropriately.
6. Your baby has the right to be cared for in a nurturing, loving environment.
7. Your baby should show evidence of thriving. Its daily schedule needs to reflect this.

Assessment components:

Baby book: Includes birth certificate, daily schedule, and 22 reflective journal entries

Parenting skills: A daily schedule was followed, care was shown in class, the baby developed an appropriate personality, the baby had appropriate clothing, there were supportive behavior reports and constraining behavior reports (i.e., negative points), and there was evidence of thriving.

Figure 9.2. "Flour baby" assessment form.

Name: _____

Baby Book: Points earned

_____   1. Birth certificate
_____   2. Describe how you feel about the birth of your baby.
_____   3. Explain how you will build a strong family for your
          baby to grow. Include all six secrets of a strong family.
_____   4. Read the article titled, *Love at First Sight,* then
          make an appropriate daily schedule for your newborn
          child (24 hours).
_____   5. Due to the demands of your baby's daily schedule,
          explain how you will manage your personal schedule
          as well as appropriately care for your baby.
_____   6. Describe how your 5-day-old baby behaves.
_____   7. Describe how you cared for your baby today.
_____   8. Interview your parents and ask them to tell you about
          yourself as a baby.
_____   9. Describe how being a parent affected your behavior
          over the weekend.
_____   10. Describe how you properly bathe a newborn baby.
_____   11. Why is parenting education important to you, your
          family, and society?
_____   12. Describe how you fulfill the roles of manager, problem
          solver, nurturer, and leader with your flour baby.
_____   13. How can parents manage the numerous tasks
          associated with meeting the needs of their children
          and their own needs?
_____   14. Which parenting role is easiest to fulfill and which
          parenting role is most difficult to fulfill? Explain your
          answer.
_____   15. Shadow a parent for a day and make an activity record
          showing what the parent does.
_____   16. Describe how you and your baby spent this past
          Sunday.

Family Unit: Points earned

_____   17. What part do family celebrations play in building
          strong families? What family celebrations do you plan
          to celebrate with your future children?
_____   18. Your baby is leaving you today. Write a story explain-
          ing what happened to the baby.

Figure 9.3. "Baby book" evaluation form.

Evaluation of Parenting Skills: Points earned

_____ Care in class

_____ Appropriate clothing

_____ Constraining behavior
       reports

_____ Baby's personality
       developed

_____ Supportive behavior
       reports

_____ Baby gained weight

Follow-Up Reflection

Write about a situation you experience.

List six characteristics of caring behavior.

Define caring and respectful behavior.

Compare your feelings when the baby was born to your feelings at the end of the project.

Explain why your feelings changed over time.

Do you think real parents experience similar feelings?

Describe the behavior you exhibited that supports child development.

Describe the behavior you exhibited that constrains child development.

What did you learn about yourself from this project?

Total points_____

Positive comments:

The faculty of the English department at Purcell Marian High School have dedicated program meetings to an ongoing seminar regarding the use of portfolios. They have been engaged in asking questions that may assist other teachers in the implementation of portfolios. Jason Haap, the teacher facilitating the discussion of portfolio issues, listed these primary issues that have emerged through their discussions:

- Why are we implementing portfolios?
- What should be contained in portfolios?
- What are the habits we want our students to have and how can that be presented through a portfolio?

When the faculty looked at these questions, other issues emerged for the department. Discussions developed about defining quality work and the writing and thinking habits students should develop. Questions evolved about the types of writing that students should produce and the reasons for selecting the writing.

These issues also have been reported in the literature. Salend (1998) offered guidelines for the effective use of portfolio assessment in the classroom. First, the teacher should identify the goals of the portfolio. For students with disabilities this could include the annual goals of the individualized education programs (IEPs) and for general education students this could include curriculum benchmarks. Next, the teacher determines the type of portfolio to be used. Swicegood (1994) identified several kinds of portfolios:

- Showcase portfolios present the student's best work and may be used to gain admission to a specialized program or school.
- Reflective portfolios help individuals think about various dimensions of student learning.
- Cumulative portfolios contain items collected for an extended period of time to verify changes in the student's work.
- Goal-based portfolios include pre-established objectives, and teachers and students choose items to match those objectives.

Next, Salend (1998) suggested that teachers establish procedures for organizing the portfolio. Items need to be organized using file folders, accordion files, binders, or boxes. After the items are organized, the authentic classroom products that relate to the objectives of the portfolio should be chosen. The significance of items should be recorded (e.g., using caption statements). Students may write letters for their portfolios, use caption-statement prompts, or use questioning prompts. The teacher should periodically review and evaluate portfolios. Salend suggested that teachers ask

- What does this portfolio reveal about the student's academic behavior and socioemotional performance and skills?

- What information does the portfolio provide with respect to the student's IEP?
- What are the student's strengths and instructional needs?
- What does the portfolio indicate with respect to the student's learning styles, attitudes, motivation, interests, cultural backgrounds, and use of learning strategies?
- Do the items in the portfolio relate to each other? What patterns are revealed?
- How can the information presented in the portfolio assist in planning the student's educational program (Swicegood, 1994)?

Teachers indicate that when scoring student work, the process opens new windows of understanding for them, which elucidate new ideas for classroom activities, potential gaps in their classroom curriculum, and, perhaps most important, insights about their students' strengths and weaknesses (Herman, 1998).

Bowers (1989) suggested that the trade-off in the shift to performance assessment is the shift to sacrificing reliability for validity. Performance-based tests do not lend themselves to a cost- and time-efficient method of scoring that provides reliable results. They actually test what is being taught and the skills prerequisite for performing in the real world.

WHAT ACCOMMODATIONS
AND MODIFICATIONS ARE USEFUL IN TESTING SITUATIONS?

CRESST (National Center for Research on Evaluation, Standards, and Student Testing, 1999) defined *accommodations* and *adaptations* as modifications in the way assessments are designed or administered so that students with disabilities and students with limited English proficiency can be included in the assessment. The Center for Innovations in Special Education (1998) stated that the purpose of an accommodation is to help each student show what he or she knows and can do and to remove the impact of the disability. The intent is to provide equal footing. Accommodations do not change what the test is evaluating. Typical accommodations include modifications in

- Time or schedule of the assessment
- Test directions
- Presentation of questions
- Student response to questions
- Test setting

The Assessment Accommodation Checklist (Elliott, Kratochwill, & Gilbertson, 1998) was developed with input from general and special educators. This instrument was designed to help maintain consistent documentation and implementation of testing accommodations for students with disabilities. The Assessment Accommodations Checklist contains 74 accommodations in these domains: 1) motivation, 2) assistance prior to administration of the test, 3) scheduling, and 4) setting, assessment directions, assistance during assessment, use of equipment or adaptive technology, and changes in format (see Table 9.3).

Our teacher contributors described several accommodations related to testing. All of the teachers mentioned extra time, change in setting, the use of a reader, and the use of a scribe. In addition, they described several format considerations. In mathematics, after teachers provided some of the students with their tests written on graph paper to help them align their figures, the students asked if all tests could be written on graph paper. Thus, an accommodation for students with special needs became a way of helping all students succeed.

In other subjects, formats originally provided for students with disabilities also became part of standard test format. For example, teachers put sections of tests in boxes, to delineate parts of the test. Typically, no more than five questions were in each of the boxes, and if matching was involved the words were provided in the box. Students were not required to use separate answer sheets. Abbreviated tests also were used, with additional modifications in language and complexity. A comparison of items is presented in Table 9.4.

Sister Kristin Matthes utilizes tests as an additional way to force students to reflect on and organize the material from the class. She will issue a blank note card and students may write down any and all of the information they choose on the card. Students must organize the material, determine what is most important, and reflect on ways to map the material. In addition, she will tell students that they only need to respond to a certain number of questions. For example, she may tell the students, "Answer 10 of these 20 questions." The students reflect on each of the questions, weigh their knowledge regarding that question, and choose whether to respond.

Table 9.3.   Accommodations in the eight areas of the assessment accommodations checklist

Area	Accommodation
Motivating	Working toward a reward for continued effort throughout the assessment
Assisting prior to administering test	Teaching test-taking skills
Scheduling	Additional time; breaking the sessions into several shorter sessions
Setting	Distraction-free space; individual administration
Directing	Paraphrase directions; reread directions
Providing assistance during assessment	Record responses for the student
Using aids	Electronic reader
Changing test form and content	Braille or large print; audiotaped questions

Table 9.4.   Examples of comparison of test forms

General test essay questions

Identify the author of *Siddhartha*. List two pieces of information about his personal background and how each is connected to something in the book.

Give two examples of how the river enters the story. Explain what it symbolizes in each example.

Give two examples of when the songbird enters the story. Explain what it symbolizes in each example.

Siddhartha is about the search for self. List and explain two insights that the book may have for a person today who is trying to understand their self more deeply.

Explain how Siddhartha's ability to love grows throughout the book. How do you know Siddhartha has finally learned to love?

Alternative test form essay questions

Identify the author of *Siddhartha*. List two pieces of information about his personal background and how each of these is connected to something in the book.

Give an example of how the river enters the story. Explain what it symbolizes in your example.

Siddhartha is about the search for self. List and explain one insight that the book may have for a person today who is trying to understand their self more deeply.

WHAT ARE ISSUES RELATED TO GRADING IN INCLUSIVE ENVIRONMENTS?

Grading students with disabilities changed rapidly in the latter part of the 1990s. Valdes, Williamson, and Wagner (1990) reported that 64.2% of secondary students with disabilities in general education were graded on the same standards as their peers without disabilities. More recent findings show that things have changed for students with disabilities in general education settings.

Bursuck, Bolloway, Plante, and Epstein (1996) completed a national survey of elementary and secondary general education teachers to determine the classroom grading practices of general education teachers, including grading adaptations for students with disabilities. They found that many teachers are willing to modify their grading criteria for students with disabilities. About 50% responded that they use the same adaptations for students without disabilities. On the whole, teachers were more receptive to passing students who made an effort. Because teachers use homework, tests, and quizzes for most of the students' grades, 1) students need strategies for taking tests and organizing their assignments, 2) homework and tests should be adapted, and 3) general education teachers need to be trained to develop valid classroom tests.

Teachers wanted grading adaptations to be considered for all students, regardless of whether they had a diagnosed disability.

Grades are not meaningful unless the criteria behind them are explicit (Bradley & Calvin, 1998). Grading modified assignments provides a significant challenge to teachers. Bradley and Calvin (1998) suggested that any grading system should provide frequent assessment; incorporate product, progress, and process evaluation; accurately report achievement to the parent and student; and provide useful feedback to help the student improve. Bradley and Calvin provided a critique of various grading practices:

- Letter and number grades, which are the most common grading practices, can be used frequently and can analyze product, progress, and process. However, letter and number grades cannot convey feedback to the student or provide insight to parents about how much the student has learned.
- Progress checklists containing criterion-related goals provide clear feedback to students and parents, and can analyze product, progress, and process. However, checklists may be time-consuming and tedious to administer and may not provide frequent assessment.
- Contracts, which establish predetermined learning goals, also assess product, progress and product. However, they do not provide feedback when the student is unsuccessful in meeting goals.
- Work samples can display progress and product but may not be effective in showing precise growth.
- Curriculum-based assessments may not depict process because many curriculum-based assessments are designed to test skills rather than concepts.
- Mastery level assessment divides the content into subcomponents with pretests and posttests.

However, many content areas go beyond learning that can be demonstrated on pretests and posttests.

- Multiple grading is used to provide feedback on various aspects of the learning criteria, with separate grades for effort, product, progress, and process.
- Portfolios provide rationales, goals, contents, standards, and judgments of the contents. In addition, they are self-reflective in nature, providing feedback to the student and parent in product, process, and products
- Rubrics provide criteria for individual standards. They delineate the exact criteria before the project is undertaken.

Bradley and Calvin (1998) made the following suggestions to "level the playing field" in evaluating the modified assignments of students with disabilities:

- Use points and percentages to grade differentiated assignments, rather than letter grades.

- Avoid using a traditional grading scale with most students and changing the grading scale for other students. Rather, set expectations and make adjustments before grades are given.
- Avoid posting grades and scores.
- Attend to the student's IEP goals and objectives.
- Provide students with opportunities to grade themselves and one another, especially in group activities.
- Use rubrics and share them with students and parents when introducing assignments.
- Use a variety of grading approaches to obtain grades.
- Avoiding grading students strictly on effort or learning behaviors.

Our contributing teachers, by virtue of the school system's report card, are locked into reporting percentage grades for each of their students. They have, however, employed modifications to account for students with disabilities. For example, the mathematics teacher awards points for making an effort on assignments and accuracy. She utilizes daily quizzes on the material from the previous day, administering them immediately after reviewing the material. The use of frequent assessment allows the students to gain more points as well as providing the teacher with information as to whether the students are understanding the material.

The use of rubrics also is pervasive among our contributing teachers. Yet, they talked about the adaptation of these rubrics—requiring greater depth and length for students who are able to produce and reducing those expectations for other students. The use of rubrics is so frequent that one of the teachers devised a blank, write-in rubric form that she would complete as she and the students collaboratively developed criteria. She duplicates it and uses it as a means for evaluation (see Figure 9.4).

WHAT ARE ISSUES RELATED TO STATE- OR DISTRICTWIDE PROFICIENCY TESTING AND STUDENTS WITH DISABILITIES?

Accountability is a system of informing those inside and outside of the educational arena about the direction in which schools are moving (Westat, Inc., 1994). One of the ways that school districts and states feel they can address the issue of accountability is through statewide or districtwide proficiency tests.

The Individuals with Disabilities Education Act (IDEA) Amendments of 1997 (PL 105-17) require that students with disabilities are included in general state- and districtwide assessment, with appropriate accommodations. States and school districts must develop guidelines for the participation of students with disabilities in alternative assessments when they cannot participate in state- and districtwide assessment programs. Special education students have three alternatives for participation in state- or districtwide testing programs:

Work and Family Assessment

Title of work:_____

Creator(s) of work:_____

Criteria/standard	Well done	Acceptable	Needs improvement	Not acceptable
1.				
2.				
3.				
4.				
5.				
6.				

Total:_____

Assessor(s)	Comments stated positively
1.	
2.	
3.	
4.	

Adolescents and Inclusion: Transforming Secondary Schools © 2001 Paul H. Brookes Publishing Co., Inc.

Figure 9.4.   Sample rubric form to be used as a means of evaluation.

- Standard testing administration offered to all other students
- The use of approved accommodations
- The use of alternative assessment designed to measure the progress of students who cannot meaningfully participate in the standard assessment program (Erickson, Ysseldyke, Thurlow, & Elliott, 1998)

The state needs to report the number of students participating in alternative assessments, and gather and analyze these data. Ysseldyke and Olsen (1999) suggested that a set of assumptions about alternative assessments for students with disabilities are emerging:

- Alternative assessments can be used in place of typical procedures when students cannot participate even with accommodations. Clear guidelines and criteria for making decisions about who participates in alternative assessments, then, must be developed.
- Alternative assessment should be relevant to the curriculum, and the focus of the curriculum for students who participate in an alternative assessment differs from the typical curriculum.
- Performance on alternative assessments can serve as a substitute for information obtained through typical methods.

In a focus group of teachers, Ysseldyke and Olsen (1999) reported that several important considerations for alternative assessments emerged. First, the focus should be on authentic skills and on assessment experiences in community and real-life environments. Second, school personnel should measure integrated skills across domains. Third, in order to be accurate, assessment methods should involve multiple measures over time. Fourth, the extent to which the school system provides the needed assistive devices, people, and other supports should be studied. Finally, the purpose of alternative assessments should be to improve results for students. The extent to which alternative assessments provide information that leads to instructional and policy decisions to improve decisions should be evaluated and used to inform decisions regarding testing programs.

The IEP represents an educational accountability system that outlines learner expectations, assessment strategies, and performance standards established through consensus among various stakeholders. It focuses on individual students, however, whereas system accountability focuses on districtwide or statewide student populations (Erickson et al., 1998). In its 1994 survey of state assessment practices for students with disabilities, the National Center on Educational Outcomes found that state special education directors could estimate participation rates for students with disabilities for only 49 of the 133 statewide tests being used during that year (Erickson, Thurlow, & Thor, 1995).

Ysseldyke, Thurlow, McGrew, and Shriner (1994) suggested that large numbers of excluded students could possibly participate in state and national assessments, especially if provided with accommodations. However, a small group of students exists (usually students with severe cognitive deficits or multiple disabilities) for whom standard large-scale testing practices and accommodations remain inappropriate. IDEA '97 includes a requirement that states have aggregate data on the educational progress and accomplishments of students who are typically included (Ysseldyke & Olsen, 1999).

Most states recognize the importance of the IEP and the IEP team in making decisions about individual student accommodations. However, Elliott, Thurlow, Ysseldyke, and Erickson (1997) reported that little space if any is provided on the IEP for making accommodation plans, and IEPs rarely provide a list of possible accommodations. Twenty-four of the states reported that accommodations during assessment are linked to those used during instruction. Although most states will not allow accommodations unless the student's IEP lists them, only four states require written documentation about assessment accommodations beyond the IEP.

Elliott and associates (1997) grouped common assessment accommodations into four areas—timing, setting, presentation, and response. In the area of timing, accommodations may include extending time for test completion, changing the time of day during which the test is administered, administering the test in several sessions over the course of one or several days, and allowing frequent breaks. Setting accommodations include administering the assessment in a small group, in an individual study carrel, in a hospital, in isolation, or in a home. Presentation of the test may include using an audiocassette, reading the test aloud, providing a large print version, repeating directions, interpreting with sign language, providing braille versions of the test, or using magnification devices. Responses may include dictating to a scribe, interpreting with sign language, using braille writers, recording answers, using a word processor, or transferring answers from the booklet to the answer sheet.

SUMMARY POINTS

- The purpose of assessment is to help teachers gather information to facilitate decision making.
- Fair assessment allows every student to demonstrate what he or she can do.
- Assessment is part of the learning process and is itself a learning experience.
- Student learning can be assessed in a variety of ways. Authentic assessment, one option, is direct examination of student performance on real world tasks.
- Accommodations and modifications are designed so that students with disabilities can be included in general assessments.
- In state- and districtwide assessment, students with disabilities 1) may participate in the standard testing administration offered to all other students, 2) use approved accommodations, or 3) use alternative assessments to measure their progress.

REFERENCES

Arter, J.A., Spandel, V., & Culham, R. (1995). *Portfolios for assessment and instruction.* Portland, OR: Northwest Regional Educational Laboratory. (ERIC Document Reproduction Service No. ED 388890)

Ascher, C. (1990). *Can performance-based assessments improve urban schooling?* New York: ERIC Clearinghouse on Urban Education. (ERIC Document Reproduction Service No. ED 327612)

Barnett, D.W., Lentz, F.E., Bauer, A.M., Macmann, G., Stollar, S., & Ehrhardt, K. (1997). Ecological foundations of early intervention: Planned activities and strategic sampling. *Journal of Special Education, 30*(4), 471–490.

Bowers, B.C. (1989). *Alternatives to standardized educational assessment.* Eugene, OR: ERIC Clearinghouse on Educational Management. (ERIC Document Reproduction Service No. ED 312773)

Bradley, D.F., & Calvin, M.B. (1998). Grading modified assignments: Equity or compromise? *Teaching Exceptional Children, 31*(2), 24–29.

Bursuck, W., Bolloway, E., Plante, L., & Epstein, M. (1996). Report card grading and adaptations: A national survey of classroom practices. *Exceptional Children, 62,*(4), 301–318.

California State Department of Education. (1994). *Science framework.* Sacramento, CA: Author.

Center for Innovations in Special Education (CISE). (1998). *Questions and answers about testing accommodations for students with disabilities: A guide for parents and educators.* Columbia: University of Missouri–Columbia, Center for Innovations in Special Education.

Cullen, B., & Pratt, T. (1992). Measuring and reporting student progress. In S. Stainback & W. Stainback (Eds.), *Curriculum considerations in inclusive classrooms: Facilitating learning for all students* (pp. 175–196). Baltimore: Paul H. Brookes Publishing Co.

Elliott, J., Thurlow, M.E., Ysseldyke, J.E., & Erickson, R. (1997). *Providing assessment accommodations for students with disabilities in state and district assessments.* Minneapolis: University of Minnesota, National Center on Educational Outcomes. (ERIC No. ED 416628)

Elliott, S.N. (1994). *Creating meaningful performance assessments: Fundamental concepts.* Reston, VA: Council for Exceptional Children.

Elliott, S.N., Kratochwill, T.R., & Gilbertson, A.G. (1998). The Assessment Accommodation Checklist: Who, what, where, when, why, and how? *Teaching Exceptional Children, 31*(2), 10–14.

Erickson, R., Thurlow, M.L., & Thor, K. (1995). *State special education outcomes: A report on how states are assessing educational outcomes for students with disabilities, 1994.* Minneapolis: University of Minnesota, National Center on Educational Outcomes. (ERIC Document Reproduction Service No. ED 385061)

Erickson, R., Ysseldyke, J., Thurlow, M., & Elliott, J. (1998). Inclusive assessments and accountability systems: Tools of the trade in educational reform. *Teaching Exceptional Children, 31*(2), 4–9.

Frechtling, J.A. (1991). Performance assessment: Moonstruck or the real thing? *Educational Measurement: Issues and Practices, 10*(4), 23–25.

Herman, J.L. (1998). The state of performance assessments. *School Administrator, 11*(55), 17–18.

Herman, J.L., Aschbacher, P.R., & Winters, L. (1992). *A practical guide to alternative assessment.* Alexandria, VA: Association for Supervision and Curriculum Development.

Individuals with Disabilities Education Act (IDEA) Amendments of 1997, PL 105-17, 20 U.S.C. §§ 1400 *et seq.*

Lam, T.C.M. (1995). *Fairness in performance assessment.* College Park, MD: ERIC Clearinghouse on Assessment and Evaluation. (ERIC Document Reproduction Service No. ED 391982)

Linn, R.E., Baker, E.L., & Dunbar, S.B. (1991). Complex, performance-based assessment: Expectations and validation criteria. *Educational Assessment, 20*(8), 15–21.

Maker, C.J. (1993). Creativity, intelligence, and problem solving: A definition and design for cross-cultural research and measurement related to giftedness. *Gifted Education International, 9*(2), 68–77.

Meisels, S.J. (1993). Remaking classroom assessment with the work sampling system. *Young Children, 48*(5), 34–40.

National Center for Research on Evaluation, Standards, and Student Testing (CRESST). (1996). *CRESST assessment glossary.* Available http://www.cse.ucla.edu/CRESST/pages/glossary.htm.

Nickell, P. (1993). *Alternative assessment: Implication for social studies.* College Park, MD: ERIC Clearinghouse on Assessment and Evaluation. (ERIC Document Reproduction Service No. ED 360219)

Rudner, L.M. (1991). *Assessing civics education.* College Park, MD: ERIC Clearinghouse on Assessment and Evaluation. (ERIC No. ED 338698)

Salend, S.J. (1998). Using portfolios to assess student performance. *Teaching Exceptional Children, 31*(2), 36–43.

Salvia, J., & Ysseldyke, J.E. (1998). *Assessment* (7th ed.). Boston: Houghton Mifflin.

Stainback, W., Stainback, S., & Stefanich, G. (1996). Learning together in inclusive classrooms: What about the curriculum? *Teaching Exceptional Children, 28*(3), 14–19.

Swicegood, P. (1994). Portfolio-based assessment practices. *Intervention in School and Clinic, 30*(1), 6–15.

U.S. Congress, Office of Technology Assessment. (1992, February). *Testing in American schools: Asking the right questions.* Washington, DC: U.S. Government Printing Office. (ERIC No. ED 340770)

Valdes, K.A., Williamson, C.L., & Wagner, M.M. (1990). *The national longitudinal transition study of special education students.* Menlo Park, CA: SRI International. (ERIC Document Reproduction Service No. ED 324 893)

Westat, Inc. (1994). *The 1994 high school transcript study.* Rockville, MD: Author.

Wiggins, G.A. (1989). A true test: Toward more authentic and equitable assessment. *Phi Delta Kappan, 70*(9), 703–713.

Witt, J.C., Elliott, S.N., Kramer, J.J., & Gresham, F.M. (1998). *Assessment of at-risk and special needs children* (2nd ed.). New York: McGraw-Hill.

Ysseldyke, J.E., & Olsen, K. (1999). Putting alternative assessments into practice: What to measure and possible sources of data. *Exceptional Children, 65*(2), 175–185.

Ysseldyke, J.E., Thurlow, M.L., McGrew, K.S., & Shriner, J.G. (1994). *Recommendations for making decisions about the participation of students with disabilities in statewide assessment programs: A report on a working conference to develop guidelines for statewide assessments and students with disabilities.* Minneapolis: University of Minnesota, National Center for Education Outcomes. (ERIC Document Reproduction Service No. ED 375588)

10

Individualized Education Programs and Legal Issues

Anne M. Bauer

Teacher Contributor: Karen Matuszek

In the past, general education teachers have sometimes been befuddled by special education paperwork and acronyms. The Individuals with Disabilities Education Act (IDEA) Amendments of 1997 (PL 105-17) describe a larger role for general education teachers, increasing the need for everyone to understand individualized education programs (IEPs) and legal issues.

The IEP has been called "the heart and soul of the Individuals with Disabilities Education Act" (Bateman, 1995, p. 1) and the "cornerstone of special education" (Tomey, 1998, p. 3). Yet, the IEP process is sometimes described by teachers as useless, time consuming, threatening, and pointless (Bateman, 1995). The IEP, to be educationally useful and legally correct, must describe 1) what needs or characteristics of the student require individualized supports, 2) how each need will be addressed, and 3) how and when the efficacy of those services will be evaluated (Bateman, 1995).

IEPs are fairly inflexible in their format and prescribed content. Areas and items that must be included are described in the federal regulations. Even "interpretations" are described in the U.S. Code. This chapter, then, may appear fairly dry because most citations come directly from the regulations. However, we are dependent on these sources to provide you with accurate information.

After reading this chapter, you will be able to

* Describe the IEP and its use in the education of students with disabilities
* Describe the components of the IEP
* Identify the rights of parents
* Identify the rights of students
* Describe the general education teacher's role in the IEP
* Describe the general education teacher's role in the development and implementation of 504 plans

To help clarify the material on IEPs, two examples to which we refer throughout the chapter are provided: IEPs for Veronica, a student identified as having learning disabilities (Figure 10.1), and Lawrence, a student with moderate mental retardation (Figure 10.2). Both of these students are in inclusive secondary schools, yet their programs vary significantly.

WHAT IS AN IEP AND HOW CAN I USE IT?

The IEP was first described in the Education for All Handicapped Children Act of 1975 (PL 94-142). The IEP was developed to serve as a guideline, rather than a contract, for individualized instruction. The school is responsible for providing the services and activities listed in the student's IEP, but it is not responsible for ensuring progress. The IEP, then, is a written commitment for delivery of services to meet the student's needs. Tomey (1998) described the IEP document as

- *Comprehensive,* covering all areas that may need support, including communication, behavior, socialization, self-help, academics, fine and gross motor skills, vocational skills, transition services, related services, and accommodations for both general and vocational education
- *Specific,* including measurable and observable goals and objectives
- *Sequential,* grounded in a developmental or functional sequence of skills
- *Realistic and appropriate,* fitting the student's current level of functioning and probable growth rate
- *Understandable,* written in a language that is comprehensible to parents and professionals
- *Mutually developed,* representing a consensus among parents, the student, and the school

Before we begin to describe IEPs in detail, it may be helpful to describe the process through which a student has been identified as needing an IEP. This is not a one-step process in which the school or the parent, acting individually or together, simply decides that a student needs help. Rather, there is a series of steps that precede the writing of the initial IEP (see Table 10.1).

The process for formally supporting a student with special education services usually begins with a period called *pre-referral,* because teachers and parents engage in these activities before the student is actually referred for evaluation for a disability. The parents and the school have the ability, however, to request an evaluation without engaging in extensive prereferral activities if a disability is suspected. If there is documentation that a series of appropriate, individualized strategies and accommodations are not successfully supporting the student, he or she may be referred for a multifactored evaluation. Parents must consent for their child to participate in such an evaluation.

Table 10.1. Steps toward identifying a student who may need an individualized education program (IEP)

Activity	Parents' role	School district's role
Prereferral	May contact school with concern May provide helpful information May request assistance with intervention May initiate referral for multifactored evaluation, if parents suspect a disability	Contacts parents for information Attempts various strategies, documenting results Uses an intervention assistance team to generate additional supports Suggests new interventions and documents results Gathers materials for referral to request multifactored evaluation if disability is suspected
Referral	Receives a copy of parent's rights Receives replies to any questions Gives permission for evaluation	Provides written information in native language regarding referral process, parent's and student's rights, and due process procedures Asks parent for consent to evaluate
Evaluation	Provides information for evaluation process, including medical, family, and educational history; student's functioning outside of school; perceptions of student's-strengths and needs	Notifies parents of who will evaluate and what types of tests or procedures will be used Collects information from parents, teachers, and others Completes evaluation activities Summarizes and interprets evaluation results Determines, with parent, eligibility for special education services
Pre-IEP meeting	Reviews parents' rights information Identifies concerns and questions Identifies potential goals	Notifies parents of IEP meeting and participants Determines mutual time and place for the meeting
During IEP meeting	Asks any questions about evaluation Shares information regarding student's strengths and needs Collaborates to develop goals and objectives Collaborates to determine special education and related services Gives permission for child to receive special education and related services	Explains evaluation results and eligibility Develops IEP (if the student is eligible); if child is not eligible, determines appropriate accomodations, modifications, or interventions; considers eligibility for services under Section 504 of the Rehabilitation Act of 1973 (PL 93-112) Notifies parents of their right to an independent evaluation if there is a disagreement about evaluation results

Name: _Veronica Porter_   Date of Birth: _9-27-86_

Grade level: _9_   _X_ Female   ___Male

Student address: _355 Crane Avenue, Apt. 2C, Smithville, 45279_

Parent/Guardian: _Samantha and Vaughn Porter_

Parent address: _same_

Home telephone: _555-1876_   Work telephone: _555-1984_

Effective dates: _8/25/01 to 8/24/02_

Additional considerations:

- Testing and assessment programs, including proficiency tests: _Veronica will participate in state proficiency testing, with accommodations of extended time and a separate testing room; she will circle her responses on the test that will be transferred to a Scantron sheet by a scribe_
- Transition from early childhood (ages 3–5) to school-age programs: _Does not apply_
- Transition services statement, no later than age 14: _See attached_
- A plan to address behavior, if the IEP and MFE team have determined this to be a concern: _Does not apply_
- Physical education must be addressed for all children and incorporated into the IEP: _Regular P.E._
- Extended school year services: _Does not apply_
- Children/students with visual impairments: _Does not apply_
- Limited English proficiency: _Does not apply_
- Communication: _Does not apply_
- Assistive technology: _Veronica uses speech recognition software to complete written assignments; she uses a microcassette recorder to record all lectures and discussions_

The student has been informed of his or her rights that will transfer to the student when he or she reaches majority. (Yes)   No

Relevant information/suggestions (e.g., medical information, other information): _Veronica takes 20 mg of Ritalin 3 times per day: at lunch time during school hours_

Figure 10.1. IEP form for Veronica.

Name: _Veronica Porter_

Present levels of development/functioning/performance:

Veronica is a ninth-grade student with at least average cognitive abilities who struggles with retention of information and written expression. She is strong in verbal expression and is skillful in interpersonal communication and interaction. Her visual organization is weak and affects her writing, including math, copying from the board, and sustaining written assignments. She fatigues easily during written work and has tremors in her hands when concentrating.

Veronica is using her plan book infrequently. She continues to have difficulty with open-ended questions and expressive written language. Veronica uses a voice-activated word processing system to organize and study her work. This helps her particularly in math and social studies. Veronica loves to read. Veronica understands math concepts, but her challenges with written work carry over into written mathematics activities.

Annual goals: *Write goals and objectives in areas of need. (What will the student be able to do in 1 year?)*

1. Veronica will increase her coping strategies and utilize supports and accommodations to organize her work and complete essential classes and assignments.

Objectives: *What are the steps or stages to each goal?*

Objective	Procedure for evaluation	Criteria	Schedule for review	Person responsible	Review of progress
1a. Veronica will use her plan book independently.	Weekly teacher check	5 of 5 days completed	Quarterly	Ms. Henshaw	
1b. Veronica will follow the proper sequence when structuring written responses.	Observations, work samples	Passing grades on papers requiring written responses	Quarterly	Mr. Andrews Ms. Brinker Ms. Kerlew Mr. Krycheck Ms. Paul	
1c. Veronica will use dictation, scribe, or a word processor when needed with minimal prompts.	Observations, work samples	Passing grades	Quarterly	Mr. Andrews Ms. Brinker Ms. Kerlew Mr. Krycheck Ms. Paul	

Figure 10.1.   *(continued)*

Services:	What special education services, including related services, are needed in implementing each goal? Include a description of the amount of services, when they will begin, and the duration of services. Note where the services will be provided.

Services	Initiation	Duration	Where provided
Modified services Oral testing Scribe Gaining access to class notes Extended time Plan book Pass/fail on assignments requiring written expression Graph paper Numbered answer sheets	8/25/00	1 year	General education classes

Transition plan
Annual goals:

1. Veronica will begin to identify jobs for which she is interested in preparing.

Objectives:

1a. Veronica will complete the Occupational Performance Survey.
1b. Veronica will identify several jobs in which she is interested and shadow individuals doing those jobs.

Objective	Procedure for evaluation	Criteria	Schedule for review	Person responsible	Review of progress
1a. Veronica will complete the Occupational Performance Survey.	Completion documented; form reviewed with Veronica and parents	Completion documented	December 1	Ms. Henshaw	
1b. Veronica will identify several jobs in which she is interested and shadow individuals doing those jobs.	Summary report	At least five jobs shadowed	June 1	Ms. Henshaw	

IEP Summary

Name: _Veronica Porter_

Extent of participation in general education environment: _100%_

Meeting participants:

Parent(s): _Vaughn Porter & Samantha Porter_

General education teacher: _Jim Andrews_

Special education teacher: _Elaine Henshaw_

District representative: _Mitch Wingfield_

Others: _____

Chairperson of the IEP team: _Hank Macleod_

__X__   *I give my consent to initiate special education and related services specific in this IEP.*

_____   *I waive my right to notification of special education and related services by certified mail.*

_____   *I do not give consent for special education services at this time.*

Parent signature: _Vaughn Porter_   Date: _8/25/01_

__X__   *I have received a copy of the parent notice of procedural safeguards.*

Parent signature: _Vaughn Porter_   Date: _8/25/01_

Name: _Lawrence de la Luz_ Date of Birth: _9-21-85_
Grade level: _10_ Female _X_ Male
Student address: _2835 Virginia, Adamstown, 63108_
Parent/Guardian: _Fran de la Luz_
Parent address: _same_
Home telephone: _555-1222_ Work telephone: _none_
Effective dates: _8/25/01 to 8/24/02_

Additional considerations:
- Testing and assessment programs, including proficiency tests:
  Lawrence will not participate in proficiency tests; rather, a behavioral
  portfolio will be maintained for him
- Transition from early childhood (ages 3–5) to school-age programs:
  Does not apply
- Transition services statement, no later than age 14: _See attached_
- A plan to address behavior, if the IEP and MFE team have determined
  this to be a concern: _Does not apply_
- Physical education must be addressed for all children and incorporat-
  ed into the IEP: _Regular P.E._
- Extended school year services: _Does not apply_
- Children/students with visual impairments: _Does not apply_
- Limited English proficiency: _Does not apply_
- Communication: _Does not apply_
- Assistive technology: _Does not apply_

The student has been informed of his or her rights that will transfer to
the student when he or she reaches majority. (Yes)   No

Relevant information/suggestions (e.g., medical information, other
information): _Lawrence has a history of seizures; he has been seizure free_
for 3 years, however, and is no longer on medication

Figure 10.2. IEP form for Lawrence.

Figure 10.2. (continued)

Name: *Lawrence de la Luz*

Present levels of development/functioning/performance:

Lawrence is a tenth-grade student who has significant talents in interpersonal communication and drama. He has participated in several school productions, memorizing dialogue that was adapted for him. He can sign his first and last name and verbally provide personal information. Lawrence requires a model to write personal information other than his name. He has some functional reading but gains most information through listening. Although he enjoys being on stage, Lawrence often fails to initiate a request for help and will sit with his task or paper. His peer buddies have, at times, "overassisted" Lawrence, and he enjoys chatting with them as they complete his work.

Lawrence has begun some work experience and is assigned to monitor tables and sweep the floor during lunch. He requires two to three reminders to work rather than socialize during the 50 minutes. He would like to join the work group that rides the public bus to McDonald's, each day for work experience. He enjoys his consumer science course and is an active participant in discussions. When provided with a task to complete independently, however, Lawrence relies on his peers and supports.

Lawrence uses a microcassette recorder to record assignments but frequently forgets the recorder in his locker or at home. When asked, he says, "Mary will write it down for my mom." He makes similar comments when asked to complete an activity in group, saying, "Ms. Houlihan will help me."

Annual goals:

1. Lawrence will increase his ability to complete tasks independently using a variety of accommodations and supports.
2. Lawrence will increase his stamina for school- and work-related tasks.

Objectives: *What are the steps or stages to each goal?*

Objective	Procedure for evaluation	Criteria	Schedule for review	Person responsible	Review of progress
1a. Lawrence will use his recorder daily for notes and assignments.	Weekly teacher check	5 of 5 days completed	Quarterly	Ms. Henshaw	
1b. Lawrence will initiate a request for help when he is unable to proceed with a task.	Observations, work samples	Passing grades on papers requiring written responses	Quarterly	Mr. Andrews Ms. Brinker Ms. Kerlew Mr. Krycheck Ms. Paul	

Objective	Procedure for evaluation	Criteria	Schedule for review	Person responsible	Review of progress
1c. Lawrence will attempt to complete tasks independently during consumer science.	Observations, work samples	Passing grades	Quarterly	Mr. Andrews	
2a. Lawrence will complete his job detail during a 30-minute lunch period with no more than one reminder to complete tasks.	Observations, number of times Lawrence is told to get back to work will be documented daily	No more than one reminder each period	Weekly	Ms. Jackson	

Services: What special education services, including related services, are needed in implementing each goal? Include a description of the amout of services, when they will begin, and the duration of services. Note where the services will be provided.

Services	Initiation	Duration	Where provided
Peer buddy assigned during consumer science, drama, and history classes Scribe to assist in recording responses Adapted assignments and readings Microcassette recorder	8/25/01	1 year	General education classes

Figure 10.2. *(continued)*

IEP Summary

Name: _Lawrence de la Luz_

Extent of participation in general education environment: _100%_

Meeting participants:

Parent(s): _Fran de la Luz_

General education teacher: _Jim Andrews_

Special education teacher: _Elaine Henshaw_

District representative: _Mitch Wingfield_

Others: _Katherine Jackson, work-study coordinator_

Chairperson of the IEP team: _Hank Macleod_

_X_ *I give my consent to initiate special education and related services specific in this IEP.*

_____ *I waive my right to notification of special education and related services by certified mail.*

_____ *I do not give consent for special education services at this time.*

Parent signature: _Fran de la Luz_   Date: _8/25/01_

_X_ *I have received a copy of the parent notice of procedural safeguards.*

Parent signature: _Fran de la Luz_   Date: _8/25/01_

Transition Plan

Annual goals:

> Lawrence will participate in activities preparing him to assume part-time employment next year.

Objectives:

1a. Lawrence will be evaluated by the Bureau of Vocational Rehabilitation (BVR).

1b. Lawrence will participate in identifying five jobs and will shadow individuals doing these jobs.

1c. Lawrence will participate in a variety of work-study jobs on the school campus.

Objective	Procedure for evaluation	Criteria	Schedule for review	Person responsible	Review of progress
1a. Lawrence will be evaluated by BVR.	Completion documented; form reviewed with Lawrence and parents	Completion documented	December 1	Ms. Henshaw	
1b. Lawrence will participate in identifying five jobs and will shadow individuals doing these jobs.	Summary report	At least five jobs shadowed	June 1	Ms. Jackson	
1c. Lawrence will participate in a variety of work-study jobs on the school campus.	Work study checklist	Satisfactory performance	Monthly	Ms. Jackson	

A fair evaluation must look at the whole child and include various environments in which the student interacts. This evaluation is called *multifactored* because it may include observations by professionals who have worked with the student; medical history that is relevant to school performance; and information and observations from the family about the student's experiences, abilities, needs, and behaviors outside of the school. The multifactored evaluation must 1) use several means of measurement, 2) be in the student's native language, and 3) be culturally appropriate (National Information Center for Children and Youth with Disabilities, 1996).

Parents are full participants in the evaluation team. They are part of the process of making the decision as to whether the student is eligible. *Eligible* means that the student's profile matches the characteristics of the disabilities defined by the state's rules and regulations for receiving special education services for a particular disability. Members of the evaluation team, including the parents, review the information that was gathered and compare the student's profile with the definition of various disabilities provided in the state guidelines for eligibility for special education services. If the student's profile meets the criteria, the team may either proceed with developing an IEP or determine a time and place for an IEP meeting. If the student's profile does not meet the criteria for one of the disabilities and he or she is not eligible for services, the team may determine appropriate modifications, accommodations, or interventions that may be conducted in the classroom without special education services. In our two examples, Veronica has met the eligibility criteria for learning disabilities and Lawrence has met the eligibility criteria for mental retardation. In addition, the team may consider whether the student is eligible for services under Section 504 of the Rehabilitation Act of 1973 (PL 93-112). Finally, the team notifies parents of their right to an independent evaluation if they disagree with the evaluation results.

IEPs are developed by a team for each student. The regulations for IDEA '97 indicate that the team must include the parents of the student and at least one general education teacher if the student is or may be participating in the general education classroom. In addition, the team must include at least one of the student's special education teachers and a representative of the school district who is qualified to provide or supervise special education and who is knowledgeable about general education curriculum and resources. In addition, an individual who can interpret the evaluation results should be present. Other individuals who have knowledge or special expertise regarding the student also may be present. If the purpose of the meeting is to consider transition services, the student should be invited. If the student doesn't attend, the school must take additional steps to ensure that the student's preferences and interests are considered. Because our example students are older than 14 years of age, their IEPs include statements about transition.

Parent participation in IEP development is emphasized throughout the IDEA '97 regulations. School districts must ensure that one or both of the student's parents are present at each IEP meeting, or have the opportunity to participate. To do so, districts must notify the parents early and meet at a mutual time and place. Parents must be provided with a written notice indicating the purpose, time, and location of the meeting and who will be in attendance, as well as their right to bring other individuals who have knowledge or special expertise about the student. When the student is 14 years old, the written notice includes statements about transition services that will be developed and a statement that the student is invited to the meeting. When the student is 16 years old, the written notice must include an indication that transition services will be considered, the student will be invited, and other agency personnel may attend. If parents cannot attend, the school district must ensure participation through individual and conference telephone calls. If the parents do not attend, the school district must document efforts that it tried to arrange a mutual time and place for the meeting, including records of telephone calls or attempts, copies of correspondence sent and responses received, and records of home visits. Interpreters are required for deaf parents or parents whose native language is not English. Parents must be given a copy of the IEP (Assistance to the States for the Education of Children with Disabilities, 1999). On our sample IEPs, parents have signed their consent on the IEP summary page.

The focus of the IEP meeting is to design a plan to meet the needs of the student. Bateman (1995) suggested beginning the development process with large pieces of newsprint. Using the newsprint to document the team's discussion, she suggested a three-step process of 1) listing the student's unique characteristics or needs that require individualization and entitle the student to special education services, 2) identifying district-provided services and modifications appropriate to address each need, and 3) writing goals and objectives that will be accomplished by the student if the services and modifications are appropriate and effective.

The student's unique characteristics and needs are described to decide the way in which special services or supports can be directed. This description of performance becomes the present level of performance on the IEP. The present level of performance "paints a picture" of the student, communicating the areas of need in a way that is easy to understand and precise enough to measure progress. Tomey (1998) suggested that the present level of performance should include strengths, needs, and data acquired from administering diagnostic procedures such as formal and informal testing, observations, anecdotal records, and interviews. The characteristics or needs may cluster. For example, Luisa may be described as 1) having difficulty copying notes from the board or the overhead projector, 2) working slowly, often restarting her paper when it appears "messy," and 3) transcribing numbers when copying mathematics problems from the book or the board. From these characteristics, the following statement for the present level of functioning emerges: Luisa has difficulty accurately copying from the board or the textbook, making three to five errors during each task. Review the present level of functioning of the two sample IEPs.

From this present level of functioning, the IEP team asks, "How will the school respond to each of these needs?" Bateman (1995) suggested that listing special education services, related services, or modifications that the district will provide could be described as "district do's." After the services have been delineated, annual goals and behavioral objectives for each need and service cluster are written. Although it seems obvious, there must be a direct correlation between the annual goals and the present level of educational performance. The annual goals answer the question, "What do we want this student to be able to do in 1 year?" (Tomey, 1998). If the learning rate is underestimated and the student achieves the annual goal(s) earlier, then new goal(s) can be added. The annual goals should be

- Stated in terms of measurable, observable behaviors, and answer the questions, "Who?" "What?" "Where?" "When?" and "How?"
- Responsive to the areas identified in the present level of educational performance
- Based on the student's present level of functioning
- Realistic to the student
- Prioritized on the basis of the student's age, amount of time left in school, and skills needed to live independently (Tomey, 1998)

Not all IEPs have the same number of annual goals, as noted on our sample IEPs. The short-term objectives or benchmarks are steps toward the completion of the annual goal. These objectives are not lesson plans but do serve as intermediate steps to the goal. Short-term objectives are based on annual goals and a sequence of skills. Similar to annual goals, short-term objectives are stated in observable, behavioral, and measurable terms and answer the questions, "Who?" "What?" "Where?" "When?" and "How?" In addition, the evaluation criterion for each objective, written in percentage of accuracy required or number of times a certain performance is required or amount of time is described. Our sample IEPs show how progress toward the objectives will be measured.

Any accommodations and inclusive supplementary aids and services needed by the student to succeed in general and vocational education should be clearly listed and described in the IEP. Tomey (1998) suggested that these accommodations may include instructional modifications, assessment modifications, adaptive equipment, or assistive technology. For example, Veronica uses voice recognition software for a word processor; Lawrence uses a micro-cassette recorder.

WHAT ARE THE COMPONENTS OF THE IEP?

The rules and regulations of IDEA '97 indicate that there are seven primary components of the IEP. These components, as described in the rules and regulations, include

1. The student's present level of educational performance, including the effect of the disability on the student's involvement and progress in the general curriculum
2. Measurable annual goals, including short-term objectives or benchmarks that address the student's needs resulting from the disability and enable the student to be involved in and progress in the general education curriculum as well as other educational needs
3. Special education services, related services, supplementary aids and services, and program modifications or supports for school personnel that allow the student to 1) advance appropriately toward the annual goals, 2) be involved in and progress in the general curriculum, and 3) be educated and participate with students with and without disabilities
4. An explanation of the extent to which the student will not participate in general education classes.
5. Any individual modifications in the administration of state- or districtwide assessment of student achievement that are needed for the child to participate in the assessment. If the IEP determines that the student will not participate in a state- or districtwide assessment, the IEP will include a statement of why the assessment is not appropriate and how the student will be assessed.
6. The projected date for the beginning of the services and accommodations as well as the anticipated frequency, location, and duration of services and accommodations
7. How the student's progress toward the annual goals will be measured and how the student's parents will be regularly informed (e.g., through report cards)

For students with disabilities who are 14 years old (or younger, if determined necessary by the IEP team), each IEP must include an annually updated statement of the transition services. Beginning at the age of 16 (or younger, if determined necessary by the IEP team), a statement of needed transitions services for the student, including, if appropriate, interagency responsibilities, must be included (Assistance to the States for the Education of Children with Disabilities, 1999).

In addition to these components, the rules and regulations of IDEA '97 describe several "special factors" that must be documented on the IEP. These factors are related to special considerations related to specific student characteristics:

- Students whose behavior interferes with learning or the learning of others, and strategies, including positive behavioral interventions, that will address that behavior
- Students with limited English proficiency and the students' language needs
- Students who are blind or have visual impairments; the appropriateness of instruction in braille and the use of braille must be described
- Students with communication issues or who are deaf or hard of hearing; their language and communicative needs; opportunities for direct communication with peers and professional personnel in the student's communication and academic mode
- Students who require assistive technology devices and services

After considering these special factors, if the IEP team determines that the student needs a device, intervention, accommodation, or other program modification to receive a free, appropriate public education, the IEP must include a statement to that effect. The general education teacher must assist in the development of appropriate positive behavioral intervention strategies and supplementary aids and services (Assistance to the States for the Education of Children with Disabilities, 1999). The discussion of special considerations is documented on the first page of each of our sample IEPs.

IEPs must be in effect at the beginning of each school year and must be implemented as soon as possible following the IEP meeting. The IEP must, according to the federal regulations, be accessible to each general education teacher, special education teacher, related service provider, or other service providers responsible for its implementation. Each of these individuals also must be informed of his or her responsibilities related to implementing the IEP and specific accommodations, modifications, and supports that must be provided (Assistance to the States for the Education of Children with Disabilities, 1999).

IEPs are to be reviewed periodically, and at least once per year, to determine whether the annual goals are being addressed. The IEP is revised when there is a lack of expected progress toward the annual goals or in the general education curriculum. If appropriate, further evaluation; additional information provided by the parents, the student, or the teachers; or changes in needs may be addressed in these revisions (Assistance to the States for the Education of Children with Disabilities, 1999).

WHAT ARE THE RIGHTS OF PARENTS?

According to IDEA '97, parents of students with disabilities have many rights and safeguards. In addition, it is clearly delineated that they should receive copies of these rights and safeguards 1) when the student is first referred for evaluation, 2) at each IEP meeting, 3) when the student is re-evaluated, and

4) at their request. This notice is supposed to be in understandable language (Assistance to the States for the Education of Children with Disabilities, 1999; see Table 10.2).

Independent Educational Evaluation

An *independent evaluation* is described by the regulations as "an evaluation conducted by a qualified examiner who is not employed by the public agency responsible for the education of the child in question" (Assistance to the States for the Education of Children with Disabilities, 1999, p. 12448). Parents have the right to obtain an independent educational evaluation of the student, and the school must provide parents with information about where they may obtain such an evaluation. If the parents disagree with an evaluation obtained by the school, they have the right to an independent educational evaluation at no cost. If the parents request this evaluation, the school must either 1) initiate a hearing to show that its evaluation is appropriate or 2) provide the independent evaluation at public expense if the evaluation meets predetermined criteria. If the hearing finds that the school's evaluation is appropriate, parents can seek an independent educational evaluation, but at their own cost. Schools also may ask the parents to describe their objections about the evaluation. If the parents obtain an independent educational evaluation at their own expense, the results must be considered by the school as they make their decisions, and may be presented as evidence at a hearing (Assistance to the States for the Education of Children with Disabilities, 1999).

Prior Written Notice

Prior written notice must be provided to the parents of a student with a disability within a responsible time before the school proposes to begin to change the identification, evaluation, or placement of a student, or refuses to initiate a change in the identification, evaluation, or placement. The notice must be written in language that is understandable to the general public and in the native language of the parents; if the native language or mode of communication is not a written language, the school should take steps to ensure that the notice is translated to the parents, that they understand the contents of the notice, and that the school has documented their efforts. Notices must include

- A description of what the school is proposing or refusing
- The school's reasons
- Other options that the school considered and the reasons those options were rejected
- Description of the evaluation procedures, tests, records, or reports that the school used as a basis for their decision
- Other relevant factors

Table 10.2.   Parents' rights under the Individuals with Disabilities Education Act (IDEA) Amendments of 1997 (PL 105-17)

Parents have the right to
- Independent educational evaluation
- Prior written notice
- Parental consent
- Access to educational records
- Opportunity to present complaints to initiate due process hearing
- Mediation
- Due process hearings, including requirements for disclosure of evaluation results and recommendations
- State-level appeals (if they apply in the student's state of residence), civil actions, and attorneys' fees

- A statement showing that the parents are protected by procedural safeguards
- Sources for parents to contact to receive help in understanding the safeguards

Parental Consent

Informed parental consent is required before an initial evaluation or re-evaluation is conducted, or special education and related services begin. Consent is not required before reviewing existing data as part of an evaluation or re-evaluation or in administering a test or other evaluation that is given to all students, unless parental consent also is sought in that situation. If parents refuse consent, the school may continue to pursue those evaluations through due process procedures or through mediation procedures. If the school can demonstrate that it has taken reasonable measures to obtain consent and the parents have failed to respond, the school may proceed with re-evaluation (Assistance to the States for the Education of Children with Disabilities, 1999). In our sample IEPs, parents sign their consent on the IEP summary page.

Access to Educational Records

Parents have the right to review and inspect all educational records for the student with respect to the identification, evaluation, and educational placement of the student and the provision of his or her free, appropriate public education. The regulations that address gaining access to educational records also describe the rights of the parent to participate in meetings. The parent has the right to participate in meetings with respect to these two areas. The school must make sure that the parents are members of any group that is making decisions about educational placement. The regulations clarify that informal or unscheduled conversations on teaching methodology; lesson plans; coordination of services; or ways to develop a plan to respond to a parent proposal are not, by definition, meetings (Assistance to the States for the Education of Children with Disabilities, 1999).

Mediation

IDEA '97 includes the use of a mediator to resolve disputes between parents and the school. This mediation process is voluntary; does not deny or delay a parent's right to a due process hearing; and is conducted by a qualified, trained, and impartial mediator who is not an employee of any local education agency or state education agency and does not have a conflict of interest. Both parties are engaged in the selection of the mediator, and the state bears the cost of mediation. Each session must be scheduled in a timely manner and held at a convenient time and place. Any agreement reached must be described in a written mediation agreement, and discussions are confidential and may not be used as evidence in subsequent due process hearings or civil proceedings. To ensure this confidentiality, all parties must sign a confidentiality pledge before mediation begins. School districts are provided with suggestions to encourage the use of mediation and may explain the mediation process to parents (Assistance to the States for the Education of Children with Disabilities, 1999).

Due Process Hearings

The impartial due process hearing at which parents or the school district present their complaints is conducted either by the state or the local school district as determined by state law or regulations. In general, at least 5 days before the hearing, the parents and the school district must present to each other all evaluations and recommendations based on the offering party's evaluations that may be used at the hearing. If either the parents or the school district fails to disclose information, they may be barred from the hearing. At these hearings, either the parents or the school district may be accompanied and advised by legal counsel or other experts; may present evidence, cross-examine, or compel the presence of a witness; and must be provided with a verbatim record of the hearing and written or electronic findings of facts or decisions.

Decisions made at a due process hearing are final unless either the parents or the school appeals the hearing. In some states, there are *state-level appeals*. When state-level appeals are not appropriate, either the school district or the parents may begin *civil action* in either a state court or the U.S. District Court. The court must receive records of the administrative procedures, hear evidence, and base its decision on the preponderance of evidence. The court may award reasonable attorneys' fees as part of the costs to the parents of a student with a disability if they win the action. Attorneys' fees may be reduced in some cases.

WHAT ARE THE RIGHTS OF STUDENTS?

IDEA '97 clarifies the rights of students when they reach the age of majority. The regulations indicate that the IEP must include a statement that the student has been informed of his or her rights that will transfer to the student on reaching the age of 21. Beginning 1 year before the student reaches the age of majority, he or she must be informed that rights will transfer to him or her (Assistance to the States for the Education of Children with Disabilities, 1999).

In terms of the transfer of parental rights at the age of majority, the school may provide any notice to both the student and the parent. However, except for notices regarding change of placement or other program changes, all other rights transfer to the student. Rights do not transfer to students who have been determined to be incompetent under state law.

WHAT IS THE GENERAL EDUCATION
TEACHER'S ROLE IN THE IEP AND 504 PLAN?

IDEA '97 increases the emphasis of the student's participation in general education. The IEP, for example, requires a description of how the student's disability affects his or her involvement and progress in the general education curriculum.

As indicated previously, the general education teacher of a student with a disability, as a member of the IEP team, must participate in the development, review, and revision of the IEP, including assisting in determining appropriate positive behavioral interventions and strategies, supplementary aids and services, or program modifications (Assistance to the States for the Education of Children with Disabilities, 1999). In addition, the general education teacher must receive a copy of the IEP.

Teacher involvement in the general education curriculum pervades IDEA '97; therefore, general education teachers should be active participants. In writing goals, the general education teacher can provide vital input into ways to address the disability to enable the student to be involved in a process regarding the general education curriculum. Because special education and related services are to be in place to allow the student to advance toward attaining annual goals and to be involved in the general education curriculum, the general education teacher again is actively engaged.

Teachers participating as team members in designing and implementing IEPs may be a developmental process. Wood (1998) reported an evolution of roles as teachers worked together to meet the needs of students with disabilities. Special educators retained discrete role responsibilities for IEP goals and objectives, out of a sense of both professional obligation and self-preservation. General education teachers suggested that their responsibilities were related to the student's social goals, appropriate classroom functioning, and maintaining classroom standards and the structured routine.

Siegel-Causey, McMorris, McGowen, and Sands-Buss (1998) suggested that general education teachers should be involved in four essential steps: planning, selecting classes, accommodating, and collaborating. In planning, the student's strengths are identified, and educational outcomes and annual goals are defined. Special education services and supports are then determined. In selecting classes, curricular areas are first identified, and then the instructional styles of teachers in potential classes are discussed. A class schedule can then be configured. In the third step, accommodating, the student's strengths are blended with annual goals for each class. Each general educator can share knowledge about the student with the class, and goals can be fit within a sample unit. Classroom placement can then be confirmed. In the final step, partnerships are established between special and general education staff for each class. Teacher and collaborative roles, information sharing strategies, adaptations, and accommodations are then discussed.

It is important that everyone leaves the IEP meeting with a sense of ownership. Kroeger, Leibold, and Ryan (1999) suggested the simple, low-tech method of using a chalkboard to anchor the process of IEP development, and to engage the general education teacher and the student. They suggested that following the introduction of all people present, the facilitator (who may be the special education or general education teacher) set the stage, verifying that everyone present can stay for the duration of the meeting and understands the process. Beginning with a list of strengths and gifts, the positive intent of the IEP process and team is established. An open-ended listing of the student's strengths is used to provide the opportunity for additions to the IEP during the meeting and future meetings. By using the chalkboard, the facilitator focuses away from the individual members of the group and engages everyone in collaborating. The facilitator continues to function as the timekeeper and periodically reviews how much of the task remains. All team members share ownership in the successful implementation of the IEP and the progress of the student because they have actively participated, not just listened and "signed off." The vision of the learner is at the heart of the IEP process, giving the student and other team members something to hold on to as needs and challenges are listed. The positive, affirming voices help the student meet the challenge of contributing to the program design. The groundwork for consensus at the meeting is collaborative problem solving. Goals, outcomes, and interventions are planned through brainstorming, evaluating each idea, designing an action plan, and laying out the way in which the plan will be implemented.

Section 504 is a nondiscrimination law, and any analysis of an appropriate education for a student with disabilities needs to include the educational opportunities provided to students without disabilities. Unlike IDEA '97, which focuses on the unique educational needs of the student, Section 504 compares the education of students with and without disabilities (Rosenfeld, 1999). A free, appropriate public education under Section 504 is defined as:

The provision of regular or special education and related aids and services that . . . are designed to meet individual educational needs of persons with disabilities as adequately as the needs of persons without disabilities are met and . . . are based upon adherence to specified procedures. (34 C.F.R. §§ 104.33[b][1])

Section 504, then, is broader than IDEA '97. Development of a 504 plan varies from development of an IEP. Blazer (1999) suggested that the beginning of the 504 plan meeting focuses on ways to "make school easier" for the student. The student can be asked to complete a worksheet or discuss, "What can my teacher do to help me learn?" Following the discussion of possible accommodations, a formal written compilation of classroom accommodations is made. The general education teacher may be asked what is working and what isn't. A systematic, comprehensive list of various accommodations may be described, with each item rated in terms of effectiveness. Following the development of the plan, the formal listing of accommodations, with the parents' cover letter explaining and documenting eligibility, is written.

SUMMARY POINTS

- An IEP is developed by a team for each student.
- The IEP includes a present level of educational performance; measurable annual goals and short-term objectives; special education services, related services, and supplementary aids; an explanation of nonparticipation in general education curriculum; the way in which state or district proficiency testing will be addressed; and a projected date for the beginning and the duration of services.
- IEPs must be in effect at the beginning of each school year and must be evaluated at least once a year.
- Parents have specific rights described by law. When the student reaches 18 years of age, these rights pass to the student.
- General education teachers are full participating members of the IEP team.

REFERENCES

Assistance to the states for the education of children with disabilities and the early intervention program for infants and toddlers with disabilities: Final regulations. (1999, March 14). 64(48) Fed. Reg. 12406–12454, 34 C.F.R. pts. 300, 303.
Bateman, B.D. (1995). *Writing individualized education programs (IEPs) for success.* Washington, DC: Learning Disabilities Association of America.
Blazer, B. (1999). Developing 504 classroom accommodation plans: A collaborative, systematic parent-student-teacher approach. *Teaching Exceptional Children, 32*(2), 28–33.
Education for All Handicapped Children Act of 1975, PL 94-142, 20 U.S.C. §§ 1400 *et seq.*
Individuals with Disabilities Education Act (IDEA) Amendments of 1997, PL 105-17, 20 U.S.C. §§ 1400 *et seq.*

Kroeger, S.D., Leibold, C.K., & Ryan, B. (1999). Creating a sense of ownership in the IEP process. *Teaching Exceptional Children, 32*(1), 4–9.

National Information Center for Children and Youth with Disabilities (NICHCY). (1996). *The education of children and youth with special needs: What do the laws say?* Washington, DC: Author.

Rehabilitation Act of 1973, PL 93-112, 29 U.S.C. §§ 701 *et seq.*

Rosenfeld, S.J. (1999). *Section 504 and IDEA: Basic similarities and differences.* (Available http://www.wrightslaw.com/advoc/articles/504_IDEA-rosenfeld.html.)

Siegel-Causey, E., McMorris, C., McGowen, S., & Sands-Buss, S. (1998). In junior high you take earth science: Including a student with severe disabilities into an academic class. *Teaching Exceptional Children, 31*(2), 66–72.

Tomey, H.A. (1998). *Individualized education program: The process.* Richmond: Virginia Department of Education.

Wood, M. (1998). Whose job is it anyway? Education roles in inclusion. *Exceptional Children, 64*(2), 181–195.

I HAVE DAYS
—Jason Haap, English teacher

I have days.

I have days when I'm the world's biggest idiot, days when it's absurd to expect a tenth grader to understand something so big and so important as "justice," days when teaching Socrates really is like speaking Greek.

I have days.

Sometimes, I assign so much writing, original essays, and original stories and original poems, it seems impossible to grade them all, much less for my students to write them all. *But they need practice writing,* I think. *It's for a good reason.*

"Did you grade our essays yet?" One day later the kids want results. With more than 100 students writing four-page papers, reading more than 400 pages of tenth-grade writing is data processing in the worst way.

Sometimes I feel like a machine.

I say the purpose of an education is not mere job preparation. I say it really is important to memorize Shakespeare because of his artistry and craft. I say a good essay is revised, really revised, at least three times. The kids think I'm crazy.

The kids think I'm crazy, and sometimes, I believe them.

I have days.

I have days when, finally, after three drafts of hellish revision, Bradley Johnson turns in the best informal essay about ink pens I've ever imagined. I have days when, suddenly, Matthew Simpson puts his hand in the air and discusses character motivation in terms of Socratic justice and intelligently explains why the individual's actions were philosophically and morally wrong.

Sometimes, after assigning original essays and original stories and original poems, Jeff Schneider, with no warning, turns everything in, shows me he actually paid attention, and all his work is quality. It may be late but it's there and it's good. *He was awake after all,* I think. *I wonder if I can keep him that way.*

"I know I've been slacking. I'm gonna really try this quarter, though." He sounds honest and I believe him. With more than 100 students, it's good to realize someone was listening, especially a slacker. I hope he stays true to his word.

Sometimes, I feel like an actual person.

The kids think I'm an actual crazy person.

The kids think I'm an actual crazy person, and I am, because you can't *not* be crazy and try to educate 16-year-olds. That's why sometimes, I find my way through the insanity and the chaos and get somewhere worthwhile.

Sometimes, I have days.

I have days.

III

Getting the Most Out of
Your Inclusive High School

A Class in Itself

—Lisa Mueller, math teacher

Sometime around the start of the third quarter this year, I began to receive little notes, folded thoughtfully into small squares and hand delivered by James himself. I would say I have received three or four to date. They are not about anything spectacular, just about his latest math lesson, or the topic of his intercession classes, or the swim team, of which he is a member. I didn't request these notes, nor did I write him first; he just drops a line once in a while to let me know what is going on.

James brings his camera with him to all school events. He can be found at pep rallies and basketball games surrounded by peers smiling for the camera. I can't even begin to count the number of pictures I have taken with James. Normally he waits by the entrance and asks people as they come in to pose in a picture with him. He then finds someone else to snap the shot. James never seems to tire of smiling.

The entire student body smiles when Christopher appears at pep rallies. It is safe to say that the boy has an immense amount of school spirit. He turns cartwheels and leads cheers at pep rallies and sporting events. When our basketball team went to the state tournament, Christopher gladly accepted the microphone in our gym and led the school through our fight song not once, but twice. He seems to have a passion for microphones because he also frequently uses the one in our cafeteria to sing Happy Birthday to his friends.

The treats in the main office are compliments of Elizabeth most days of the week. She is the person responsible for refilling Ms. Foster's candy jar, as long as she is not held up in the hallways catching up on the latest happenings. Elizabeth is always wearing a smile and always inquires as to how my day was.

Purcell Marian is a class in itself, I believe, not solely because of people such as James, Christopher, and Elizabeth, but in part for the way they are treated by the rest of the students. It is not unusual to see one of our varsity basketball players sit with Christopher at lunch for a few minutes, just to chat. He even wished him Happy Birthday using the microphone at lunch the other day. At least 50 people a day receive hugs from another student, yet no one tells him to stop. After beating Bellbrook en route to the state tournament this year, the team climbed the ladder to cut the net so that they could keep it. Without question, the team manager climbed up along with senior sensation Jaime to make his cut.

To smile, I believe, is one of the most important lessons I have learned from attending school with students with special needs. Something terribly awful must happen to wipe the smile from Paula's face. From the special student I have learned that there are always things to appreciate. Smile, even if those things seem small and insignificant.

To have a passion for what I love and believe in is another lesson I have observed at Purcell. Caleb will gladly risk being late for homeroom if it means he can get his hands on a book. His desire to read is incredible. His passion for books is greater than some people's will to succeed. If people sought their dreams with the same passion Caleb displays, there would be no stopping them.

Without the inclusion of people with special needs, I don't believe that the education I have received at Purcell Marian would be of the same quality or depth that it is. I say this because I believe education includes more than what you learn from an algebra or history textbook. I believe that social lessons and life lessons are equally important. I don't believe a person can be fully educated without being exposed to many different types of people. From each individual, there is something to be learned, even if it is small or goes unnoticed.

11

Joining Up

Becoming a Member of an Academic Department

Richard Hague

Editor's note: In our time at Purcell Marian High School, the collaboration among members of the various academic departments emerged as a key element in the teachers' efforts to meet the needs of students. In teacher education programs, however, the emphasis usually is on the classroom, with little attention paid to the department. In this chapter, Richard Hague, chair of the English department, provides insights to novice teachers as they become members of the school community at the classroom, department, and school levels.

Education classes in college may or may not prepare teachers well for the classroom. But regardless of how much we have read, talked, observed, cooperated, and student taught, when we find ourselves in a room of our own for the first time with a bunch of young people about whom we know nothing, the real teaching begins. Teaching is mostly learning, and learning consists mostly of trial and error. The setting for learning is the sometimes frighteningly intense or the profoundly boring place called *the classroom*.

What do teachers learn? First, we learn who we are in relation to our subject and to our students. "Real learning does not happen until students are brought into relationship with the teacher, with each other, and with the subject" (Palmer, 1993, p. xvi). You'll have to read *To Know as We Are Known: Education as a Spiritual Journey* (Palmer, 1993) to understand all of the complexities of these relationships and the difficulties that we face in establishing them. If you do, you will save years of unproductive anguish in your teaching career. So, the learning we do as teachers is not only in our subject area and its related skills, but in the habits of our mind, in our psychological and spiritual stance, and in our relationships to each other as we explore learning.

What trials do teachers face? We face trials of all of the theories that we have learned during our contact area and education classes. For me, those trials have involved theories about how best to teach writing; theories about memory; and theories about learning, cognition, and creativity. For others, the theories may involve human nature, group dynamics, and discipline in the classroom. In addition, others may require a critical look at unexamined or largely unarticulated theories about ourselves and why we think we're teaching. (If we don't have a few theories—especially why we think we're teaching—we need to write or read something about each of these topics, and we need to take what makes sense to us and try it out in our classrooms. The information that doesn't make sense to us, we need to ignore. More importantly, if we can't give any nongeneric, richly convincing answers to why we are teaching, maybe we shouldn't be.)

What errors do teachers make? We make errors in finding and cultivating the right relationship between ourselves, our subject, and our students; in taking care of ourselves in this psychologically dangerous profession; in not using our failures to grow and become better; in not bringing our strengths to the forefront because we don't think our personal strengths have much to do with our life in the classroom; in matters of fact and logic; and in, and omissions of, sympathy and compassion.

A secondary school academic department exists not only as an administrative entity but, more important, as a set of people with shared experiences. They have accumulated experience about what works and what doesn't work in the school and what the students in the school need. Because no two schools are alike and because every school creates its own culture, the only people who can tell us about our school are our colleagues. Not relying on their knowledge would be like throwing away all of our textbooks at the beginning of each class in college or throwing away all of our tools at the beginning of a plumbing project.

My observer one semester, Erin Stafford, a graduate student in education at Xavier University in Cincinnati, asked a good question near the beginning of her work with us: "What expertise does each of the English teachers have?" For example, Erin wanted to know who the expert in writing was, who knew a lot about American literature, or who ran the extracurricular activities associated with the English department. These types of questions will get us talking to other members of the department, and the questions will expose some hidden talents and interests that might be helpful for teaching. Relax. You do not have to be an expert as a first-year teacher. It is helpful if you are curious and open.

A note of warning: I would not expect a new department member to try to do all of the activities suggested in this chapter. Think of this as a menu from which you can choose, selecting those exercises and activities that appeal most to you or that seem to match up to your own learning style. Remember that teaching is a complex occupation that requires not only a great deal of specific knowledge, but also a great deal of instinct.

EXERCISE: *Within the first week of your teaching, begin a log, a diary, or a journal to have an intellectual, emotional, and spiritual record of your first year. Keep track of the conflict between what you expected and what actually happened, between what you learned in college and how it played out in the classroom, and between what you didn't learn in college but what seems of great importance now. Show the difference between getting the map—being taught theory and practice in the classroom—and being there—the actual hassles and triumphs of the work. Equally important, keep a record of your successes, no matter how small they might seem. Think of teaching as an adventure, a journey whose end cannot be predicted. Think of teaching as an ongoing conversation in which you are a participant, obligated to tell others what you have experienced.*

ARGUMENT IS GOOD, NOT BAD

When I refer to *argument,* I mean it as Socrates would have meant it—argument as a way toward the truth. I often tell those students who seem put off by my challenging their beliefs and attitudes that if they go to college and don't get into an argument in their classes, they have wasted their money. School should be a place of friendly, ongoing argument. I once read a description of Ireland that called it "a conversation in the shape of a country." School should be an argument in the shape of an institution. So, when your department chair is talking to you about your teaching practice, and he or she seems to be getting into a position where you might want to argue, go ahead and give it your best shot. Try to defend the assignment that you gave that laid out everything the writer was supposed to do, leaving no room for error. Try to justify the lengthy lab assignment that you thought would lead students to some significant and perhaps even startling discovery, not just to what many of them already knew. If you lose the argument, that's great, because that means one more powerful notion or accurate account of actual teaching experience has prevailed; you're better off for knowing it. If you win the argument, you get to feel good and competent, and if your department chair is dedicated to excellence, you will have made a great impression. There is a lot to be said for dialect, argument, and opposition. They are tools for toughening the mind.

Jason Haap, one of the two youngest members of my department, has been willing to ask questions every day. I can't count the number of times we've had a discussion that was, in part, an argument, and both of us have learned a lot during these exchanges. They are intellectually playful arguments, mostly full of "what-ifs" and "I thinks." As a result of them, I have been forced to articulate more clearly to myself some of my own thoughts about teaching and about running a department; likewise, because of them, Jason has occasionally changed his mind and practice, always revising toward sharper and more effective teaching.

Because of Jason's questions and the questions of other younger department members, we have begun to study how to use writing portfolios. At first, we had to argue whether we even wanted portfolios; once the argument took place, we had to decide how we were going to use them: as repositories of students' best work? As records of students' mastery of the various stages of the writing process? As a collection of assignments we give as a department? The ways of using portfolios vary, and how they are used is directly connected to how writing will be taught in school. As department chair, I handed Jason the job of researching portfolios for us and of facilitating a series of department meetings during which we would all participate in generating our portfolio philosophy. Then, because all things are connected, I knew we would have to discuss the curriculum implications of what we decided about portfolios. Jason's "local" handling of these meetings gave me an opportunity to sit in as a participant, rather than as department head, and get a "global" look at the issues. As a result, I have begun to generate a scope and sequence for writing that will match up with the actual needs of our students and with what we are actually teaching. Too many plans work down from the top, or from the abstract; this one is working its way up from the faculty and the classroom, where the actual teaching happens.

Another one of Jason's pet ideas is that English teachers should write. They should practice what they preach. If they require creative writing from their students, they should practice creative writing themselves, struggling with the same issues that their students struggle with, so they are able to better discuss and understand their students' problems. Jason came in with some writing experience, but soon after joining us he signed up for two local writer's support and critique groups and began to attend their meetings. He investigated the publishing business and put together short collections of poems and sent them out for publication. He took creativity workshops and workshops designed to teach him how to use drama and movement in his classes. He began to help his students mount poetry performances and short exhibitions. He took part in an exhibition himself. If teachers require historical research from their students, perhaps we should practice historical research ourselves. If teachers require community service from their students, perhaps we should participate in community service ourselves. If questions exist in your department and have not yet led to constructive arguments, instigate them yourself.

Frequently, before I saw the need to explain this phenomenon of self-investigation about myself ahead of time, my students accused me of being uncooperative. I would not answer questions that I thought would be fruitful for them to answer themselves. I wanted them to think through and discover the answer rather than unwittingly hand over to me all of the fun of the "aha!" moment. Or, I would question unexamined notions or half-baked ideas that students had, always with the goal of pushing them deeper into their ideas, their complexities, and their implications. Of course, students often saw this not as education but as stinginess or arrogance on my part. "Just give me the answer, Mr. Hague. It's so much easier for the both of us." If teaching and learning were merely exchanges of superficial questions and factual answers, then it certainly would be a sorry business. In writing this poem, I articulated to myself certain ideas abut teaching and learning that I had not articulated before in exactly the same way.

The Advocate Speaks in the Poem's Defense
for Mike B.,
who asked me not to badger him

Not everything you'll meet
is a meek squirrel,
or a birthday puppy,
eating from your hand.
Truth is not fish thrown to seals.
Not everything is nice.
Not everything is easy.
For example this poem,
that badger, that grizzled
squat beast
of claws and grumbles,
often seems mean
and strange.
It digs under the door of your notions,
wrecks the tidy room
of your truth,
bucks you out of the nursery
of your ideas,
rolling you angry and cursing
into a life as strange
as metamorphosis.
It wants you to think,
sweat, wrestle with angels,
bleed words, change
your ways.
It wants you to be delivered.

But, if you don't want to be delivered,
don't want to burst new
into the world
like a great poem or idea,
like a shower of meteors
lighting some novel way
through the dark,
then here's what to do:

Hide out.
Skip town.
Close the blinds
of your fugitive motel
like the shutter of a mind.
Live on Pepsi and trivia,
drown in "Dawson's Creek."
Give up.
Believe what TV tells you.
Whine when it isn't true.
Uselessly complain.

Then you'll be
your own life's helpless infant forever,
the false nurse of ignorance
clutching you close,
the twin who's your fear
holding you back.

But if a good life
is worth it,
if adventure is the point,
and the shape of your life
is not a fixed course,
boring before it begins,
but a river of many bends,
a new world every turn—
mystery and confusion,
discovery and possible glory—
then live like the badger,
badgering.
Don't think straight

like everyone else,
but think around all corners,
think clear through things
head-first, full-speed,
knowing they can't stand up
if they're generic, cheaply gained
or lies.

Climb an idea
further
than anyone else,
be stubborn and relentless,
see from the top of it,
scout ahead of the rest.
Or travel down it,
burrow and explore,
tracing its roots
deep into the ground.
See for yourself if they're healthy.

Study dirt.
Know earth.
Dig gardens.
Scorn money.
Eat books.
Show your teeth
to the enemy.
Find work that does good for many.
Love truth
like a beautiful sister.

Grow large,
travel strange roads,
president of the world
that you rip and praise,
question and upend,
the world that you wander
to know;
find the self
that you're born
to come home to.

EXERCISE: *What are the competing educational theories in your school? Whole-language versus phonics? Lecture and delivery-system model versus student-as-worker? Teacher-centered versus student-centered learning? Where do you stand on these issues? Have an extended discussion (yes, maybe even an argument) with a peer or veteran over the subject. Later, watch your students closely and elicit commentary and reflection from them, finding out what they think about your teaching and about their own learning.*

EXPECT A MENTOR: IF YOU DON'T GET ONE, ADOPT ONE

Our school has instituted a mentoring program for new teachers. But each new teacher is *assigned* a mentor, and that, of course, does not always result in the best match between the mentor and the one being mentored. These situations have a way of working themselves out, though. So, if you are attracted to the views, attitudes, or reputation of a veteran faculty member, even if you are slightly awed by him or her, go ahead and see if something can come of it. You'll know soon whether the relationship will work, and if it does work, the veteran will be flattered and well disposed to listen to you at length. If the relationship is really going well, the distinction between professional mentoring and friendship will begin to blur, and going for a plate of quesadillas or barbecue wings after school on Friday will be a dual event, profitable from the professional and social side.

One of the signs of real learning is that different aspects of life begin to be integrated; teaching, living, learning, and growing become intertwined. I was chosen by Jason to be a mentor. In 1999, a new young teacher, Anthony Corder, joined the faculty. He's a former student of mine and member of the religion department. Jason and Anthony have struck up a friendship that is, in part, a mentoring relationship. All three of us go out occasionally after school for a holiday of the mind. We laugh a lot, and rather than engaging in the usual venting so often practiced by frustrated or exhausted teachers, we make a point of keeping the discussion focused on some aspect of teaching or learning. It's a self-assigned curriculum of professional development, using the resources that we can be for each other. We talk about books that we have assigned one another to read, and we analyze the school culture in the light of several themes: race relations, the expectations the school has or fails to have concerning "general," so-called "non–college-bound students," or the need for a more connected interdisciplinary curriculum.

When Bryan Ammer, another younger member of the English faculty, first joined us, he and I had long conversations about a number of issues. He was not backward about wanting to talk, and I learned a great deal. Along with Cathy Kennicott, Betsy McNally, and Laura Rupp, also younger members of the department, Bryan volunteered to prepare and present a faculty exhibition in 1998. This was daring on his and all of their parts; they knew that their performance was going to be given before either the whole faculty or the parents of prospective advance placement students. From August to December, while handling full teaching loads, coaching school teams, and engaging in other extracurricular activities, they pored over books, poems, videos, artwork, as well as teaching themselves PowerPoint technology. At last, they presented 60-minute performances. Clearly they had learned, from the inside out, the kinds of obstacles that their students would face in the same task. Together, they had "walked the walk and talked the talk" as students might say. Once the group dynamics worked themselves out, they mentored one another, in a manner of speaking, and the experience was invaluable to them and to the school's program of change.

So, if you are not assigned a mentor by your school, dig around until you hear of someone on the faculty who might have something to offer. You don't even have to approach him or her formally; ask if every now and then it would be all right to drop in after school for a chat. In most cases, there will be no objection; most veteran teachers are veterans because they have, over the years, learned how to be approachable and useful. If there is no culture of mentoring in your school, however, do not hesitate to suggest that a program be established. Schools are busy and conservative places, for the most part, where, as Joe Rogus (1990), longtime professor of educational administration at the University of Dayton, said to our faculty during an opening day in-service, "The immediate crowds out the important." Good ideas do not necessarily get recognized, let alone acted on. You might have to be the one to suggest, and perhaps even institute, a mentoring program.

> **EXERCISE:**   *After you've been teaching for a semester or two, choose a problem that you have faced as a teacher. Perhaps it is a problem of technique—how to vary your classes while keeping higher-order thinking skills before your students—or perhaps something about the school's unwritten rules about race has got you troubled. Spend a semester or a year reading, talking, and writing about the problem and about what you have learned and find someone to whom you can present it—your mentor, your principal, or a committee you belong to at school.*

BE A CONTINUAL LEADER

Speaking as a department chair, I expect that members of my department will continue to learn. This does not only mean, of course, that they take the licenser-driven courses and workshops, but that they are intellectually alive when it comes to pedagogy and their subjects. Part of what I have begun to do is to ask for a copy of each teacher's lesson plans and reflections. I have already learned a lot from reading these, and they give us an opportunity for dialogue and thought about the most important things of teaching and learning. These reflections, instituted by our principal, Jan Kennedy, provide a window into my colleagues' styles, concerns, and habits. From them, I get a sense of what works and what doesn't work for them. Here's an example of Jason Haap's (2000) reflections, which I find especially interesting and plan to include in the latest update of my *Exhibition Papers,* a guide to mounting and evaluating an exhibition of learning:

Toward the beginning of the third quarter, my thinking came to a temporary standstill while I was trying to conceive of how the idea of justice *could be expanded beyond where my students had taken it. Once the students had their heads around Socrates, I felt inclined to move forward. Last year, I did not get so far.*

So, during conversations with Dick [Hague] and Anthony [Corder], I found some additional readings, like Lawrence Kohlberg's ideas on moral development and reasons, and Martin Luther King Jr.'s Letter from a Birmingham Jail. *From these readings we began to develop a list of the "loaded words," ideas for any in-depth conversation about "justice." Some of my favorites from the enormous list include "patriotism," "betrayal," "friendship," "truth," "conscience," and "reality."*

For the last week or so, three of my sophomore classes have embarked on independent group study projects. The idea is to give them experience to further their background knowledge on a topic of their choice—focusing on the process of learning as opposed to obsessing over a presentation. One of my students was having trouble locating information on "conscience." As I perused my bookshelf to see what resources I may have had in the room, I found two books. The second is on loan from Anthony, entitled Forming a Catholic Conscience, *and the student found the chapter "Conscience" obviously useful. The first book I looked through, though, was called* Maps of the Mind. *This is something a friend gave me 2 years ago and I never really paid it much attention. It has neat pictures; I sometimes use for poetry assignments.*

While paging through the contents, I was momentarily impressed with the chapter called, "The Tree with Poisoned Fruit," an essay on the Eden story. I added it to my "tree folder." [The tree refers to a course Anthony and Jason proposed for next year—an interdisciplinary elective in English and religion focusing on the central symbol of the tree—its religious, literary, legendary, and cultural significance.] Then what happened next was, in my opinion, remarkable.

A few pages later in the contents I read another chapter heading, "The Ascent From Plato's Cave: Moral Development from Piaget to Kohlberg." While I had always focused on Chapter 3 of The Republic, *I had forgotten all about Plato's "Allegory of the Cave." I thought it would be an excellent way to continue with the character of Socrates. As with Kohlberg, who says our level of moral reasoning advances when someone at a higher level challenges our thinking, Socrates, in* The Republic, *likens enlightenment to a cave-dweller emerging into the blinding light, seeing reality for the first time, and once accustomed to the light, being unable to return to the dark illusion of his or her former reality.*

As I read through the essay which links Kohlberg to Socrates, two people we are already familiar with, I discovered a part of the essay where Kohlberg interprets the thinking of Martin Luther King, Jr., from Letter from a Birmingham Jail. *How incredible! The fourth quarter had unfolded, quite coincidentally, in front of my very eyes, and everything was, though unbeknownst by me, already connected.*

I love that kind of stuff. This is an excellent example of what Emerson called "Man Thinking," and offers insight into Jason's learning style. It also opens a window into his classroom practice and his cognitive habits. He participates in learning as an adventurer participates in a quest; he trusts that whatever happens will be a part of the meaning of the journey; he has learned to "expect the unexpected." You even get the sense that in the process of writing his narrative of what happened, Jason discerns more accurately the "meaning" of it, and is engaged in the act of writing-to-learn that we want our students to experience. If some of Jason's excited trust in the process passes from him to his students as he works along with them, if they begin to expect a connection between the stories and poems they read, between their own experiences and their reading, even between the disciplines that are symbolically held separate from one another by the walls of separate classrooms and the curricula of separate departments, then they will have experienced something energizing and liberating about learning.

EXERCISE: *Write a story about a moment of discovery in your own teaching, making it happen for your reader as it happened for you. Articulate to yourself during the telling of this story what lessons about learning and teaching emerged. Remember that because learning is trial and error, this story need not be one of a success. Perhaps you discovered a flaw in your thinking or teaching practice, or a quirk of your personality that is not productive, or a mistake or unexamined assumption in your own thinking about teaching and learning. In your story, show how you came to this realization, and articulate to yourself and your reader how your teaching practice might change as a result of this realization.*

COMPILE A PORTFOLIO ABOUT YOURSELF EACH YEAR

Compiling a portfolio about yourself might be nothing more than a collection of programs from workshops that you attended; honors you or your students won; newspaper articles about you, your programs, or your students; photographs of class activities, science fairs, or field trips; or anything else that creates the fullest picture of your teaching and learning. In addition, you might want to include a written reflection or analysis of the portfolio, celebrating the strengths without overlooking the gaps—the things not represented that you want to work on next year.

For a long time, I gave little thought to the importance of having a list of goals for each teaching year. But I have found that a list of goals—even two or three items—gives some focus to my efforts each year, and gives me a rough yardstick with which to measure myself and my practice at year's end. These goals can be personal (e.g., "I will read three new books on race relations this year because I see that there are gaps in my understanding of intolerance") or professional (e.g., "I will take a course in astronomy in preparation for proposing an interdisciplinary course called 'The Sky'"), or departmental (e.g., "I will prepare and present a department in-service on portfolios because we seem to want to use them but don't know how"). In your annual portfolio, collect the outcomes of your objectives and reflect on them. Have a file on yourself and track your own development.

> **EXERCISE:** *Imagine that you are the chair of your department and you must evaluate every teacher annually. Create the teacher-evaluation rubric that you think would recognize and value your strengths. Offer it to your department chair as the "tool" with which to evaluate you.*

KEEP THE LEVEL OF DISCUSSION HIGH

Because of the nature of the beast and because teaching is a high-risk job, psychologically speaking, the temptation is great to drop out of the tough discussions and engage in small talk and chatter over the lunch table or in the faculty room. There is nothing wrong with this, but if indulged in habitually it robs you and your colleagues of small but useful chances for professional growth.

Jason and I deliberately have had serious discussions over lunch. Jason and I read a couple of books together. Then, seated at one end of the lunch table in the faculty room, we discussed them in tones loud enough to be overheard. This may have been construed as impolite and boorish behavior, but so what? If we were taken to court, no jury in its right mind would have convicted us. They would probably have said something along the lines of, "It's about time."

If we are to convince our students that we are people in the habit of using our minds, we are doing the equivalent of what the poet John Keats was getting at when he said that he tried "to load every rift with ore." Why can't we aspire to that kind of habitual intensity and singleness of purpose that makes a discussion at lunch a learning experience?

EXERCISE: *It is widely accepted that "changing the bias"—if by no other means than going to places different than the usual classroom—can improve learning. Set up a series of learning lunches with a student or group of students who have a special problem or a particular driving interest. Seek out that department member who may have expertise in the area and invite him or her to the lunch, too. It's not necessary to go outside the normal lunch room. In fact, having "power-lunching" teachers and students visible to onlookers might provide a provocative spectacle good for the general learning environment.*

MAINTAIN RESPECT FOR YOURSELF AND YOUR PROFESSION

Do not believe what the newspapers often say about teachers: that we are not doing our jobs, that students who are failing their proficiency exams are solely our problem, that the violence of schools is solely our problem, and so forth. In his book *The Art of Teaching*, Gilbert Highet (1950/1989) wrote,

> The best school in the world will scarcely save the boy who hates the school and the purpose it serves and the society that created it. No attempt to "make learning relevant" will permanently bridge the gap between the classroom and the juvenile gangster. This problem must be solved by the municipal authorities, the churches, the police, the local political organizations, by the rest of the citizens, and by the parents themselves. The best work is already being done by the teachers and the policemen, and all the rest of the problem remains for others to solve. (p. 30)

Although we might argue with some of Highet's statements, nevertheless, he is right to recognize that teachers and schools cannot solve the problems alone.

So, let's not get defensive when proficiency scores aren't all we had hoped. Let's analyze who fails the tests and what these students have in common with one another. Then, let's suggest to the legislators and all of the others on Highet's list of responsible parties what might be done in realms other than education. Let's not assume poverty, abuse, and ethnic isolation as our own problems and then punish ourselves with things that are beyond our control.

Related to this is the problem created for the teacher by our culture's extreme sense of entitlement. No one would expect to be able to walk into a doctor's office and get an immediate opinion on a medical matter without an appointment. So it should be with us; our students and our teaching schedules are our appointments, and any interruption of them by parents, other students, administrators, and legislators should not be accommodated. If we do not protect our professional space, it will be distorted and devalued.

Do not, in an attempt to fit in or to be well liked, stifle your intentions and aspirations. In the final balance, I prefer department members who are a little creatively "wild" than those who are quietly docile. The profession is at an important historical period and needs to be active and fluid in challenging itself. Teachers can't afford complacency or timidity. A good department member carries the habit of a constructive argument everywhere he or she goes.

This does not mean, of course, arguing only for argument's sake. Have a plan and a vision of the profession that shapes your thinking.

DO YOUR OWN ASSIGNMENTS

I can't think of any suggestion that will immediately point out to you where your assignments are flawed than this one: Whenever possible—and perhaps even when nearly impossible—do your own assignments. You will discover what your students may struggle with as you try to do the assignments. You will discover where your assignments are unclear, too broad, or too narrow. This applies in any subject—if you assign a science project, you ought to publicly do one yourself as an example for your students. If you assign a research paper in social studies, you should do one yourself—using the same resources your students use and dealing with the same difficulties they encounter. Then you will be more able to talk to them about their learning, and they might see you more as a co-learner and less as the sole authority. We want to teach the democracy of ideas and not suggest that there is only one holder of knowledge—the teacher.

Also, if there are certain assignments or skills that are a traditional part of your department's curriculum (e.g., science projects, research papers, video projects), do not let them become fossilized or impervious to revision. As a new colleague you may have a perspective on an old curricular chestnut that veteran members have simply maintained out of habit. Perhaps you are closer to the newest research on brain-compatible teaching, for example, and can offer some ideas on how to design learning so that it engages multiple intelligences, rather than simply verbal or mathematical skill.

Be diligent in your effort to make other department members aware of what you know and of what new practices may prove useful. Again, don't be shy. The profession needs energy; it needs stirring up, even a bit of revolution here and there.

PLAY

Outside of native intelligence, rich preparation in your teaching field, an apt personality for the work, self-forgiveness, and a sense of adventure, the most important characteristic of the successful, even exemplary department member, is an ever-growing understanding of the importance of play. It is from *play*—which I informally define in an educational context as the habit of fiddling around with your teaching practice, trying new strategies, flying sometimes by the seat of your pants—that undiscovered innovations might arise. Maybe you will discover a knack for drawing cartoons, or you realize that your experience in mountaineering becomes a model for teaching and learning writing or that the meander of a river becomes an essay about writing and learning. Try to connect apparently unconnected realms (e.g., the tree and religion, science and music, geometry and history). Take some chances in your teaching; go outside the canon and select areas to study with your students that have been infrequently studied before. Once, when I was teaching a senior advanced placement course in world literature, I decided to use *Zorba the Greek*. I'd never taught it before, nor had I seen it on many high school reading lists. As we studied it and were caught up in its passion and language, I nevertheless found it necessary to make an apology to the students, a rationalization of why I had asked them to read it. A few months later, the following poem by my student, Anne Endress (1989), appeared in the school's literary magazine:

Teaching the Risqúe

I mean,
how do you go about explaining
that Everything they know is false
and ought to be thrown out like
old baby diapers?

They'll laugh at you like agnostics,
or just silently stone you, if you're lucky!

Few will understand that simply getting there
gets you nowhere
if you don't move in a
dancing way.

Many people will remember the famous "teach me to dance" scene in *Zorba* in which the emotionally uptight Boss at last opens himself to the fullness of life when Zorba teaches him to dance on the ocean shore. It is a moment of epiphany for the Boss, an example of a time when learning reaches most deeply into the soul. It is a moment of the most important kind of play.

FINAL WORDS

There are no final words, of course. Since the time of The Academy at Athens, teaching and learning have been open issues, changing with their times and with their historical and cultural contexts. As I write this, technology is a major issue in education, as are the various theories emerging from research on the brain and on such concepts as multiple intelligences. There are challenges being mounted against standardized tests, charter schools, and proficiency examinations. It's a lot to keep up with, but very exciting. Within the profession we desperately need first-hand accounts of teaching and learning, given by teachers and learners. Jason Haap filmed, edited, and burned onto a CD a 25-minute documentary on exhibitions in Purcell Marian High School. Featuring footage of the actual exhibitions, follow-up interviews with students talking about the process, and a bit of snazzy narrative and musical overlay, the video is the first of what I suspect will be an ongoing archive of learning. There are still gaps in the story, of course. We need one of these videos from the teacher's point of view, exposing the paradigm shift that may be necessary for a veteran teacher to give up the control that has customarily been delegated to him or her in the classroom. The video could discuss how to hand control of the classroom over to the students so that they might experience learning and discovery firsthand—so that they might experience and learn to deal with the frustrations of sorting through the clutter and apparent chaos at the beginning of any real learning experience.

So, one of the roles a department member can play is as a researcher and storyteller. Anecdotal evidence is always better reading (or viewing) than dry data, and, if nothing else, it gives the teacher good practice at writing and reflecting on his or her teaching. Its potential public nature keeps you connected with the ongoing conversation about education.

> **EXERCISE:** *Think of your teaching year as an example. Of what, exactly, is it an example? Is it an example of a teacher trying new things because he or she seems to be called to overcome student resistance or disengagement? Is it the tale of error and learning? Is it a solo performance in which you are the star? Is it a collaborative story, with the teacher and students involved in the process, negotiating and revising all along the way? Is it a comedy? A tragedy? A melodrama? An inconclusive tale, filled with sound and fury? A confession of error and conversion, in the spirit of St. Augustine? Every one of our teaching years is, after all, a kind of narrative. What kind is yours? What is its theme?*

REFERENCES

Endress, A. (1989). Teaching the risque. *Hackberry: Purcell Marian's Literary Magazine, 2,* 4.

Haap, J. (2000). *Lesson plans and reflections.* Cincinnati: Purcell Marian High School.

Hague, R. (1998). The advocate speaks in the poem's defense. *Writing on the Edge, 9(2),* 24–26.

Highet, G. (1989). *The art of teaching.* New York: Vintage Books. (Originally published in 1950).

Palmer, P.J. (1993). *To know as we are known: Education as a spiritual journey.* San Francisco: HarperCollins.

Rogus, J.S.M. (1990, August). *Opening day inservice presentation.* Cincinnati: Purcell Marian High School.

12

Everybody Can Play

Anne M. Bauer
Roseanne Bays

*Teacher Contributors: Dave Campbell,
Allan Karol, Jan Kennedy, Tom Stickley*

There is more to going to high school than going to class. Dave Campbell, director of campus ministries, during orientation at Purcell Marian High School, tells incoming freshmen, "Take risks. Get involved. If you leave right at the last bell, your memories will only be about classes, not about people."

Participating in extracurricular activities has positive implications for all students. Garton and Pratt (1991) contended that active participation in out-of-class activities is important to healthy psychological development. If the available activities fail to meet the student's social and individual needs either because the activities aren't accessible to the student or they lack interest for the student, progress through adolescence may be judged as unsatisfactory. For students with disabilities, participation in extracurricular activities has the potential for even greater impact; a student's current level of involvement in sports and group activities may predict perceived future community involvement (Kraemer, Blacher, & Marshal, 1997).

The Individuals with Disabilities Education Act (IDEA) Amendments of 1997 (PL 105-17) support the inclusion of students with disabilities in extracurricular activities and specifically refer to their participation. In addition, participation in extracurricular activities may have positive effects on the quality of life of students with disabilities. The potential benefits of participation in extracurricular activities include 1) enhanced self-esteem and self-confidence, 2) increased social interaction and opportunities for friendships, 3) enhanced feelings of belonging and acceptance, 4) increased autonomy, independence, and self-direction, and 5) an expanded range of leisure skills that may lead to lifelong participation (Heyne, 1998). Participating in extracurricular activities may, thus, have a tremendous long-term impact on the lives of individuals with disabilities (Demchak, 1994). In addition, a major goal for students with disabilities is to enhance their interactions and their involvement with peers, family, and community members; participating in extracurricular activities may enhance the opportunity to work toward this goal (York, Vandercook, & Stave, 1990). In a retrospective study, college students with physical and sensory disabilities reported that participation in sports and fitness activities helped them become more socially competent, taught them that they could attain goals, and provided social interaction (Blinde & Taub, 1999).

Although participation outside of the classroom is important to membership in the school community, there has been little research related to engaging students with disabilities in extracurricular activities. Individuals with physical disabilities, for example, have reported that they believe that individuals without physical disabilities discount and overlook their physical ability to participate in sport and physical fitness activity (Taub & Greer, 1998). Students without disabilities are more likely to be involved in activities than their peers with identified disabilities (Murtaugh, 1988). Students in smaller schools tend to participate in a greater number and variety of extracurricular activities (Holland & Andre, 1987). Participation in sports and physical activities is viewed as one possible way to empower individuals with disabilities (Blinde & Taub, 1999). In this chapter, we discuss some of the issues involved when everybody plays. After reading this chapter, you will be able to answer the following questions:

- What are the challenges confronting an activity moderator in an inclusive high school?
- What is partial participation, and what is its role in relation to high school students?
- How can student participation in extracurricular activities be supported?

CHALLENGES CONFRONTING AN ACTIVITY MODERATOR

Our teacher contributors described a "make it work" attitude toward including students with disabilities in their activities. Tom Stickley, history teacher and football coach, reiterated his commitment to the mission statement and the climate of inclusion, where you "work hard to help everyone fit in." Allan Karol, theatre teacher, concurred, indicating that inclusion in extracurricular activities is part of the general atmosphere of the school. In an inclusive high school, inclusion goes beyond the classroom into all aspects of high school life.

Traditionally, however, students with disabilities have been excluded from sponsored extracurricular activities such as sports events and dances unless a parent provided support during the activity (Walker, 1990). This use of parents, however, is artificial—few parents are present in high school activities—and may interfere with the typical interaction that takes place among participants. For teenagers, the presence of parents may be uncomfortable for students with and without disabilities. Although in the past, students may have participated in "special" activities, a new emphasis on providing support for individuals with disabilities within common programs rather than segregated activities has emerged (Walker & Shoultz, 1996). At Purcell Marian High School there are no "special" clubs or sports for students with disabilities. All students are strongly encouraged to participate in clubs or sports.

The challenges of engaging students with disabilities in extracurricular activities is not simply a student issue. There are several aspects that need to be addressed, including issues related to parents of students with disabilities, student skill and experience, moderator skill and experience, and the nature of high school activities.

Parents may not always advocate for their child's participation in sports. Block (1995) suggested that advocating for extracurricular opportunities may take a back seat to advocating for services addressing academic and other life skills issues. In addition, parents may be discouraged by coaches and administrators who identify possible safety aspects of participation. Participation in sports and activities places a burden on parents in terms of transportation because activities may be after school or on weekends. Another burden is the expense of equipment and materials. Jan Kennedy, the school principal, recognized the problems of having to "come back" after school for practices and activities. Several activities, such as theater, band, and school publications (e.g., yearbook, newspaper), are scheduled as classes during the school day so that students with transportation problems may participate.

Student skill and experience also may be a challenge for moderators as they attempt to include students with varying levels of ability. Students with disabilities may have little experience in participating in clubs, working on theatrical productions, or playing sports. Prior to high school, youth sport coaches may be apprehensive about having a child with a disability on the team. By the time the students reach adolescence, there may be a significant discrepancy in the skill level between students with and without disabilities because of lack of experience and participation (Peniston, 1998; Rizzo, Bishop, Hwang, & Grenfel, 1995). Youth sport involvement is essential because many prerequisite skills and concepts are taught at the youth sports level. For students with disabilities, high school may be their first exposure to art club, computer club, pep squad, or theatrical productions. Whereas the other students have developed expectations and comfort about such activities, students with disabilities are beginning fresh.

Perhaps the greatest challenge facing activity moderators is their own lack of preparation or experience in working with individuals with disabilities. Kozub and Porretta (1998) reported that although a majority of coaches in high schools felt that students with disabilities should be allowed to participate and had a right to participate, most had no prior experience with athletes with disabilities. Moderators also may anticipate that students have some basic skills in the activities prior to high school and may be uncomfortable with their ability to work with students who are truly newcomers to the sport or activity. Teachers, coaches, and moderators usually have, in their own education, been prepared to apply developmental educational models (Krebs & Block, 1992). In developmental models, students traditionally have been required to master "prerequisite skills" before being taught more complicated or advanced skills. The problem is that many students may never master these "prerequisite skills" and are not given the opportunity to participate in any way. For these students, "pre" means never. Coaches and moderators are confronted with the challenge of identifying roles for students to participate, rather than "bringing them along" in skill development.

The nature of high school activities themselves may pose a challenge for moderators and coaches. Desiring to win rather than encouraging the participation of all students may put coaches, parents, and alumni in stressful situations. Having to limit roster sizes supports the notion that winning is important. However, Kozub and Poretta (1997) argued that "cutting" based on ability is not an optimal situation for many athletes, including students without disabilities. Only playing the "best and brightest" is difficult for students with and without disabilities.

Creativity is demanded of activity moderators when including students with disabilities. Allan Karol suggested that one challenge is helping students incorporate new behaviors that are slightly beyond their current repertoire. Another challenge is helping students generate a difficult skill for a new situation.

PARTIAL PARTICIPATION

Participating in extracurricular activities is, in itself, important. Garton and Pratt (1991) found a close relationship between the frequency of participation in activities and interest in those activities. Greater participation is reflected in higher interest. In other words, the more you do, the more you enjoy the doing. Tom Stickley, football coach and history teacher, emphasized the need for students to get involved so that they "do something these 4 years, so they don't look back at them and think they wasted them."

Students with disabilities, however, may not have acquired all of the skills needed to participate independently in a sport or extracurricular activity (Krebs & Block, 1992). For these students, partial participation may emerge. The principle of partial participation states that, regardless of the extent of the disability, individuals can be taught to participate in a variety of activities to some degree, or the activities can be adapted to allow participation (Baumgart et al., 1982).

Partial participation may involve students with disabilities participating in an activity in a variety of ways. Tom Stickley has involved students on the football team who play regularly (he told one student that if he worked out in the weight room all summer he would be allowed to play, and coach and athlete were true to the agreement), spend time on the bench, and help with water and equipment. Allan Karol engaged students in drama productions in chorus parts, technical support, speaking roles, or as the assistant stage manager. All roles and levels of participation are valued, and all students are recognized with athletic letters or listings in the program. Partial participation is grounded in what Allan Karol described as "varying degrees of direction and supervision." He suggested that all students require direction and supervision to some different extent, but the intensity of that direction and supervision varies. The ultimate goal, however, is to have each student in a role in which he or she can participate independently.

Partial participation is based on the value that "everyone plays." In addition, partial participation allows students to participate in age-appropriate activities. Walker and Edinger (1988) had several suggestions for facilitating the participation of individuals with disabilities:

- Moderators should learn about the student participants who do not have identified disabilities and provide those typical students with a way to connect with the students with disabilities. Highlighting the skills of students without identified disabilities, and using them as models and teachers, can increase the participation of students with disabilities.
- As a moderator, you may need to model interactions for the other participants and assist them in communicating with the student with disabilities. You will need to model how to respond appropriately to behavior that is not desirable during the activity.
- Interactions among the students should emerge naturally rather than the moderator trying to control what happens. Savard (1988) talked of "backing off," letting "kids be kids" (p. 40). Students without disabilities may provide cues to the students with disabilities related to expectations for behavior and participation. In the past, the guidelines for the behavior of students with disabilities have been more strict than that of students without disabilities. For example, when meeting at a park, the adolescents may run to the swing set just to swing and "mess around." The student with disabilities may be told by his or her support person that such behavior is inappropriate and that he or she is too old for such an activity. Another example is that two typical students may get into a heated argument, resolve the issue, and proceed, whereas a student with disabilities may be prevented from further participation to avoid "fighting."
- If support people are used rather than natural supports, the support person should notice and promote opportunities for interaction. Nonverbal interactions, even those as simple as sitting together, should be encouraged. The support person should only enter the interaction when needed,

however, because the presence of additional adults may make the natural interactions among students difficult.

- Moderators should provide opportunities for students to have fun, get acquainted, and increase their interpersonal attachments.

Even with partial participation, individualized and flexible support may be necessary. Partial participation can take many forms, ranging from cheering for the team, serving as a team manager, or serving a role "behind the scenes." The key to partial participation is that help is offered only when needed. As Allan Karol suggested, use as few modifications as possible. Too much visibility for support persons may create barriers between the student with disabilities and other participants (Schleien, Ray, & Green, 1997). In some situations, however, a support person may be essential for the student's full participation (e.g., a sign language interpreter for a student whose primary language is American Sign Language).

SUPPORTING STUDENT PARTICIPATION

Axelson (1986) contended that when activities are oriented around the concept of a disability, they tend to be defined by the boundaries of what the individual can currently do, rather than what they could do or what they would like to do. Allan Karol, in his role as drama coordinator, reported a similar experience. He indicated that he changed his practice of putting people into categories or expecting certain behaviors based on certain labels. Participation, rather than "participation for someone with a disability," became the key. This application of the process of normalization reported by Schleien and associates (1997) is of central importance in involving individuals with disabilities into recreation programs.

Another way of engaging students with disabilities is through a "life-skills model." Krebs and Block (1992) described this model as involving students with disabilities in real-life skills that are chronologically age appropriate, functional, and community based. They suggested the following:

- Identifying community-based sport and fitness facilities. Find places where students may continue their skill development after school or during summer vacation. This may require working with community-based facility staff, helping them support the student as he or she participates.
- Conducting an ecological inventory and discrepancy analysis of the environment in which the student is expected to function, and comparing the student's skills with those needed to perform each activity
- Determining the amount of support the student will need and identifying who will provide that support. It is important to be explicit in terms of how much support is going to be provided by whom.

- Including leisure, sports, and fitness activities in the individual transition plan for each student. Parents and other family members can help implement these goals by engaging the student in community-based activities.
- Implementing and evaluating the program

Careful, systematic planning is needed in all efforts to support students (Stainback & Stainback, 1990). As Allan Karol indicated, this involves continual consultation with other teachers, participation in individualized education program development, and working collaboratively with parents. Activity moderators and coaches may learn a great deal about the student by observing him or her in a class or during lunch. These observations may provide insights into how to increase the student's independent participation in the activity.

In addition, in some situations the moderator or coach may need to back up and teach the basic skills. As discussed previously, students with disabilities may have had limited experiences prior to high school. Identifying one sports play that the student can execute or a necessary but simple role for the student to fill in the activity or organization may be helpful. Through teaching this one play or skill, the student may be able to participate independently in some way.

As a moderator or coach, you also may need to make "everybody plays" part of your team or organization climate. Simply allowing students with disabilities to be "on the team" and "dress out" without ever playing is not an inclusive practice. Finding the appropriate role for students to actively participate may take creativity and commitment.

Natural supports remain the first choice for supporting students with disabilities. For example, if a student with a hearing impairment is playing soccer, the player nearest him or her may be responsible for gaining the student's attention so that he or she knows the whistle has blown and play must stop. The student standing next to the student with a disability on the stage may be responsible for helping the student off of the stage.

SUMMARY POINTS

- Participation in extracurricular activities is important to the development of students with and without disabilities.
- Moderators and coaches may lack experience and preparation for working with students with disabilities. In addition, students with disabilities may have had little experience in the activities in which they want to participate in high school.
- Partial participation involves students participating in an activity in a variety of ways.
- Engaging students with disabilities in extracurricular activities may require systematic planning.

- Moderators or coaches may need to modify activities to include teaching more basic skills to students with disabilities.
- Natural supports remain the first choice for supporting students with disabilities.

REFERENCES

Axelson, P.W. (1986). Facilitation of integrated recreation. In C. Sherrill (Ed.), *Sport and disabled athletes* (pp. 81–90). Champaign, IL: Human Kinetics.

Baumgart, D., Brown, L., Pumpian, I., Nisbet, J., Ford, A., Sweet, M., Messina, R., & Schroeder, J. (1982). Principle of partial participation and individualized adaptations in educational programs for severely handicapped students. *Journal of The Association for the Severely Handicapped, 7*(2), 17–27.

Blinde, E.M., & Taub, D.E. (1999). Personal empowerment through sport and physical fitness activity: Perspectives from male college students with physical and sensory disabilities. *Journal of Sport Behavior, 22*(2), 181–202.

Block, M.E. (1995). Americans with Disabilities Act: Its impact on youth sports. *Journal of Physical Education, Recreation, and Dance, 66*(1), 28–32.

Demchak, M.A. (1994). Helping individuals with severe disabilities find leisure activities. *Teaching Exceptional Children, 27*(1), 48–52.

Garton, A.F., & Pratt, C. (1991). Leisure activities of adolescent school students: Predictors of participation and interest. *Journal of Adolescence, 14,* 305–321.

Heyne, L.A. (1998). Therapeutic recreation in the schools: Teaching students to play. *TASH Newsletter, 24*(4), 10–12.

Holland, A., & Andre, T. (1987). Participation in extracurricular activities in secondary school: What is known, what needs to be known? *Review of Educational Research, 57*(4), 437–466.

Individuals with Disabilities Education Act (IDEA) Amendments of 1997, PL 105-17, 20 U.S.C. §§ 1400 *et seq.*

Kozub, F.M., & Porretta, D.L. (1997). Cutting athletes from sports teams: An issue of "ability" and "disability." *Future Focus, 17*(2), 10–13.

Kozub, F.M., & Porretta, D.L. (1998). Interscholastic coaches' attitudes toward integration of adolescents with disabilities. *Adapted Physical Activity Quarterly, 15,* 328–344.

Kraemer, B.R., Blacher, J., & Marshal, M.P. (1997). Adolescents with severe disabilities: Family, school, and community integration. *Journal of The Association for Persons with Severe Handicaps, 22*(4), 224–234.

Krebs, P.L., & Block, M.E. (1992). Transition of students with disabilities into community recreation: The role of the adapted physical educator. *Adapted Physical Activity Quarterly, 9,* 305–315.

Murtaugh, M. (1988). Achievement outside the classroom: The role of nonacademic activities in the lives of high school students. *Anthropology and Education Quarterly, 19*(4), 382–395.

Peniston, L. (1998). *Developing recreation skills in persons with learning disabilities.* Champaign, IL: Sagamore Publishing.

Rizzo, T.L., Bishop, P., Hwang, J., & Grenfel, J. (1995). Will everybody play? Attitudes of soccer coaches toward players with mild mental retardation. *Research Quarterly for Exercise and Sport, 66,* 4–87.

Savard, C. (1988). Taking part in the dream. In G. Allan Roeher Institute (Ed.), *The pursuit of leisure: Enriching the lives of people who have disabilities* (pp. 39–42). Downsview, Ontario, Canada: G. Allan Roeher Institute.

Schleien, S.J., Ray, M.T., & Green, F.P. (1997). *Community recreation and people with disabilities: Strategies for inclusion* (2nd ed.). Baltimore: Paul H. Brookes Publishing Co.

Stainback, W., & Stainback, S. (1990). *Support networks for inclusive schooling: Interdependent integrated education.* Baltimore: Paul H. Brookes Publishing Co.

Taub, D.E., & Greer, K.R. (1998). Sociology of acceptance revisited: Males with physical disabilities participating in sport and physical fitness activity. *Deviant Behavior, 19*(3), 279–302.

Walker, P. (1990). *Resources on integrated recreation/leisure opportunities for children and teens with developmental disabilities.* Syracuse, NY: Syracuse University, Center on Human Policy.

Walker, P., & Edinger, B. (1988, May). The kid from Cabin 17. *Camping Magazine,* 19–21.

Walker, P., & Shoultz, B. (1996). *Community integration report: Supporting children and youth with disabilities in integrated recreation and leisure activities.* Syracuse, NY: Syracuse University, Center on Human Policy.

York, J., Vandercook, T., & Stave, K. (1990). Recreation and leisure activities: Determining the favorites for middle school students. *Teaching Exceptional Children, 22*(4), 10–13.

13

Inclusion Is More than Disability

Experiences of Successful African American Students

Louis A. Castenell, Jr.
Rachel Davis-Haley

Public schooling in America is a primary focus of educational research. Data and research findings inform us about relationships among students, teachers, administrators, and parents. These reports and studies generally conclude that schools replicate existing social structures in terms of achievements, teacher expectations, and quality of parental involvement.

The purpose of this chapter is to describe the contextual experiences of African American students in an inclusive high school. Two graduates, one male and one female, of a high school recognized for its commitment to academic excellence and diversity, describe the impact of their high school on their lives. After reading this chapter, you will be able to answer the following questions:

- What are the real issues related to racism and education?
- What is unique about the African American male experience?
- What are the issues concerning the "invisibility" of African American females?
- What are the experiences of African American students in the schools?
- How can teachers develop the full potential of African American students?

RACISM

Racism and the resulting social inequality exist within our society and, by extension, within our schools. *Racism* can be defined as attitudes, actions, or institutional structures that subordinate a person or group because of their color (Goldberg, 1996).

Individual racism is the belief that one's race is superior to another (racial prejudice) and the subsequent behavior that suppresses members of the so-called inferior race (Ibrahim, 1996). Such racism may be based on the incorrect assumption that physical attributes of a racial group determine the social behavior of its members, as well as their psychological and intellectual characteristics (Robertson, 1987, cited in Ibrahim, 1996).

"Institutional racism consists of those established laws, customs and practices that systematically reflect and produce racial inequalities, regardless of whether the individuals maintaining those practices have racial intentions" (Ibrahim, 1996, p. 12). Perhaps the most pernicious form of institutional racism can be conceptualized as everyday racism. Essed posited that historical racial intercourse produces contemporary social interactions that reflect unequal power:

> Once we recognize that racial oppression is inherent in the nature of the social order, it becomes clear that the real racial drama is not racism but the fact that racism is an everyday problem. When…racism is transmitted in routine practices that seem "normal," at least for the dominant group, this can only mean that racism is often not recognized, not acknowledged—let alone problematized—by the dominant group. To expose racism in the system we must analyze ambiguous meanings, expose hidden currents, and generally question what seems normal, or acceptable. (1991, p. 10)

Individual and institutional acts and policies can occur with or without intent or conscious prejudice and may be based on ignorance (Knowles & Prewitt, 1969, cited in Bennet, 1993). Although it is useful to explore definitions of racism, and the different ways racism is perpetuated (e.g., individuals, institutions), it also is necessary for individuals to explore their own understanding and relationship to racism before meaningful action-oriented antiracist work can occur.

Bringelson (1996) and Frankenburg (1996) discussed how "whiteness" has been constructed as the baseline norm. They reflected on their own experiences as Caucasians. The authors concluded that "whiteness" is a position of privilege that consequentially shapes their perspectives from the views of others. The socialization of this process causes society in general to overlook cultural practices and multicultural curricula that may be important to minority cultures. "I'm just normal" is a common uncritical perception that many Caucasians who have limited contact with others possess, according to Tatum (1997).

Tatum (1997) has extensively investigated this social phenomenon. She is convinced that our national dialogue on race relations must include Caucasians who understand their racial identity before we can seriously discuss antiracist pedagogy. As Lawrence and Tatum stated, "when white teachers fail to acknowledge their own racial identity, this lack of knowledge becomes a barrier for understanding and connecting with the developmental needs of children of color" (1997, p. 163). Similarly, Caucasian teacher educators who deny their cultural status contribute to the inadequate preparation of teachers for today's classroom. Color blindness is not a virtue but a disability. Building on Helm's work (1990), Lawrence and Tatum proposed three critical steps to be completed as a necessary prelude to antiracist behavior:

1. Become aware of one's position as a Caucasian person in the social order.
2. Learn to accept this aspect as meaningful and personally salient.
3. Internalize a realistic and positive view of the self.

Teachers

Eighty percent of all teachers in America are Caucasian (Chavez, 1995). Hence, minority students can expect to be taught by a significant number of Caucasian teachers. Tettegah (1996) reported on a number of studies linking one's racial identity and values systems. She argued that one's racial identity affects the development of racial attitudes toward oneself and others; thus, racist attitudes historically noted among the general population of the United States are just as common within its teacher populations. Furthermore, these attitudes may have a significant influence on interactions between Caucasian teachers and students from different racial or ethnic backgrounds and may ultimately affect educational outcomes.

Viadero (1996) posited that whenever two distinct cultures are bumping up against one another, an invisible wall is formed that stands in the way of learning and communication. She presented evidence that predominantly Caucasian educators have been slow to recognize that their own backgrounds and the culture of the school have a bearing on learning.

In addition to knowledge and technique, one's personal qualities and character determine to a considerable degree a teachers' effectiveness in the classroom (Banner & Cannon, 1997). It is difficult for students to learn when teachers fail (intentionally or not) to embrace the worth of each and every learner regardless of differences and abilities. Students, especially those who feel or look different, are especially sensitive to the verbal and nonverbal behaviors of teachers. This becomes particularly problematic when Caucasian teachers feign color blindness, conceptualize racism as having a strictly individual pathology rather than a cultural or institutional one, and deny the existence of racism and their associated race privilege (Clarke & O'Donnell, 1999).

Identity Formation

In America, the process of identity formation is developmental and usually begins during adolescence. Identity formation for African Americans is the product of interactions among several cultural factors, cognitive developmental processes, and social experiences (Whaley, 1993). Tatum (1997) posited that an individual's identity formation is affected by the larger society's response to the various ethnic or racial groups of which these adolescents are members.

Individual adolescents often infer similar treatment toward them by virtue of their membership in the group. The process of identity formation for African American students usually begins in adolescence with an episode in which the adolescent is made aware of common racial stereotypes and cultural presumptions. This episode (e.g., being asked to leave a video store because there are too many people inside the store, being stopped by the police when driving an expensive or flashy car) triggers the evaluation, reflection, and analysis of past experiences leading adolescents to begin the life-long process of developing their identities. African American students are more influenced by their immediate cultural contexts than the context of their school culture. Whenever there is a disconnection between school culture and minority social culture, school-based communication suffers.

SCHOOL EXPERIENCES OF AFRICAN AMERICAN MALES

Nowhere is the disconnection between school culture and minority social culture more obvious than in the plight of African American male adolescents. It is nearly impossible to read any body of research literature that does not conclude that African American male adolescents are significantly lagging in achievement and "acceptable social behavior" as compared with Caucasian male adolescents and male adolescents in most other groups. In fact, they have been described as an endangered species (Gibbs, 1998). Hopkins (1997) featured a positive portrayal of African Americans' gains in recent years. The statistical reality of the lack of progress or gains for African American males is sobering. For instance, African American males were less likely to attend college in 2001 than in 1981. African American males, according to Gibbs, are perceived as young, hostile, and impulsive. Hopkins cogently concluded, "this relationship of Black males and school authority can best be characterized through the powerlessness, hopelessness, and invisibility of Black males" (1997, p. 64). Research reports, however, that African American males are part of a larger group of minority students who exercise a wider range of coping strategies than Caucasian students (Steward et al., 1998). For example, African American males were found to minimize problems by making fun, joking, talking to parents, and focusing on self-reliance. Another coping mechanism is invisibility. In addition, some of these students try to disappear by acting in a race neutral manner and privately pursuing their interests in academic gains. Fordham (1996) referred to this concept as *racelessness*.

SCHOOL EXPERIENCES OF AFRICAN AMERICAN FEMALES

Although African American males have received the bulk of writers' attention, the plight of African American females merits special attention. The experiences of the students featured in this chapter point to the importance of race and gender as critical constructs in determining the prospects of African American males and females whose individual needs and abilities may not have been met in their respective educational arenas. In reviewing the research literature relating to the experiences of African American females, we discovered that not only have African American female students been excluded and omitted from the discussion in the research literature but also their invisibility stems from the invisibility and omission of the experiences of all females in educational literature.

In the 1990s, researchers focused on African American females' experiences in American classrooms and found that they occupy more disparate academic and social locations than female members of other ethnic groups in elementary school classrooms (Grant, 1984, 1992; Irvine, 1990). Irvine (1990), for example, discovered that African American female students received less academic feedback than their male counterparts in the classroom. She further observed that African American female students in upper elementary grades were provided fewer opportunities to respond in classrooms and received less teacher feedback than female students in lower elementary grades.

The nature and amount of student–teacher interactions is an area that has been researched by Scott-Jones and Clark (1986). One-to-one student contact with teachers in most elementary, middle, and high schools seems to be reserved primarily for male students. African American girls were more likely to repeat a grade than any other cultural group and were most likely to initiate interaction with teachers. But they received less reinforcement from teachers than any other group of students in classes and often found themselves rebuffed by the teacher for their efforts (American Association of University Women, 1992). For example, African American female students were encouraged to act as "social agents" and "go betweens" in the academic environment. When African American females were provided with the rare opportunity to act as academic consumers, teachers provided them with fewer opportunities to respond and less scaffolding than other members of the class. Although African American female students did not receive academic encouragement from teachers like their Caucasian females, it was revealed that teachers sought African American female students out for nonacademic matters—running errands, cleaning up, calming other African American students, and assisting in handling disruptive African American males. The research found that Caucasian females received tasks from teachers that involved higher degrees of responsibility (Grant, 1984, 1992; Scott-Jones & Clark, 1986).

Washington's (1982) research also cast light on the school experiences and the interaction patterns of African American female students when she reported on the effects of teacher perceptions on the learner. In her study involving 64 first- and fourth-grade teachers, Washington found African American female students were not the objects of positive teacher perception. The 64 first- and fourth-grade teachers perceived Caucasian females more positively than they did African American females and in larger proportions that greatly exceeded their representation as students in integrated classrooms. More disturbing was Washington's finding that schools rewarded students on neatness, conformity, concepts of beauty, appearance, attitudes, language, and behaviors that are culturally defined by the majority group. Therefore, Caucasian students received more praise.

Ford (1993) assessed the perceptions that African American middle school students had about the achievement ideology and to what degree they believed their social, cultural, and psychological perceptions affected underachievement and overachievement. She set out to answer the following questions: To what extent do gifted African American students differ from other students in their perceptions of social, cultural, and psychological attainment of underachievement, and do these differences vary by academic programs and gender?

Ford (1993) studied perceptions because they provided real information about real influences on the lives of African American students and because this research approach provided new perspectives on students' social cognition and their interpretations of their social worlds. By directly asking students about their perceptions, Ford found little room for researchers to speculate about the causes of over- and underachievement in African American student populations. Nor was there a need to guess at why African American students tend to adopt the persona of "racelessness and acting white" in schools that were associated with the majority culture.

Most students, with the exception of gifted African American female students, reported that they received encouragement from school personnel to achieve more in school. Students believed that hard work and effort were contributors to social advancement and upward mobility. Gifted students had the highest belief in the achievement ideology. Gifted African American females were more optimistic than were average and above average students when responding to the following statement, "I worry about kids teasing me when I do my best in school." These results point to the paradox that African American students believed in the achievement ideology but did not necessarily put forth the effort to achieve academically in school.

Grant (1984, 1992) also provided information about the status of African American females in academic arenas. In her study, Caucasian female students were presented with numerous positive opportunities to demonstrate their academic skills. However, African American female students viewed their academic experiences negatively because of the lack of emphasis placed on their academic progress. Follow-up discussions on these findings with teachers revealed the existence of a fixation on the social experiences of African American females rather than on their academic progress (Ayers, 1992; Grant, 1984, 1992; Jeffries, 1993; Philipsen, 1993; Sims, 1983).

To gain insight into why African American and Hispanic females tended to have fewer opportunities to respond and participate in classroom learning activities, Ayers (1992) studied the participation and achievement of Virginia's secondary African American and Hispanic female students in mathematics, science, and advanced technologies. He found that these students were provided with fewer opportunities to respond and got less encouragement to be active participants in classroom academics. A question facing today's educators is what can be done to improve educational opportunities for African American and Hispanic females?

In "Those Loud Black Girls: (Black) Women, Silence, and Gender in the Academy," Fordham (1993) found that invisibility and silence were traits that African American girls adopted at Capital High to cope with their positions in the academy. Their silence supported the claim of invisibility:

> The most salient characteristic of the academically successful female at Capital High is a deliberate silence, a controlled response to their evolving, ambiguous status as academically successful students. . . . Developing and using this strategy at the high school level enables high achieving African American females to deflect the latent and not too latent hostility and anger that might be directed at them were they to be both highly visible and academically successful. Invisibility is a highly valued prerequisite for academic success. (Fordham, 1993, p. 17)

Although African Americans typically have been educated in American Catholic schools only since the 1950s, evidence reveals that African American students in Catholic schools fare better academically than their public school counterparts (York, 1996). In a review entitled "The Academic Achievement of African Americans in Catholic Schools: A Review of the Literature," York painted a picture of the status of minority students who are enrolled in Catholic schools. Despite the limited number of research studies focusing on their academic experiences, York's review revealed achievement gains in African American students resulting from controlled environments and strong family support.

York's (1996) review revealed that minority students had higher achievement gains as students enrolled in Catholic schools than their public school counterparts. Catholic schools with the largest enrollment of African American students are located in the Southeast, Midwest, and the Great Lakes regions of the United States and tend to have smaller class sizes. African American students enrolled in Catholic schools also had fewer attendance and discipline referrals when compared with their public school counterparts. African American students enrolled in Catholic schools made greater gains on achievement measures in both college preparatory programs and vocational programs. York's review also revealed that African American students enrolled in Catholic schools are more likely to continue attending Catholic schools than any other students, even if their parents, who tend to be non-Catholic, have vastly different incomes. Parents of African American Catholic school students tend to be more educated than their public school counterparts. York found that when studying African American students' achievement in Catholic schools, researchers chose to study school factors. They seemed to be less interested in how family factors contributed to students' success.

Although the research on African American students educated in Catholic contexts is scarce and suggests a more supportive and enhanced learning experience, little is written about the actual school experiences of African American students. The remainder of this chapter describes two African American students' experiences in one Catholic high school.

AFRICAN AMERICAN STUDENT EXPERIENCE

The two students featured in this section were in their third year of undergraduate studies at a private, historically black university in the southeastern United States when this chapter was written. Both students matriculated through high school in the advanced and college preparatory tracks and are children of well-educated, middle- to upper-income families. The female student (Brittney) is a biology-premed student and her male classmate (Charles) is an English major. Both students report having at least a B average and both have plans for postbaccalaureate schooling.

Each student participated in an in-depth interview. The taped interviews were transcribed and analyzed by the co-investigators to uncover the students' experiences while enrolled as high school students. The analysis and interpretation process consisted of reading and examining the interview data and formulating tentative assertions. These tentative assertions were tested against the interview transcripts in a hermeneutic cycle (i.e., an interpretive process in which the data collected is continual analyzed, interpreted, and explained) that resulted in the emergence of two constructions of one possible view of the experiences of these students. Several themes and assertions that gave insight into the experiences of Brittney and Charles were constructed after a careful analysis of the data. As the data analysis revealed, the students' experiences fell into two categories: social and academic. Academically, Brittney and Charles reported that they were achievers and were supported by teachers. When asked if they felt free to respond in the school environment and whether their teachers actively assisted and answered their questions, Brittney responded, "Yes, for the most part, my personality made me ask questions whenever I didn't understand something. Some teachers may have felt strained to move on, but I felt like a lot of questions I did ask were ones that the other people had. If a lot of money was being paid for my education, I was going to take the time to get the concepts. Most of my teachers were very responsive to my questions." Charles also agreed that the teachers were responsive and reported that he felt comfortable going to them for help when necessary.

When asked if diversity was welcomed, they were hesitant but both responded yes. Both Brittney and Charles agreed that they felt the school's administration wanted to make sure that students learned about other cultures but that the administration was unsure of how to go about making this a reality. They believed that the administration (e.g., teachers, counselors, principal) was open and responsive to diversity, but left the responsibility of disseminating the information to the students. In other words, the African American and Hispanic students were responsible for teaching the majority Caucasian students about diversity.

When asked whether the students talked about non-Caucasian cultures in classes, Brittney responded, "Yes, especially when every other page would say, 'nigger, nigger'. . . . That caused a lot of controversy [here she is responding to a class assignment in which they read the novel *The Adventures of Huckleberry Finn*]. . . .That was American literature class. The surprising thing was that my teacher wasn't shocked because it was a traditional book that everybody read. He didn't understand why I didn't want to read a book that said, 'nigger, nigger, nigger.'" She further stated that the teacher then threw the ball into her hands after seeing how upset she was. He instructed the African American students in her class to devise a project in which they were to deal with the controversy of the book. They earned extra credit for the project, but the students created the project. Charles responded, "Yes, we did surveys that we talked about people's opinions about the book. I remember some of the people being really disturbed about some of the comments and some which basically conveyed an attitude of 'we don't care.' Which I guess was a teenage thing. It seemed like the teacher thought it was a good idea to do something creative with a controversial idea." Brittney added, "I think that was his tension.... The project started out with getting some newspapers and magazine articles and reading about it. We took it to another level by doing a survey and relaying how we felt personally about it. And that added a little bit, something he wasn't expecting."

Although the students reported that the administration was supportive of the ideas of inclusion, they were disappointed that they were responsible for creating the activities and bringing awareness to the faculty and staff. The faculty wasn't aware of the inappropriateness and offensiveness of some passages of *The Adventures of Huckleberry Finn*. An interview with one of the parents also revealed an administration that was interested in diversity but was at times challenged by lack of information and the complexity of the school environment.

IMPLICATIONS FOR TEACHERS

In view of the literature and the perceptions of African American students and their parents, several implications emerge:

1. Teachers must be open to the perceptions of parents and students. Parents of African American students can make significant contributions in terms of helping faculty and administrators understand their experiences and that of their children. Race must be as open a topic as disability, gender, or other issues that affect the way the school works. Teachers and ad-

ministrators should recognize their own limits, and not be intimidated by educated, assertive African American families. Teachers and administrators may need to admit the limits of their own education and experience, and recognize the significant contribution that these families may make.

2. Adhering to majority culture practices may have the unintended effect of cultural and intellectual genocide. Given Charles and Brittney's raw talent, they were underachievers—they had parents who were educated, committed, involved, parents who were concerned that their children were not achieving to their fullest potential. For example, their parents wanted to see counselors forge new relationships with many competitive institutions of learning (on behalf of their children) and encourage their children to apply to these institutions and to do their best to qualify for admission to these schools. The significant role of parents and family in the success of African American students should be recognized.

3. Teachers must be aware of identity formation in African American students. Teachers must take a leadership role in class discussions pertaining to race relations and accept input from African American families, avoiding any sense of "racelessness."

SUMMARY POINTS

- Racism exists on an individual and institutional level and may occur with or without intent.
- Educators from the majority culture may be slow to recognize that their own backgrounds and the culture of the school have a bearing on the learning of their African American students.
- Although the media and research has explored the significant educational issues related to African American males, African American females have been "invisible."
- Teachers must take a leadership role in class discussions pertaining to race relations and accept input from African American families, avoiding any sense of "racelessness."

REFERENCES

American Association of University Women Educational Foundation & the Wellesley College Center for Research on Women. (1992). *How schools shortchange girls: The AAUW report. A study of major findings on girls and education.* New York: Marlowe & Co.

Ayers, D. (1992). *A study of the participation and achievement of black, Hispanic and female students in mathematics, science and advanced technologies in Virginia secondary schools.* Richmond: Virginia Department of Education.

Banner, J., & Cannon, H. (1997). The personal qualities of teaching: What teachers do cannot be distinguished from who they are. *Change, 29*(6), 39–42.

Bennett, L., Jr. (1993). *The shaping of black America* (Rev. ed.). New York: Penguin Books.

Bringelson, C. (1996). Do you see what I see? Viewing racism through white teachers narratives. In C.A. Grant (Ed.), *National Association for Multicultural Education proceedings* (pp. 101–105). San Francisco: Caddo Gap Press.

Chavez, R.C. (1995). *Multicultural education in the everyday: A renaissance for the recommitted.* Washington, DC: AACTE Publications.

Clarke, C., & O'Donnell, J. (1999). *Becoming and unbecoming white: Owning and disowning racial identity.* Westport, CT: Bergin & Garvey.

Essed, P. (1991). *Understanding everyday racism: An interdisciplinary hearing.* Thousand Oaks, CA: Sage Publications.

Ford, D.Y. (1993). Support for the achievement ideology and determinants of underachievement as perceived by gifted, above-average, and average black students. *Journal for the Education of the Gifted, 16*(3), 280–298.

Fordham, S. (1993). "Those loud black girls": (Black) women, silence, and gender "passing" in the academy. *Anthropology and Education Quarterly, 24*(1), 3–32.

Fordham, S. (1996). *Blacked out: Dilemmas of race, identity, and success at Capital High.* Chicago: Chicago Press.

Frankenburg, R. (1996). When we are capable of stopping we begin to see: Being white, seeing whiteness. In B. Thompson & S. Tyagi (Eds.), *Names we call home: Autobiography on racial identity* (pp. 127–148). New York: Routledge.

Gibbs, J.T. (1998). *Young, black, and male in America: An endangered species.* Dover, MA: Auburn House.

Goldberg, D. (1996). *Anatomy of racism.* Minneapolis: University of Minnesota Press.

Grant, L. (1984). Black females' "place" in desegregated classrooms. *Sociology of Education, 57*(2), 98–111.

Grant, L. (1992). Race and the schooling of black girls. In J. Wrigley (Ed.), *Education and gender equity* (pp. 91–113). Bristol, PA: Falmer Press.

Helm, J.E. (1990). *Black and white racial identity: Theory, research, and practice.* Westport, CT: Greenwood Publishing Group.

Hopkins, R. (1997). *Educating black males: Critical lessons in schooling, community, and power.* Albany: State University of New York.

Ibrahim, A.M. (1996). *Racism in Canadian schools.* Toronto: Harcourt Brace.

Irvine, J.J. (1990). *Black students and school failure: Policies, practices, and prescriptions.* Westport, CT: Greenwood Publishing Group.

Jeffries, R.B. (1993). To go or not to go: Rural African American students' perspectives about their education. *Journal of Negro Education, 62*(4), 427–433.

Lawrence, S.M., & Tatum, B.D. (1997). Teachers in transition: The impact of antiracist professional development on classroom practice. *Teachers College Record, 99*(1), 162–178.

Philipsen, M. (1993). Values-spoken and values-lived: Female African Americans' educational experiences in rural North Carolina. *Journal of Negro Education, 62*(4), 419–426.

Scott-Jones, D., & Clark, M.L. (1986). The schooling experiences of black girls: The interaction of gender, race, and socioeconomic status. *Phi Delta Kappan, 67*(7), 520–526.

Sims, R. (1983). Strong black girls: A ten year old responds to fiction about Afro-Americans. *Journal of Research and Development in Education, 16*(3), 21–28.

Steward, R.J., Jo, H.I., Murray, D., Fitzgerald, W., Neil, D., Fear, F., & Hill, M. (1998). Psychological adjustment and coping styles of urban African American high school students. *Journal of Multicultural Counseling and Development, 26,* 70–82.

Tatum, B.D. (1997). *Why are all the black kids sitting together in the cafeteria?: And other conversations about race.* New York: Basic Books.

Tettegah, S. (1996). The racial consciousness attitudes of white prospective teachers

and their perceptions of the teachability of students from different racial/ethnic backgrounds: Findings from a California study. *Journal of Negro Education, 65*(2), 151–163.

Viadero, D. (1996). Culture clash. *Education Week*, 39–42.

Virginia Department of Education. (1992). *A study of the participation and achievement of
black, hispanic, and female students in a mathematics, science, and advanced technologies in Virginia secondary schools.* Richmond: Author. (ERIC Document Reproduction Service
No. ED 354 296)

Washington, V. (1982). Racial differences in teachers perceptions of first and fourth
grade pupils on selected characteristics. *Journal of Negro Education, 51*(1), 60–72.

Whaley, A. (1993). Self-esteem, cultural identity and psychosocial adjustment in African American children. *Journal of Black Psychology, 19*(4), 406–442.

York, D.E. (1996). The academic achievement of African Americans in Catholic
schools: A review of the literature. In J.J. Irvine & M. Foster (Eds.), *Growing up African American in Catholic schools* (pp. 11–46). New York: Teachers College Press.

14

Where Do Students Go After High School?

Anne M. Bauer

Teacher Contributors: Doug Kennedy, Karen Matuszek, Margaret Jenkins

Many students consider the completion of high school as the beginning of their adult life. Public education ends. Students are confronted with choosing vocational training, furthering their academic education, getting a job, and living independently. Unfortunately, secondary education has not been adequate for many students to make the transition to independence and adulthood (Blackorby & Wagner, 1996). These choices are even more difficult for students with disabilities and require even more planning. In addition, there are legal requirements related to this planning for students with disabilities (National Information Center for Children and Youth with Disabilities [NICHCY], 1999a).

One of the primary purposes of the Individuals with Disabilities Education Act (IDEA) of 1990 (PL 101-476) is to "ensure that all children with disabilities have available to them a free appropriate public education that emphasizes special education and related services designed to meet their unique needs and prepare them for employment and independent living" (20 U.S.C. §§ 1401, 300.1[a]). Section 300.347(b) requires that, beginning no later than age 14, each student's individualized education program (IEP) include specific transition-related content and, beginning no later than age 16, a statement of needed transition services. Unfortunately, this attention is not given to many students without identified disabilities. High schools often direct most of their efforts toward the 25% of students who will graduate from college (Peters, 1994). Students who do not plan to pursue a 4-year degree after college often are placed in a "general track," and expectations for their academic achievement tend to be low. Although concerns may emerge about students who are not college-bound, even successful students are sometimes stymied by changes when they leave high school (Paris, 1995).

After reading this chapter, you will be able to answer the following questions:

- What are transition services plans?
- What are some issues and tensions that emerge during the transition from school to work and the community?
- How can you support parents and students in confronting the transition to work?

TRANSITION SERVICES PLANS

Although we discuss transition for all students later in this chapter, we begin with the legal mandates for students with identified disabilities. The Individuals with Disabilities Education Act Amendments (IDEA) of 1997 (PL 105-17) defined transition services as

> A set of coordinated activities that is: Outcome oriented, promoting movement from school to post school activities, including postsecondary education, vocational training, integrated employment (including supported employment), continuing and adult education, adult services, independent living, or community participation; based on individual student needs; includes instruction, related services, community experiences, and the development of employment and other post school adult living objectives; and inclusive of daily living skills and functional evaluation if appropriate. (20 U.S.C. §§1401[30], Sec. 300.29)

Special education may be a transition service if it is provided as specially designed instruction or related services required to assist a student with a disability to benefit from special education.

Transition plans become an issue for students when they reach 14 years of age, and services are to be in place when the student reaches 16 years of age. Transition services may not all be designed and implemented by the school; public agencies may participate, and the plan should include each participating agency's responsibilities or linkages before the student leaves the school setting. The annual goals (including benchmarks or short-term objectives) and services for a student must include the instruction and educational experiences that will assist the student to prepare for transition from secondary education to postsecondary life (NICHCY, 1999b).

Borgen and Amundson (1995) identified several strategies for designing transition plans that support students in a smoother transition:

- *Developing multiple plans.* Most young people leave high school with a narrow plan of action and few alternatives. Students should learn to have flexible thinking to assess their options.
- *Developing self-advocacy and marketing skills:* Students need strong communication skills, self-confidence, and the ability to adapt to organizations.
- *Managing changing relationships.* Adolescents are challenged by the emotional and social changes that surround them. The friends who provided support

also are moving on. Parents are needed for emotional, material, and information support, but young people may view parents as a challenge to their own sense of identity.

- *Meeting basic needs.* Young people have strong needs for community, a sense of meaning, physical and emotional security, and basic structure in their relationships and living. Young people need help in identifying how they are meeting their current and future needs.

- *Coping with stress.* Adolescence is stressful. Adolescents seem, by their own nature, to find themselves in difficult situations. Strategies for stress management, including relaxation techniques, positive "self-talk," and use of support systems, should be taught.

- *Coping with loss.* Young people are influenced by various personal losses involving a death in the family, parental separation, and divorce. Borgen and Amundson (1995) argued that adolescents need help in handling loss and grieving.

- *Designing bridging programs.* Many young people have little "hands-on" experience as they attempt to enter employment. Many are afraid of moving into postsecondary education or training programs.

- *Providing information and information access.* Information about careers and employment is changing at a rapid rate. Students must have relevant information, and the skills to assess the information.

NICHCY (1993) argued that transition plans should include information from each of these domains: 1) employment; 2) postsecondary educational activities; 3) independent living; 4) eligibility for various adult services; and 5) community participation, including recreation and leisure activities. These areas may be assessed through a variety of questions (see Table 14.1).

Karen Matuszek suggested that, consistent with legal mandates, transition planning should begin when students begin high school. She described a general framework for students with identified disabilities. When students are freshmen, observations and student interest inventories are used to begin to identify student preferences. As sophomores, students take a career exploration course one semester, in which individuals from the community describe various jobs, followed by a one-semester course in independent living. In addition, sophomores complete a formal interest and aptitude survey. As juniors, students are assigned a work-study job on campus, with efforts to meet students' interests. For example, students may work in the cafeteria, the office, or the book depository, with supervisors completing a quarterly evaluation. Through these jobs, students generate a portfolio and build their résumés.

There is a particular emphasis on the transition to work for seniors. Although agency turnover and the overlap of agencies presents a challenge, transition ideas include plans generated by the student, parent, teacher, and community-based programs. All seniors participate in a 3-week community-based work evaluation and explore career choices at a community work re-

Table 14.1.   Questions for the assessment of transition plan areas

Domain	Assessment questions
Employment	In what type of work is the student interested?
	Considering the nature of the student's disability and his or her job interests, is competitive or supported employment more appropriate?
	If the student is interested in a particular occupation, does he or she have the skills and abilities needed to succeed?
	Does the student know what employee behaviors are considered important for successful employment and does he or she demonstrate them?
	What school activities are needed for the student to acquire these work-related skills and behaviors?
	What programs are needed for the student to acquire these skills and behaviors before he or she exits high school?
	What accommodations might be needed on the job?
	Does the student need to learn effective study habits?
	Are there job tryouts that would be helpful?
	Are arrangements or accommodations needed during college board or SAT testing?
Postsecondary educational activities	What postsecondary institutions offer the training or education desired?
	What accommodations and support services are needed?
	What postsecondary institutions make the appropriate supports available?
Independent living	Where will the student live?
	What daily living skills are still needed in the areas of personal hygiene, household chores, shopping, and managing finances?
Eligibility for adult services	For what services may the student be eligible?

source center. Students participate in community-based workshops in self-sufficiency and self-advocacy. By the time students are seniors, they have completed consumer science courses available to all students. Examples of consumer science courses are 1) school to career, 2) resource management, 3) parenting, and 4) financial planning. In addition, seniors participate in one semester of "Jobs for Cincinnati Graduates" (a school-to-work program described later in this chapter) and complete a semester of community service to add to their résumés. Students participate in part-time jobs in the community.

When they are seniors, students meet with directors of vocational education programs. Within this structure, individualized transition plans are described in each student's IEP.

ISSUES AND TENSIONS THAT EMERGE DURING THE TRANSITION FROM SCHOOL TO WORK AND THE COMMUNITY

The transition from school to work and the community does not bode well for students with disabilities. The Harris Survey (Louis Harris & Associates, 1998) on the current status of Americans with disabilities reported significant gaps between the employment rates of individuals with and without disabilities. Only 29% of individuals with disabilities of working age (18–64 years) worked full or part time, compared with 79% of individuals without disabilities. About one third (34%) of adults with disabilities lived in households with total incomes of $15,000 or less, compared with 12% of those without disabilities. One in five individuals failed to complete high school, compared with one in ten of individuals without disabilities. Among adults with disabilities who worked full time, fewer than one half (46%) said that their work requires them to use their full talents or abilities, and 47% indicated that the jobs they can get don't pay enough. Only about one in three (33%) adults with disabilities was very satisfied with their quality of life, as compared to 61% of adults without disabilities. This gap has widened since 1996.

Functional Versus Academic Curricula

One of the arguments against inclusion for students with disabilities in secondary school is related to the need for individuals with disabilities to learn functional rather than academic skills. Supporters of inclusive secondary schools, however, question the need, or even the right, to separate students with disabilities for these programs. Stainback, Stainback, and Stefanich (1996) recognized that one set of objectives in academic classes can't be expected to meet the unique learning needs of all students—the knowledge that can be gained is of value. They suggested that "there is more to life for anyone than learning only to make a sandwich or sweep a floor" (p. 15). Stainback and associates argued that we are underestimating and limiting students by assuming that the only things that they can learn are those that are useful to them. In addition, they suggested that separating students creates a subgroup that shares few common experiences and understandings with the people with whom they are expected to live, play, and work in the community.

Shapiro-Barnard (1998) also supported the need for inclusion over separate, functional programs. She argued that the only place where students with disabilities can learn what they need to in order to live in the community is in the general education classroom. She contended that functional programs link the student's disability with the student's access to knowledge, which is an unsound educational practice.

Consumer science and career exploration courses, which are open to all students, can be a significant means of including all students in an appropriate curriculum. The course in life planning, taught by Margaret Jenkins, is an example of coursework that provides support to students in their transition from school to work and in the community. Through this course, students develop a life-management plan and explore life choices and personal strengths and limitations. An emphasis is on short-term and long-term personal goals, and changes that may have an impact on those goals and life-management plans. Students explore the use of time, money, and resources, and develop a set of criteria for evaluating their choices. A particular emphasis in the course is taking personal responsibility for life choices. Examples of the questions that students explore are provided in Table 14.2.

THE ROLE OF PARENTS

Students with disabilities are required by law to receive transition services. In planning the type of transition services, the IEP team considers options such as postsecondary education, vocational training, employment, independent living, and community participation. The services are meant to be a coordinated set of activities based on the student's needs. In addition, these services must take into account the student's preferences. Tension may arise from differences of opinions between parent and student.

IDEA '97 more clearly delineated the transfer of parents' rights to the student when he or she reaches the age of majority under state law. Both parents and students must be notified of the rights that will be transferred at that time, with students receiving notification at least 1 year before they reach the age of majority. A statement must be included in the IEP that the student has been informed of these transferred rights. After the student reaches the age of majority, the school must provide any notices required by law, such as a notice regarding upcoming IEP meetings, to both the student and the parents. In many states, however, all rights transfer, and parents receive no further information. If the student is found to be incompetent under state law, rights remain with the parents or the appointed guardian. IDEA '97 recognizes that not all students may be able to provide informed consent with respect to their educational program even though they have not been determined to be incompetent under state law. States have procedures for appointing parents or another individual to represent the student's educational interests. This transfer of rights is a big step, and parents and students need to be prepared (NICHCY, 1999a). Although parents may not be legally responsible for decisions related to transitions when their children reach the age of majority, Izzo and Shumate (1991) made a strong argument for their active involvement. They argued that parents do the following:

Table 14.2.   Questions explored by students during a life planning course

Personal development	What are my interests, skills, and resources?
	What is most important to me as a person?
	Long-term goals: What would I like to work toward this year? In 5 years? 10 years? 20 years?
	Short-term goals: What can I do toward my long-term goals today? This week? This month? This year?
	Resources: What resources will I need to take action? How can I best use the resources I have?
	How can I improve or cultivate resources?
Interpersonal relationships	What are the characteristics of the relationships I would like to have with others?
	In what settings will relationships be important?
Family	What contributions do I want to make to a family?
	What are the characteristics of family relationships I would like to establish?
Wellness	What is my present level of wellness?
	What can I do to improve or work toward good health?
Education	What are my present goals with regard to education?
	How can I continue learning throughout life?
Career	What career best matches my interests, skills, and needs?
	What steps can I take to achieve my career goal?
Financial	What level of financial resources will I need?
	What values will guide my financial decisions?
Community	What contributions would I like to make to the community?
	What resources do I have to contribute?

- Know their children better than anyone else and are critical resources in planning
- Can be effective in maintaining continuity of training
- Serve as advocates, often getting things done that professionals desire but are constrained to accomplish
- Can act as role models
- Can act as a community support

- Can coordinate services for their child, ensuring more effective and positive results
- Serve as nurturers and caregivers to provide support and encouragement

Parents may have a difficult time during the students' secondary school years as they begin to realize that their dreams of independence and postsecondary education for their children may not be realized. Karen Matuszek suggested that parents sometimes have a difficult time accepting recommendations for options that do not include full-time competitive employment. Ongoing communication through meetings, conferences, and materials may assist parents in identifying positive goals for their children.

Self-Determination

Self-determination and self-advocacy skills are necessary for students as they make the transition from school to work or the community. NICHCY (1993) suggested that four fundamental skills related to self-determination and self-advocacy for students include

1. The ability to assess themselves, including their skills and abilities, and the needs associated with their disability
2. Awareness of the accommodations that they need because of their disability
3. Knowledge of their rights through legislation such as the Americans with Disabilities Act (ADA) of 1990 (PL 101-336) and Section 504 of the Rehabilitation Act of 1973 (PL 93-112)
4. The self-advocacy skills necessary to express their needs in the workplace, in educational institutions, and in community environments

The supportive, inclusive high school may in itself prove a challenge to students as they begin to serve as their own advocates. Students may identify their desire for a competitive job, and in fact be hired. They may refuse a job coach and be fired. Unfortunately, for some students, it takes a few failures for them to realize that recognizing their own needs for support is as important for them as "calling the shots" in their own lives.

SUPPORTING STUDENTS AND PARENTS IN CONFRONTING THE TRANSITION TO WORK

There are several first steps that each individual can make regarding transition. Students may begin by writing down long-term goals and monitoring their IEP and transition plans. Students should learn about their disability, learn how to explain their strengths to people, and learn to request reasonable accommodations. Family members can observe their child's independent living skills, work behaviors, social involvement, and dreams and hopes. They can actively seek information by calling their child's teacher, looking in the telephone directory, and working on financial planning. In addition, parents can help the child learn about his or her disability, give him or her chores at home, and role-play different situations. Teachers should talk with students and families about transition services, and they should teach students about their rights under the law. In addition, teachers need to prepare their students with simple activities that will familiarize them with the IEP process and prepare them as full participants (NICHCY, 1999a).

Transition plans are developed by a team, and describe services from a wide range of professionals and individuals. Students and parents, however, continue to have their primary contact with teachers. Secondary teachers can help ease the transition for secondary students through a variety of practices. These practices, described by Cicamanec and Boston (1996), include

- Structuring classroom activities to integrate academic skills with skills required for successful employment
- Providing information about careers and school-to-work opportunities to parents and students, and helping them make their decisions based on their interests and aptitude
- Forming partnerships with business people, technical workers, and others from the public and private sectors to provide resources and enhance classroom activities
- Broadening their knowledge of various vocations and providing contextual learning activities for students
- Assessing students' knowledge and skills in a variety of ways

As discussed previously, family involvement in the transition to work is essential. Whitney-Thomas and Hanley-Maxwell (1996) found that as the transition approaches, parents of students with disabilities feel greater discomfort and pessimism than do parents of students without disabilities. They have a less positive vision, and the transition may be as problematic for parents as it is for the students. Students themselves, however, report that family involvement in their transition is important to them (Morningstar, Turnbull, & Turnbull, 1995). Morningstar and associates found that students reported that parents and extended family members influence their career vision. Students expressed a desire to live close to their families and a need to use their families rather than professionals as role models. A critical theme that emerged was a lack of systematic attention to the process of planning for the future, with the majority of students identifying family members as their support during the transition process. Students reported that they are seeking autonomy in making certain kinds of decisions but also desire ongoing support from their families. Devlieger and Trach (1999) reported similar results of parents and focus people being more involved in transition than agency personnel.

When school and agency efforts were employed, placement often resulted in sheltered employment, whereas personal or parental efforts resulted more often in self-employment and continuing education.

In recognition of the need to engage individuals with disabilities and their families in the transition process, personal futures planning has emerged. Personal futures planning recognizes that the individual with a disability and his or her family should be engaged in determining the services and supports needed and wanted (Mount, 1992). Making Action Plans (MAPs; formerly known as the McGill Action Planning System; Vandercook, York, & Forest, 1989) is a personal futures planning process in which the primary emphasis is on the involvement of students with disabilities in the school community. MAPs is structured around seven key questions that structure planning:

- What is the student's history?
- What is the dream or vision for the student?
- What is the nightmare–the least desirable outcome–for the student?
- Who is the student?
- What are the student's strengths, gifts, and abilities?
- What are the student's needs?
- What would be the student's ideal day, and what must be done to make this happen?

Rather than being based on the curriculum or the special education program, MAPs bases educational planning on a vision for the student. This personal futures planning becomes a lifestyle planning process in which the student's desirable future, necessary activities and supports, and developing resources are needed (O'Brien & Lyle, 1997). The quality of life for the student is measured through 1) the student's presence in the community, 2) the amount of choice given the student, 3) the student's competence, 4) respect given to the student, and 5) student participation in the process and community.

Hutchins and Renzaglia (1998) suggested the use of interviews to explore concerns and issues related to current and future vocational instruction and experiences. The interview contains six sets of questions:

1. *Parental expectations* questions help identify family members' attitudes and goals for future employment for their child. Specific questions involve the student's current responsibilities at home, interest in student employment, where the student will live after graduation, resources available, and the amount of time the family wishes the child to spend on a job.
2. *Experiences and preference* questions focus on work experiences and family perceptions of the student's satisfaction and success in those experiences.
3. *Personal needs* questions gather information about the personal care or communication needs of the child.

4. *Family support* questions discuss the family's role, such as parents' assuming responsibility for reporting absences or monitoring personal appearance.
5. *Transportation issues,* discussed next, often appear to be a primary barrier for gaining access to and maintaining long-term employment. Parents are asked to indicate where they live and where they anticipate the child will live after graduation.
6. *Wages and benefits* questions should also be addressed during vocational education.

The use of this interview prevents professionals from making assumptions about student and family wishes related to employment.

Community Services

A wide array of services and community agencies may be included in the student's transition plan. One of the most common agencies is the vocational rehabilitation agency. Vocational rehabilitation agencies, funded by federal and state money, have their own criteria for eligibility, and not all students receiving special education may be able to receive vocational rehabilitation services. Some of the services that vocational rehabilitation may be able to provide to students are presented in Table 14.3.

In addition to vocational rehabilitation services, there often are specific service agencies for students with mental retardation or mental health concerns. These agencies provide specific services, often on a sliding payment

Table 14.3.   Common services of vocational rehabilitation agencies

Employment services	Vocational guidance and counseling
	Assessments (e.g., medical, psychological, vocational) to determine vocational potential
	Job development, placement, and follow up
	Technological services and adaptive devices, tools, equipment, and supplies
Postsecondary services	Apprenticeship programs, often sponsored by Departments of Labor
	Vocational training
	College training toward a vocational goal
Adult and independent living services	Housing or transportation supports needed to maintain employment
	Interpreters
	Orientation and mobility training

scale. These programs may assist individuals in supported and sheltered employment, or in competitive employment with assistance. These agencies provide a greater emphasis on independent living services, often providing case management, therapeutic recreation, respite care, and residential services.

Independent living centers are community-based agencies typically run by individuals with disabilities and are available in most large urban areas. Although some programs do have a fee, independent living centers usually provide advocacy and independent living services at no cost. They may provide information and referral services regarding employment and postsecondary education and assist students in identifying mentors with disabilities. In addition, they often provide advocacy training, peer counseling, housing assistance, training in skills of independent living (e.g., attendant management, housing, transportation, career development) and information and referral services.

The Social Security Administration also is often involved as students move toward independence. These federally funded programs are often of great support for individuals with more severe disabilities. Several programs are available for people with disabilities, including Social Security Disability Insurance (SSDI) and Supplemental Security Income (SSI). SSDI benefits are paid to individuals with disabilities apparent before the age of 22 if at least one of their parents had worked a certain amount of time and paid Social Security taxes but now has a disability, is retired, or is deceased (National Association of State Directors of Special Education, 1990). SSI provides funding to individuals who are in financial need and have a disability. When a child reaches the age of 18, the Social Security Administration no longer considers the income and resources of parents when determining if the child is eligible for benefits. Under SSI, individuals older than 18 are eligible to receive monthly payments if they 1) have little or no income or resources, 2) are considered to have a medical disability or are blind, and 3) earn less than a certain amount (NICHCY, 1994). Social Security may provide work incentive programs, including case benefits while working, Medicare or Medicaid, or help with extra work expenses. Postsecondary services include financial incentives for further education and training.

School-to-Work Initiatives

The School-to-Work Opportunities Act of 1994 (PL 103-239) was enacted to establish a national framework for development of school-to-work opportunities. Congress found that three fourths of secondary students in the United States enter the work force without baccalaureate degrees, and many without entry-level occupational skills. Unemployment is high, and earnings of high school graduates have been falling relative to earnings of individuals with more education. In the changing workplace, the act was designed to support students in achieving high academic and occupational standards. In addition, it allows students to acquire the knowledge, skills, abilities, and information about and access to the labor market to make a successful transition from school to work or to further their education and training. This act was designed to increase opportunities for all students to participate in a performance-based education and training program that

- Enables students to earn portable credentials, licenses, and certificates that move with them from job to job or state to state, preparing them for first jobs in high-skill, high-wage careers
- Facilitates the creation of a universal, high-quality, school-to-work transition system
- Uses workplaces as active learning environments and makes employers joint partners in education
- Promotes the formation of local partnerships linking the worlds of school and work
- Helps all students attain high academic and occupational standards
- Integrates academic and occupational learning
- Motivates students by providing enriched learning experiences and assistance in obtaining good jobs
- Exposes students to a broad array of career opportunities
- Increases opportunities for minorities, women, and individuals with disabilities by enabling them to prepare for careers that are not traditional for their race, gender, or disability.

"Jobs for Cincinnati Graduates" is such a school-to-work program. Doug Kennedy, the vocational specialist for the program, builds a 2-year relationship with program participants. The specific goals of "Jobs for Cincinnati Graduates" include

- Offering seniors the opportunity to make a commitment to their future careers
- Maintaining regular contact with employers to explore and develop opportunities to assist in meeting hiring needs
- Offering training, counseling, placement, and follow up with the guidance of employment specialists
- Developing employability skills and positive attitudes that employers have identified as a priority
- Encouraging initiative, leadership skills, and community responsibility through membership in the student-run Cincinnati Career Association
- Providing continuous follow up for 1 year after graduation to assure a successful school-to-work transition and job retention

"Jobs for Cincinnati Graduates" is a three-part program in which 40–45 seniors participate during their entire senior year and for 1 full year after graduation. All students participate in a nonacademic elective class that involves training workshops addressing career development, employability, and workplace survival skills. In addition, students are members of the Purcell Marian Career Association, which focuses on career development and civic, social, and community service activities. In terms of follow-up activities, graduates are contacted monthly (weekly if they are still seeking employment) to provide a successful transition from high school to college, vocational school, work, or the military. Job placement assistance is provided and résumés are updated. Graduates' employees are regularly contacted. A sample of the employability skills developed through the workshop class are included in Table 14.4.

Bailey and Merritt (1997) suggested that school-to-work initiatives are beneficial to all students—including those who are college-bound. They indicated that these programs help students clarify their personal goals and identify their purpose for going to college. In addition, they broaden and inform students' choices for careers, and help students develop self-confidence by giving them learning responsibilities in the broader community outside of school. School-to-work programs boost students' earning power by giving them some work-based learning experience, and offering hands-on learning opportunities.

There are, however, several barriers to these initiatives. Brown (1998) argued that attitude is a major stumbling block. Some employers lack confidence that their involvement with schools will be cost effective, and are discouraged by the costs of bringing students into the organization and training. Not all parents are receptive to removing their sons and daughters from familiar school classes to adult workplaces. Parents may perceive that school-to-work initiatives are a threat to college preparation and attendance. Postsecondary educational programs and institutions may shy away from such programs because of the extra work and collaboration. Teachers also may be concerned, fearful of the changes that must occur in their classroom planning.

Table 14.4.   Sample employability skills addressed by "Jobs for Cincinnati Graduates"

Shaking hands
Job sources
GNAP (Greeting, name, affiliation, purpose)
Applications
Résumés and cover letters
Telephone calls
Pre-employment tests
Interviewing—questions, appearance, how to "strike out" (make a bad impression)
Hiring decisions

SUMMARY POINTS

- The transition from school to work and community is a challenge for all students.
- IDEA requires transition-related content on the IEP beginning when the student is 14 years old, with services required by the time the student is 16 years old.
- Transition plans should include several areas, including employment, postsecondary education, independent living, adult services, and community participation.
- Although parents can be a significant support to their child's transition to work and the community, there is sometimes tension between parent and student during the transition process and in relation to the student's future.
- School-to-work programs may be a significant support for all students as they move from school to work and the community.

REFERENCES

Americans with Disabilities Act (ADA) of 1990, PL 101-336, 42 U.S.C. §§ 12101 *et seq.*

Bailey, T., & Merritt, D. (1997, March). School-to-work for the college-bound. *Centerfocus, 16,* 7, 11.

Blackorby, J., & Wagner, M. (1996). Longitudinal postschool outcomes of youth with disabilities: Findings from the National Longitudinal Transition Study. *Exceptional Children, 62,* 399–413.

Borgen, W.A., & Amundson, N.E. (1995). *Models of adolescent transition.* Greensboro, NC: ERIC Clearinghouse on Counseling and Student Services. (ERIC No. ED 401502)

Brown, B.L. (1998). *What's happening in school-to-work programs?* Columbus, OH: ERIC Clearinghouse on Adult, Career, and Vocational Education. (ERIC No. ED 414435)

Cicamanec, K., & Boston, C. (1996). School-to-work transition in the K–12 classroom. *ERIC Review, 3*(2), 12–13.

Devlieger, P.J., & Trach, J.S. (1999). Mediation as a transition process: The impact on postschool employment outcomes. *Exceptional Children, 65*(4), 507–523.

Hutchins, M.P., & Renzaglia, A. (1998). Interviewing families for effective transition to employment. *Teaching Exceptional Children, 30*(4), 72–78.

Individuals with Disabilities Education Act (IDEA) of 1990, PL 101-476, 20 U.S.C. §§ 1400 *et seq.*

Individuals with Disabilities Education Act Amendments of 1997, PL 105-17, 20 U.S.C. §§ 1400 *et seq.*

Izzo, M.V., & Shumate, K.E. (1991). *NetWORK for effective transitions to work: A transition coordinator's handbook* (Targeting Employment Series). Columbus: Center on Education and Training for Employment, The Ohio State University. (ERIC No. ED 332 033)

Louis Harris & Associates. (1998). *Harris Survey on the current status of persons with disabilities in American life: Executive summary of survey findings.* Washington, DC: Author.

Morningstar, M.E., Turnbull, A.P., & Turnbull, H.R., III. (1995). What do students with disabilities tell us about the importance of family involvement in the transition from school to adult life? *Exceptional Children, 62*(3), 249–260.

Mount, B. (1992). *Personal futures planning: Promises and precautions.* New York: Graphic Press.

National Association of State Directors of Special Education. (1990). *Life after school for children with disabilities: Answers to questions parents ask about employment and financial aid.* Washington, DC: Author. (ERIC Document Reproduction Service No. ED 329-072)

National Information Center for Children and Youth with Disabilities (NICHCY). (1993). *Transition services in the IEP.* Washington, DC: Author.

National Information Center for Children and Youth with Disabilities (NICHCY). (1994). *Options after high school for youth with disabilities.* Washington, DC: Author.

National Information Center for Children and Youth with Disabilities (NICHCY). (1999a). *Briefing paper: Individualized education programs.* Washington, DC: Author.

National Information Center for Children and Youth with Disabilities (NICHCY). (1999b). *Options after high school for youth with disabilities.* Washington, DC: Author.

O'Brien, J., & Lyle, C. (1997). *Framework for accomplishments.* Decatur, GA: Responsive Systems Associates.

Paris, K.A. (1995). *Critical issue: Improving school-to-work transition for all students.* Madison, WI: North Central Regional Educational Laboratory.

Peters, L. (1994). From school-to-work and back again. *Rural Audio Journal, 2*(3), 1–14.

Rehabilitation Act of 1973, PL 93-112, 29 U.S.C. §§ 701 *et seq.*

School-to-Work Opportunities Act of 1994, PL 103-239, 20 U.S.C. §§ 6101 *et seq.*

Shapiro-Barnard, S. (1998). Preparing the ground for what is to come. In C.M. Jorgensen, *Restructuring high schools for all students: Taking inclusion to the next level* (pp. 1–14). Baltimore: Paul H. Brookes Publishing Co.

Stainback, W., Stainback, S., & Stefanich, G. (1996). Learning together in inclusive classrooms: What about the curriculum? *Teaching Exceptional Children, 28*(3), 14–19.

Vandercook, T., York, J., & Forest, M. (1989). The McGill Action Planning System (MAPS): A strategy for building the vision. *Journal of The Association for Persons with Severe Handicaps, 14,* 205–215.

Whitney-Thomas, J., & Hanley-Maxwell, C. (1996). Packing the parachute: Parents' experiences as their children prepare to leave high school. *Exceptional Children, 63,* 75–87.

MANAGER MAKES DIFFERENCE FOR PURCELL

—Mark D. Motz, sports reporter, Community Press

He was so excited his hands trembled a bit before the Boys Division II state basketball finals.

He needed some help holding the notebook in which a shaky hand scratched out answers to questions.

"We will win," wrote Danny Neyer of the Purcell Marian squad, just before it took the floor March 25.

Just by his being there, he already had won.

As had his team.

And even though the scoreboard said otherwise—the Cavaliers lost a 76-74 overtime thriller to Warrensville Heights—the Purcell Marian basketball program can't be anything but a winner for embracing a boy like sophomore Danny Neyer.

He sat on the end of the Cavalier bench all season and never once made it onto the floor.

No points.

No rebounds.

Enough assists, however, to make John Stockton look like a Piker.

Neyer has cerebral palsy and acute hearing loss which has affected his speech, making the writing of answers his best form of communication.

No matter.

He is the team manager and the team made him one of them.

So much so that Neyer climbed the ladder with senior captain Jaime Cooper [due to his cerebral palsy, he is unable to climb without physical support] to clip the last strand of net when the Cavaliers beat Dayton Christian in the regional tournament.

"It is the best thing," Neyer wrote of his trip up the ladder.

"For all the ability those kids have, they are very aware not everyone has that ability," said Karen Matuszek, director of the Purcell Marian special needs program in which Neyer is enrolled. "It would have been very easy for them to forget about Danny in their excitement of that moment, but they've gone out of their way to include him."

Neyer's parents, Lisa and Don, agree.

They are westside folks, living deep in the heart of Elder country, who spend a lot of time and effort getting Danny to and from Purcell Marian every day.

"We don't bleed purple anymore," Lisa said. "Purcell is a little treasure we found. Just hearing his name announced at the district championship, we both cried."

This article is reprinted with permission from the Community Press, Cincinnati, Ohio.

Don Neyer said he never imagined his son would be part of a Final Four team, and is thankful for the change.

"The team is just wonderful," he said. "They include him in everything. He loves it and he loves all of them."

Danny wrote his favorite player is high-flying junior Keith Jackson and the best part of being with the team is when "the players give me high fives."

"He always loved sports," Matuszek said. "He knew he wouldn't be able to make a sports team here. So he decided he wanted to be a manager."

What he became was an inspiration.

And when I said his best means of communication was writing, I lied. It's his touch.

"You look over at him and he's never down," Cooper said. "You come out of the game with a foul or after doing something dumb, and he gives you five. It gives you inspiration and makes you thankful for what you have and makes you want to do that much more because you can."

Xavier University Basketball coach Skip Prosser often quotes the Ralph Waldo Emerson line, "Our chief want in life is somebody who will make us do what we can."

Neyer is that somebody for the Cavaliers.

And they are all winners for the association.

Index

Page numbers followed by *t* denote tables; those followed by *f* denote figures.

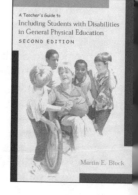